The
Norman Achievement
1050 - 1100

The
Norman Achievement
1050 - 1100

DAVID C. DOUGLAS

Fellow of the British Academy
Emeritus Professor of History in the University of Bristol

UNIVERSITY OF CALIFORNIA PRESS

BERKELEY AND LOS ANGELES · 1969

University of California Press
Berkeley and Los Angeles, California

© 1969 David C. Douglas

Librarv of Congress Catalog Card Number 74–88028

SBN 520–01383–2

Printed in Great Britain

For
ANN DOUGLAS
From Her Father

CONTENTS

LIST OF ILLUSTRATIONS

LIST OF ILLUSTRATIONS

ABBREVIATIONS

The following abbreviations are used in the footnotes. For some other books short titles are employed, and these are fully extended in the bibliography, where further information is also given of the editions used.

Alexiad	The *Alexiad* of Anna Comnena.
Amatus	*Histoire de li Normant* by Amatus of Monte Cassino. [Cited by book and chapter. For editions see bibliography.]
Amer. Hist. Rev.	*American Historical Review*
A.S. Chron.	Anglo-Saxon Chronicle. [Cited by version and annals.]
Bayeux Tapestry	This is cited by reference to the plates in the Phaidon Press edition of 1957.
Carmen	*Carmen de Hastingae Proelio*, often attributed to Guy of Amiens. [Cited by verse.]
Cod. Dipl. Barese	*Codice Diplomatico Barese*, 18 vols (1897–1950).
D.B.	Domesday Book, 2 vols, Record Commission (1783).
Eng. Hist. Rev.	*English Historical Review.*
Flor. Worc.	Florence of Worcester, *Chronicon ex Chronicis* [Cited by annals.]
Fulcher	Fulcher of Chartres, *Gesta Francorum Iherusalem Peregrinantium*. [Cited by book and chapter.]
Gesta	*Gesta Francorum et aliorum Hierosolimitanorum*. [Cited by book and chapter.]
Glaber	Rodulf Glaber, *Francorum Historiae*. [Cited by page from the edition by M. Prou (1884).]
Jaffé–Loewenfeld	*Regesta Pontificum Romanorum*, ed. Ph. Jaffé. 2nd edition by Loewenfeld, Wattenbach and others. 2 vols (1885–8).
Hefele–Leclerc	*Histoire des Conciles* by C. J. Hefele. [Edited and translated into French by H. Leclerc.]

Leo of Ostia	*Chronica Monasterii Casinenis* by Leo of Ostia (or 'of Marsi'). [Cited by book and chapter.]
Lupus	Lupus Protospartarius (of Bari), *Chronicon*. [Cited by annals.]
Kehr, *Regesta*	*Regesta Pontificum Romanorum – Italia Pontificia* vol. VIII: *Regnum Normannorum* (1936).
Malaterra	Geoffrey Malaterra, *Historia Sicula*. [Cited by book and chapter.]
Mon. Ang.	W. Dugdale, *Monasticon Anglicanum*, new edition, 6 vols. in 8 (1817–30).
Mon. Germ. Hist. S.S.	*Monumenta Germaniae Historica: Scriptores.*
Ord. Vit.	Ordericus Vitalis, *Historia Ecclesiastica*. [Cited by volume and page from the edition by M. Le Prévost and L. Delisle, 5 vols (1838–55).]
Pat. Lat.	*Patrologia Latina Cursus Completus*, ed. J. P. Migne.
Proc. Brit. Acad.	*Proceedings of the British Academy.*
Quellen und Forschungen	*Quellen und Forschungen aus Italienischen Archiven und Bibliotheken.*
R.A.D.N.	*Recueil des Actes des Ducs de Normandie (911–1066)* ed. M. Fauroux.
Rec. Hist. Croisades Occ.	*Recueil des Historiens des Croisades: Historiens Occidentaux*, 5 vols (1844–95).
Rec. Hist. Franc.	*Recueil des Historiens des Gaules et de la France* ('Dom Bouquet'), 24 vols of varying dates.
Regesta Regum	*Regesta Regum Anglo-Normannorum*, ed H. W. C. Davis and others.
Rohricht, *Regesta*	*Regesta Regni Hierosolymitani*, 2 vols (1893–1904).
R. Hist. Soc.	Royal Historical Society. [The *Transactions* are cited by series and volume.]
Starrabba, *Contributo*	B. Starrabba, *Contributo allo Studio della diplomatica Siciliana dei tempi Normanni: Diplomi di Funadazione delle chiese episcopale* (1893).
Watterich, *Vitae*	*Pontificum Romanorum – Vitae*, ed. J. M. Watterich, 2 vols (1862).
Will. Apul.	William of Apulia, *Gesta Roberti Wiscardi*. [Cited by book and verse. For editions see bibliography.]
Will. Jum.	William of Jumièges, *Gesta Normannorum Ducum*, ed. J. Marx (1914).

Will. Malms.   William of Malmesbury. [His *Gesta Regum* is cited from the edition by W. Stubbs, 2 vols (1887, 1889).]

Will. Poit.   William of Poitiers, *Gesta Guillelmi Ducis Normannorum et Regis Anglorum*. [Cited by page from the edition by R. Foreville (1952).]

PREFACE

To retell in detail the story of any of the Norman conquests would be a tedious and profitless occupation, and the more limited purpose of the present book is indicated in its first chapter. The comparative study which follows is, I hope, firmly based upon original testimony, but I am also under heavy obligations to modern scholars. Among these, my debt to the work of Ferdinand Chalandon, C. H. Haskins and Carl Erdmann will be immediately apparent, as will be my obligation to Professor Claude Cahen, Miss Evelyn Jamison and Sir Steven Runciman. Mr Philip Grierson of Gonville and Caius College Cambridge, Mr R. W. Southern, President of St John's College Oxford, and Professor L.-R. Ménager of the University of Aix-en-Provence have most kindly helped me with advice on particular questions. Especially do I offer my thanks to Professor David Knowles, who read the whole book in typescript, and, with characteristic generosity, gave me the benefit of his criticism and counsel. Nor do I forget how abundantly I am indebted not only to all the writers whose books I have cited, but also to all those colleagues and friends (some, alas, now dead) who over the years have so sympathetically sustained my work. If I have failed to profit from so much kindness from so many quarters, the fault is assuredly mine.

The maps are largely due to Mr William Bromage, and my obligations in connexion with the illustrations are individually recorded. I acknowledge with thanks the permission given me by Messrs Routledge and Kegan Paul to quote short extracts from the translation made by E. A. S. Dawes of the *Alexiad* of Anna Comnena, and in like fashion I am indebted to Messrs Chapman and Hall for allowing me to cite some verses of the *Chanson de Roland* from the translation by C. K. Scott Moncrieff. My friends on the staff of the Library of the University of Bristol have helped me throughout with their usual unfailing courtesy, and it is with particular pleasure that I take this opportunity of thanking my own Publishers for the skill and care they have once again devoted to the presentation of my work.

Finally, it must be added that this protracted undertaking might never have been begun, and would certainly not have been brought to a conclusion, had it not been for the inexorable and continuous encouragement of my wife and daughter. A public expression of thanks would here be entirely out of place. Such as it is, the book is theirs as well as mine.

D. C. D.
Bristol, 1969

The
Norman Achievement
1050 - 1100

Chapter 1

THE BACKGROUND TO ACHIEVEMENT

I

In the whole course of European history there have been few movements more remarkable than the sudden expansion of Norman power that took place during the latter half of the eleventh century. Between 1050 and 1100, the Normans – men from a single province of France – conquered England, and extended their dominion over southern Italy and Sicily. They carried their interests into Spain, and to the borders of Scotland and Wales. At the same time, they fostered the rising fortunes of the Papacy at a critical period in the history of Christendom, and they became deeply involved with the politics of Byzantium. Finally, before the eleventh century had closed, the Normans were taking a special part in the First Crusade, and during its progress they established in Syria the Norman principality of Antioch. Such an achievement has naturally attracted the close attention of historians, and there is assuredly no need to retell in detail the story of any of the Norman conquests. But it may be interesting, none the less, to make some comparisons between them; to examine their common causes and consequences; and to inquire how far the manifold activities of the Normans between 1050 and 1100 can all be regarded as having everywhere formed part of a single endeavour.

Such, at all events, is the purpose of this book, and the present state of Norman historical scholarship perhaps justifies the attempt. Norman studies have in truth been extensive and profound, but they have also for the most part been curiously segregated. Thus the Norman conquest of England,[1] the Norman conquests in Italy and Sicily[2] have all been the object of prolonged and intensive investigations, and scarcely

[1] Some of the work relating to the Norman Conquest of England is listed on pp. 427–47 of Douglas, *William the Conqueror* (1964). The earlier controversies are surveyed in Douglas, *Norman Conquest and British Historians* (1946).

[2] The enormous bulk of the literature that has been devoted to the history of the Normans

3

less attention has been paid to the Norman relations with the Papacy and to the Norman contributions to the Crusades.[1] But comparatively few efforts have been made in recent years to relate together these scattered exploits of a single people. It is now more than fifty years since C. H. Haskins produced his *Normans in European History*, with the comment that 'no account of the whole subject has yet been attempted from this point of view',[2] and while this notable book still retains its freshness and value, it covers a millenium of Norman history in a short space, and much has of course been added to our knowledge since it appeared. Again, while every student of the Normans in Mediterranean lands must depend upon the magisterial work of Miss Evelyn Jamison, most of her reflexions on the interconnexion between the various activities of the Normans, were contained in a single lecture which was in great part concerned with the twelfth century, and which was itself delivered in 1938.[3] Since that time, despite the wide sweep of M. Andrieu-Guitrancourt's treatment of Viking and Norman history,[4] the segregation of Norman studies has continued, and it may be thought that, so far as the eleventh century is concerned, a closer association should now be made between them.

It is of course as legitimate as it is usual to assess the historical importance of the Normans in connexion with the secular and ecclesiastical institutions which they modified, or in relation to the later development of the countries which they conquered, and which afterwards absorbed them. Nevertheless, it may also be true that the influence which the Normans exercised at this time upon England and Europe, upon Rome and Byzantium, upon Christendom and Islam needs to be re-examined from the point of view of the Normans themselves, and that only thus will its quality be fully appraised. A truer assessment of the Norman contribution to European history may now perhaps be attained if the

in the south is indicated by the bibliography given in F. Chalandon, *Domination Normande en Italie et en Sicile*, I (1907), pp. v–xciii. That bibliography, like the great book in which it is contained, has never been superseded, but it may now be supplemented by the bibliographical information contained in Guillaume de Pouille, *La Geste de Robert Guiscard*, ed. M. Mathieu (1961). Mention must also be made of the graphic descriptions given as long ago as 1902 by F. Marion Crawford in the second volume of his *Rulers of the South*; by J. B. Villars in his *Les Normands en Méditerranée* (1951); and very recently by Lord Norwich in his delightful *Normans in the South*, vol. 1 (1967).

[1] On this see S. Runciman, *History of the Crusades*, I (1951), pp. 342–60.

[2] *The Normans in European History* (1915), p. vii.

[3] 'The Sicilian Norman Kingdom in the minds of Anglo-Norman contemporaries' (*Proc. Brit. Acad.*, xxiv (1938), pp. 237–286).

[4] *Histoire de l'empire normand et de sa civilization* (1952).

Norman achievement between 1050 and 1100 be reconsidered in its totality.

The close interconnexion between all the enterprises undertaken by the Normans in this period can at once be suggested by a bare recital of a few selected dates. Robert Guiscard, son of Tancred of Hauteville-le-Guichard near Coutances, and later duke of Apulia, started his fantastic career in Italy in 1047 – the same year as that in which the young Duke William the future conqueror of England ended his bastard minority, and began his effective reign in Normandy after the battle of Val-ès-Dunes. Duke William obtained the promise of the English royal succession from King Edward the Confessor some two years before the Norman victory over Leo IX at Civitate in 1053, which initiated the new relations between the Normans and the papacy that were later to prove so influential in England, in Constantinople, and at Rome. Again, the capture of Bari by the Normans, which marked the end of Byzantine administration in Italy, took place only five years after the battle of Hastings; and in the next year just before William the Conqueror started his advance into Scotland, the Normans took Palermo from the Saracens. That was in 1072, and the following year Archdeacon Hildebrand who had sponsored the alliance between the papacy and the Normans ascended the papal throne as Pope Gregory VII. These chronological connexions could in fact be very widely illustrated. Robert Guiscard captured Durazzo and began his invasion of the eastern empire only four years before William the Conqueror, in 1085, returned hastily from Normandy to England in order to repel a threatened invasion from Scandinavia, and to plan the Domesday Survey. By 1091 all Sicily had been subjected to the rule of Guiscard's younger brother, Roger the 'Great Count'. And very soon the sons of both Robert Guiscard and William the Conqueror, Bohemund and Robert Curthose, were to be associated in the First Crusade.

Here, it would seem, was a vast movement of inter-related endeavour which should be studied as a unity. Despite all that has been written about the Normans no complete explanation has ever been given why this small group from northern France was able in fifty years so rapidly to extend its dominion. Was this sudden explosion of power due to some quality in the Normans themselves, or to the military techniques which they employed, or to the 'Holy Wars' which they so successfully waged to their own advantage? Or was it due to the sudden emergence from this province of a fortunate constellation of outstanding leaders such as William the Conqueror, Robert Guiscard, Count Roger of Sicily or Bohemund of Antioch? Or have other reasons to be sought to account for the Norman achievement, which between 1050 and 1100 permanently affected so many lands, and which reached a climax on Christmas Day 1066 when a Norman duke was hallowed king of the English in the abbey church of St Peter at Westminster?

II

Of the greater Norman leaders of this age, William the Conqueror was the most important, Robert Guiscard the most dominant, Count Roger of Sicily the most politic and Bohemund the ablest soldier in the field. All four of them however possessed certain qualities which they had in common. They were all in varying degrees personally repellent, cruel and coldly unscrupulous. They were all men of great ability and vastly ambitious. Endowed with keen if sometimes restricted political vision, they all pursued their purpose with inflexible determination. It was by sheer force of character that they severally rose from perilous beginnings to reach the pinnacles of power. Above everything, they were masterful: fit leaders for the astute and vigorous company of Norman magnates who surrounded them. The Norman achievement can assuredly not be explained without frequent reference to their characteristic acts.

But Norman enterprise during the latter half of the eleventh century is not to be appraised solely, or even chiefly, by reference to outstanding personalities. Indeed, its chief interest derives from the fact that it was inseparably connected with wider movements which at this time were giving a new turn to the growth of Europe. The half-century which elapsed between 1050 and 1100 witnessed for example a fundamental alteration in the balance of political power in northern Europe, and in the relations of Latin Europe with the Teutonic and the Scandinavian lands. It also saw a transformation in the relations between the eastern and western Empires and between the eastern and western Churches. It saw the papacy rise to a new peak of power, and it watched the forces of the Cross and the Crescent being brought first into more direct juxtaposition, and later into armed conflict. And in all these movements the Normans were directly involved; to all of them they made their own particular contribution; and none of them would have taken the same course apart from Norman intervention. This is, of course, not to say that Norman influence, thus exercised, was good or bad, beneficial or deleterious. But the Norman intervention was in each case of decisive effect, and its results were to prove enduring. The Norman achievement was fulfilled during years that were critical in the growth of Europe, and in countries whose fate was crucial to the formation of the European identity.

To draw lines across the time chart is a profitless occupation since it blurs the essential continuity in human affairs, and masks the constant interaction of ideas and acts, out of which the fabric of human society is perpetually being woven afresh. None the less, Marc Bloch, the great French historian, was surely right when he selected 1050 as a suitable date for marking the beginnings of social changes which 'transformed the face of Europe',[1] and certainly in the regions which were to be specially affected by the Normans the developments which occurred during these years were wholly remarkable. In the second quarter of the eleventh century for example, England might almost have been regarded as forming part of the Scandinavian world. Large areas of the country had been subject to settlement from the Baltic lands, and England herself had for a time formed part of the Scandinavian empire of Cnut the Great. Until after 1070 there was always a threat that a Scandinavian dynasty might be restored in England. Thereafter, however, all this was to be changed. Quite apart from the effects which the Norman Conquest was to have on the internal state of England, the advent of the Normans linked England to a province of France in such a way that for the remainder of the Middle Ages the filiations of England were to be deflected away from Scandinavia, and towards Latin Europe.

These changes were certainly to be of profound effect, and their consequences were to extend far beyond England. Neither France nor the western empire, nor the Baltic countries, nor the papacy, nor even Byzantium, could ignore the new grouping of political forces which was thus foreshadowed in the north, and the implications of the Norman Conquest of England were in truth to be felt even oustide the sphere of politics. Indeed it might reasonably be suggested that the alteration to the balance of power consequent upon the Norman impact upon England was among the causes of the special characteristics of the culture of Western Europe in the twelfth century.[2] The Normans, by linking

---

[1] *Feudal Society* (trans. L. A. Manyon) (1961), p. 89.
[2] R. W. Southern, *Making of the Middle Ages* (1953), pp. 15 et seq.

England more closely to Latin Europe, may have helped the Romance-speaking lands to achieve that dominance in western culture which they exercised during that brilliant and productive period. At all events, the great monastic movements of the twelfth century, crusading sentiment and troubadour song, the new universities and the learning that was taught therein, the new humanism, and, later, the new theology, came, in the main, from regions west of the Rhine and south of the Alps – from a world which was centred upon France and Italy, and which included the England which the Normans conquered.

Equally remarkable were the transformations which, during these same decades, took place in the political relations of those countries which bordered on the Mediterranean sea, and in these too the Normans were to play an essential part. At the beginning of the eleventh century, the whole Mediterranean world was dominated by three powers none of which belonged to western Europe.[1] There was the Christian eastern empire with its capital at Constantinople comprising the Balkans and Asia Minor, and extending westward towards southern Italy and eastward into northern Syria. Secondly, there was the Fatimite khalifate with its capital at Cairo, dominating not only Egypt but also Palestine and all Africa north of the Sahara as far as Tunis, and controlling also Sicily with Malta and Gozo. Finally, there was the Spanish khalifate with its capital at Cordova, dominating not only much of the Iberian peninsular, but also what is now Algeria and Morocco, and extending south – through Mauretania towards Senegal. The balance of power between these three great powers was, moreover, to fluctuate. During the first quarter of the eleventh century, after the deaths of the great khalifs, Al Azis of Cairo (996) and Al Mansour of Cordova (1002), Islam was to be weakened by dissensions, whilst the power of Byzantium was to grow steadily under the 'Macedonian' emperors until the death of Basil II in 1025.[2] By that time, the eastern empire, having stabilized its northern and eastern frontiers, was firmly established both in south Italy and in Syria, and it was in virtual control of the eastern Mediterranean. On the other hand, Sicily remained an outpost of Islam, whilst the eastern empire was itself beginning to be threatened by internal unrest, and would soon have to face a savage Moslem attack from the Seljuk Turks.

In this teeming Mediterranean world therefore – the cradle land of

[1] See C. Dawson, 'The Moslem west' (*Medieval Essays* (1953), pp. 117–34.)
[2] Cf. H. Diehl, *History of the Byzantine Empire*, trans. G. B. Ives (1925), pp. 72–111.

Christian culture – western Christendom had little or no share in 1050. No western power at that time could dispute the dominance of Islam at sea in all the area westward from Sicily to the Straits of Gibraltar. The bells of Santiago still decorated the principal mosque of Cordova; and Moslem ships made continuous raids of the coasts of Liguria and Provence.[1] Even the re-establishment of Byzantine authority in south Italy had been won at the expense of the West, and had been marked in particular by the defeat of the German, Otto II, at Stilo in 987. Rome, itself, was in eclipse, and could not vie in secular importance with Constantinople, Cairo or Palermo, whilst the papacy had become victim to secular corruption and the sport of Roman factions. The pontificate from 1012 to 1024 of the vigorous Benedict VIII (who very rashly welcomed the first Normans in Italy) was interposed between two sad periods of political degradation in the history of the papacy.[2]

The conditions existing in the Mediterranean world in 1050 could in fact be contrasted most sharply with those which were to prevail there at the close of the eleventh century: when Byzantine administration had been ousted from Italy, and Saracen rule from Sicily; when the papacy was rising to a new peak of authority and political power; and when western Christendom, having once more become a force in the Mediterranean, was preparing to take the offensive against Islam. And in effecting this momentous transformation, the Normans will be found to have been perhaps the strongest single agent. Just as, in the North, Norman enterprise was to alter the relations between England, Latin Europe, and the Scandinavian countries, so also, in the Mediterranean zone, the same enterprise would bring about changes of equal consequence to the future of Europe.

III

The background to the Norman achievement cannot, however, be adequately described without some reference to the political motives which pervaded eleventh-century Europe. But to analyse these is not easy. Not only is the age remote, but the part played by the Normans in its affairs has been continuously interpreted in the light of later controversies respecting politics or religion. The close association of

---

[1] Dawson, op. cit.; A. R. Lewis, Naval Power and Trade, pp. 197, 198; S. Runciman, Crusades, I, pp. 88, 89.
[2] Cf. Gregorovius, Rome in the Middle Ages, IV, pt i, pp. 1–54.

the Normans with the political advance of the papacy has inevitably inspired later polemics based on the effects of Norman action upon western Christendom, the eastern Church, and the Moslem world, whilst the Norman conquest of England has for centuries served as a text for political and social sermons. Few of the great controversies which harrassed England in the seventeenth century were debated without some reference to the Normans, and the heat which was then engendered has not entirely departed from Anglo-Norman studies today.[1] Correspondingly, in France, William the Conqueror has been hailed as a national hero, and also denounced as a champion of super-stition and as an enemy of the people. Statues have been erected in his honour, whilst Calvinists and revolutionaries have desecrated his tomb and scattered his remains. In England, the contrasted treatment meted out to the Conqueror has been scarcely less remarkable. For here he has been regarded both as one of the founders of English greatness, and also as the author of one of the most lamentable of English defeats.[2]

But such controversies which have loomed so large in later studies of the Normans have little relevance to the thoughts and emotions of eleventh-century men. In particular, it would be hard to discover in Europe at that time any sentiments which could legitimately compare with modern nationalism. There was then no disposition of any of the contending groups in southern Italy or Sicily to create a state based upon national feeling, and few traces of any such motives could be found in the contemporary politics of northern Europe. It is true that in the Anglo-Saxon annals, and in the *Song of Roland*, there are passages which point to the existence of common sentiments among the inhabitants respectively of England and France,[3] but these found little expression in the politics of the age. Between 1025 and 1070 England was ruled by kings of three different racial stocks, and she was constantly subjected to civil strife. In France, during the same period, the authority of the Capetian royal house hardly stretched south of the Loire, and in the north men found their primary secular loyalties in the ancient and warring provinces to which they belonged: in Anjou and Normandy, for instance, or in Brittany or Blois. Neither France nor England could be properly considered in the eleventh century as nations in the modern sense of the term.

[1] Douglas, *English Scholars* (1939), ch. vi.
[2] Douglas, *William the Conqueror*, pp. 3–6.
[3] E.g. A.S. Chron. 'C', 'D' and 'E'. s.a. 1052; *Chanson de Roland, passim.* Cf. J. Bédier, *Légendes Épiques*, III, pp. 391–455, and contrast F. Lot in *Romania*, LIV (1928), pp. 274, 275.

The absence of national sentiment in eleventh century Europe might in fact be plentifully illustrated. If modern terms be used, there were 'Englishmen' fighting on both sides at the battle of Stamford Bridge in 1066, and Greeks were engaged against Greeks at Bari in 1071. Men from England served under William the Conqueror in his campaign against Exeter in 1068, and again in Maine in 1073, whilst Roger, the son of Tancred of Hauteville, was the ally of the emir of Syracuse before he attacked the Saracens in Palermo in 1071.[1] Similarly, during his early career in Spain the Cid seems to have been as ready to fight in alliance with the Moors, as in association with his fellow Spaniards, and, throughout the latter part of the eleventh century, Lombards, Danes, Anglo-Saxons and Normans served together in amity in the armies of the Eastern Emperors. Finally, the famous conflict between Normans and English at Hastings in 1066 was renewed at Durazzo in 1081, but then for very different reasons, and in 1099 Edgar Atheling, the last representative of the Anglo-Saxon royal house, is to be found co-operating with Robert, the eldest son of William the Conqueror, in Syria.[2] Such episodes are interesting in themselves, and they point to a general conclusion. All Norman enterprise between 1050 and 1100, was interconnected, but neither that enterprise, nor the Norman world which it created were inspired by national sentiment. Nor was there anything which could properly, or with precision, be called a national resistance to the Normans in any of the countries they conquered.

To penetrate into the authentic atmosphere in which the Norman conquests were made, it is thus necessary to discard many notions begotten of modern politics. And it is scarcely less essential at the same time to give full weight to many powerful motives, both rational and irrational, which then had far more influence on western Europe than they do today.[3] The physical background to human existence was then itself so very different. In the absence of adequate protection, the changes of nature, storm and tempest, floods and drought, even the dark and cold of winter, were menacing; and calamities sometimes appeared to follow one another with distressful frequency. Famine and epidemics were common. The years 1044 and 1083 were, for example, notorious for scarcity, and in 1075 and 1094 there were particularly savage onslaughts of the plague. Europe, in fact, then experienced

---

[1] Below, pp. 57, 58.

[2] Runciman, *op. cit.*, I, pp. 227, 228.

[3] M. Bloch, *op. cit.*, pp. 59–79; Alphandéry et Dupront, *Le Chrétienté et l'idée de Croisade* (1954), pp. 43–6.

many of the physical hardships that now afflict less fortunate lands. Infant mortality was staggeringly high, and the average age of death, by modern standards was very low.

A sense of personal insecurity was thus inevitably pervasive, but it was a special mark of the age that the hazards of life then seemed to stretch far beyond the boundaries of the physical world. Seldom have men been more conscious of the supernatural than in western Europe between 1050 and 1100. Just as man's body was ever being threatened by the visible assaults of nature, so also might his salvation be destroyed by unseen powers if he fell victim in the endless war which raged between Good and Evil. Care must, of course, be taken not to exaggerate the prevalence of a mental attitude which is in any case hard to define, but it remains true that this age in western Europe was marked not only by a ruthless realism, but also by a vivid apprehension of the invisible, and by a widespread reliance on means of support which were held to be more potent than human effort.

This attitude is not to be defined simply as the product of an 'age of Faith' (or of superstition). For the matter was more complex. The eleventh century produced its saints as well as its ruffians, its practical politicians as well as its visionaries, and if at this time in Europe the basic truths of Christian doctrine were unquestioned, men's approaches to religion differed widely. Learned theologians were at work debating the logical foundations of Christian theology to the end that orthodoxy might in due course be more clearly defined, and at the same time the laity were constrained by force, mansuetude, or love, to resort regularly to their parish churches where they could hear the Mass recited more or less correctly. And beyond all this, there was a popular religion[1] – a folklore composed of many elements but impregnated with Christian symbolism – which saw the hand of angels or devils in every event, and which watched for signs and portents in all the unusual phenomena of nature – in Harlequin's ride across the October sky, in comets and animal monstrosities, in dreams and visions. Why distinguish too closely between the seen and the unseen, when the material world might itself be nothing but a curtain behind which was proceeding an unending struggle for the souls of men? And how could men escape damnation save by exceptional acts or with special help?

Hence the extraordinary penances which marked the age, and the arduous expiatory pilgrimages to distant shrines. Hence too the

[1] M. Bloch, op. cit., pp. 80–7.

passionate pleas for the intercessions of holy men, and the eagerness to obtain miracle-working relics even at the cost of violence or theft. Perhaps, indeed, the struggle between the powers of Light and Darkness was even now approaching its culmination, and perhaps the visible world (itself so partial in its significance) was itself on the point of dissolution. There is little evidence of any general belief that the end of the world was to come at, or about, the Millenium, or of any general relief when that term was safely passed. But there is no doubt that terrors of this nature repeatedly afflicted particular regions of western Europe during the eleventh century, and often for strange causes: a wicked ruler who must surely be the final anti-Christ; or a special disturbance of nature or even a particular coincidence in the festivals of the Church.[1] Hell was assuredly difficult to escape, and who could tell when the Day of Wrath would dawn?

This temper conduced to widespread emotional instability in eleventh-century Europe. It must also be held to explain many of the strange passions, and the sudden shifts of conduct, which will be found to mark both the progress of the Normans, and the reactions of those with whom they were brought in contact. Duke Robert I for example, the father of William the Conqueror, was a young lustful and ruthless prince who was successfully reducing his turbulent duchy to order when he suddenly determined to mend his soul by departing to Palestine on the pilgrimage from which in fact he was never to return. Again, Simon de Crépi, count of the Vexin consolidated his power by winning in profitable marriage Judith the daughter of the count of Auvergne. But he chose the occasion of his wedding night in 1078 to vow himself and his wife to perpetual continence, and departed forthwith to become a monk in the abbey of Saint Claude in the Jura.[2] To men such as these a pilgrimage might be as important as a war, or a monastic vow as compelling as the establishment of order, and it may be recalled how many of the warrior lords of this age retired after their

[1] Shortly before the beginning of the eleventh century for example, Abbo, abbot of Fleury noted that there was spreading a general belief that the end of the world would come when the Annunciation coincided with Good Friday (*Pat. Lat.*, vol. CXXXIX, col. 472). Abbo may have been anticipating the year 992 when this coincidence did in fact take place. It has of course often subsequently recurred—notably in 1065 and 1910. On the latter occasion, some may recall that there was then constantly repeated in London the rhyme:

> When our Lord falls on our Lady's lap
> England shall have a dire mishap

On this occasion however the portent was held to refer not to the end of the world but to the death of King Edward VII.

[2] Douglas, *William the Conqueror*, p. 235.

strenuous lives to spend the evening of their days in monasteries.[1] It would, moreover, be wrong to ascribe such acts simply to hypocrisy or a craven fear of Hell. Whatever eleventh century magnates lacked, they were, generally speaking, replete both with energy and with courage. Yet such contradictions marked the age. To take the most obvious example: extremes of devotion and brutality marked the progress of the First Crusade, but to discount the sincerity of the devotional zeal exhibited for instance during the siege of Antioch would be as uncritical as to ignore the monstrous massacre which disgraced the capture of the city.[2]

Strong tides of contrasted passions swept through the world in which the Norman conquests were made, and the Normans themselves were affected by them. This is the age in which began to be perfected the romances of Charlemagne and of Arthur, when were written the moving *Miracles of the Virgin*,[3] when Cluniac monasteries multiplied through France and beyond, when John of Fécamp composed his notable prayers, and when St Anselm prepared his most enduring treatises. But it was also an age marked by spectacular butchery, by the 'Harrying of the North' in 1070, for instance, by the pillaging of Rome in 1084, by the bloodstained sack of Jerusalem in 1099, and by murders as disgusting as those of the Atheling Alfred in 1036, or of Beorn in 1049 in the ships of Earl Sweyn. Even apart from such terrible examples the contrasting emotions of this period could be illustrated in many episodes which, somewhat trivial in themselves, are for that very reason, the more illuminating. For example, when in 1096 the French crusaders reached Rome, they were discouraged to find the whole basilica of St Peter's, with the exception of one tower in the hands of the armed supporters of the anti-pope; and they were further shocked when these snatched from the altar the offerings of the pilgrims, and hurled stones upon them.[4] Never perhaps was there a closer intermingling of the earthy and the sublime than in this positive and most tumultuous age.

Nevertheless, although the ideas and emotions dominant in western Europe between 1050 and 1100 appear in some ways so removed from

---

[1] Douglas, *William the Conqueror*, p. 376.

[2] 'All the streets of the city were full of corpses so that no one could endure to be there because of the stench, nor could anyone walk along the narrow paths of the city except over the bodies of the dead.' *Gesta Francorum*, VIII, c. 20.

[3] Cf. R. W. Southern in *Medieval and Renaissance Studies*, IV (1958), pp. 83–200.

[4] Fulcher of Chartres, VII, cc. 2, 3.

those prevalent today, the primary motives which then inspired men to action were such as are common to all periods, and the continuing relevance of the events which then took place needs no further emphasis. The connexion between England and Europe, the control of the Mediterranean, the relations between eastern and western Europe, the schism between the eastern and western Churches, are topics whose interest has not faded. Nor have the lust for dominion and plunder, or the cruelties which it inspires, been noticeably diminished with the years.[1] Even the manner in which the transformations of the eleventh century were brought about may sometimes suggest some surprising analogies. The eleventh century is not the only period when western European men have found value in the anxious analysis of dreams, or discovered presages of misfortune in coincidences in the calendar. Such examples may however seem of slight account but others could be noted of larger import. No century has for instance been more afflicted with ideological warfare than the eleventh – except perhaps the twentieth – and the reliance then placed on supernatural assistance in wars described as 'holy' has some strange parallels in very modern times.[2] Again, a characteristic of the Normans was the use they made of propaganda which they employed in a manner almost reminiscent of the pulsating and deceiving air of Europe since 1938. The paradox of history is here. Deep is the chasm between the centuries, but by bridging it a man may return home.

IV

Many of the problems connected with the causes and consequences of Norman enterprise between 1050 and 1100 still await solution, and some of them are probably insoluble. A comparative study such as this

[1] Few public crimes in the eleventh century excelled in horror those committed at Buchenwald or Katyn Wood, while in 1945 perhaps as many people perished in a single night at Dresden as during the whole 'harrying of the North' by William the Conqueror in 1069–70.

[2] The eleventh century can claim no monopoly of the idea. The classical example of a Holy War (apart from the Crusades) is the armed expansion of Islam in the seventh and eighth centuries. But the idea was then old, and it has persisted. Twentieth century examples could be multiplied. The report of the Angels of Mons which swept through England in 1914 could have been taken from any of the chronicles of the wars of the Normans. Again, the ideological content of the warfare between Hitler and Stalin needs no emphasis, and it may be remembered that on 19 May 1940 one of the most famous speeches of Sir Winston Churchill concluded with a quotation from Maccabees, and an oblique reference to the Crusading motto: DEUS VULT. In June 1967, according to reports, the Holy War was preached (on opposite sides) by rabbis in the synagogues of London, and by muftis in the mosques of Damascus.

can, however, at least be illustrated by much contemporary testimony. In this connexion, pride of place must be given to a number of narratives which were written by men who were specially connected with the Normans, or who possessed a special admiration for what the Normans accomplished. These writers were not only familiar with their subject, they were also acquainted with the motives that inspired the chief actors in the drama. They cannot, of course, be regarded as impartial, and for that reason they must always be approached with caution. But their narratives admirably reflect the manner in which the Normans of this age *wished* their endeavours to be regarded.

The main description of the Norman impact on England before 1072 is given in three sources which supply a Norman version of what then took place. The first is a panegyric of William the Conqueror written between 1072 and 1074 by his chaplain William of Poitiers.[1] This has survived in only one manuscript, and its conclusion is lost. But it is of importance since the author had special opportunities for gaining information, and an unrestrained fervour in presenting the Norman case – often indeed with deplorably exaggerated rhetoric. The second of these sources is a Latin poem (*Carmen*) about the battle of Hastings,[2] which was for long considered to have been written by Guy, bishop of Amiens before 1068, but which is now sometimes (but by no means always) assigned to a later date.[3]

Finally, there is the Bayeux Tapestry.[4] So many theories have been advanced about this wonderful work that it would be rash to dogmatize too freely. It is generally believed, however, that the man who commissioned this work was the Conqueror's half-brother Odo, bishop of Bayeux and earl of Kent. The great artist who made the designs may have been either Norman or English, but the stitchwork itself was probably executed in England, and was finished, it would seem, not very long after the events it depicts. It takes rank, therefore, with the narrative of William of Poitiers and with the *Carmen* as a source of Anglo-Norman history at this time. These authorities, which stand in a close, though imperfectly defined relation to each other, together offer to the historian an admirable opportunity of watching one of

---

[1] Ed. R. Foreville (1952). Reference must also be made to the chronicles of William of Jumièges (ed. J. Marx, 1914).

[2] Printed in *Chroniques anglo-normandes*, ed. F. Michel, III (1840), pp. 1–23.

[3] A new edition is being prepared.

[4] Edited with full pictorial illustration by F. M. Stenton and others (1957), in *English Historical Documents*, vol. II; and by E. Maclagen, King Penguin Books, 1943.

the culminating episodes in the Norman achievement at close quarters from the Norman point of view.

Equally informative in the same enthusiastic sense was the eleventh century commemoration of Norman enterprise in the south. Thus between 1071 and 1086 there was written an admiring history of the Normans in Italy by Amatus, a monk of Monte Cassino,[1] and though the Latin original of this has been lost,[2] it survives in a French translation that was made in the fourteenth century. In these circumstances, the history of Amatus has naturally been the object of controversial criticism, but it is now generally accepted as an authentic eleventh century authority, and it has even been hailed by an expert critic as 'the best source of the Norman conquest in Italy'.[3]

Amatus, whose heroes were Richard, the first Norman prince of Capua, and Robert Guiscard, the first Norman duke of Apulia, does not, however, stand alone. Between 1095 and 1099, or very shortly afterwards, William styled 'of Apulia' (about whom nothing personal is known, but who was probably a Norman living in Italy), composed, in admirably correct Latin, an epic poem on the deeds of Robert Guiscard,[4] and this he dedicated to Guiscard's son, Roger, nicknamed 'Borsa' (or 'money-bags'). Then, before the eleventh century had ended, Geoffrey Malaterra, who seems to have been a monk of St Evroul in Normandy before he migrated to the south, wrote his important *History of Sicily*[5] with particular reference to the heroic deeds of Guiscard's youngest brother, Roger, later to be known as the 'Great Count'. It was a notable series and it was to be notably concluded by the liveliest account that was given of the First Crusade. This was the anonymous *Gesta Francorum*,[6] which was certainly written by a Norman from southern Italy who served under another of Robert Guiscard's sons, namely Bohemund of Taranto, and who was concerned, above all, with the interests of his master, and the exploits of his compatriots.

The relationship between the work of Amatus, William of Apulia and

---

[1] The best modern edition is Amato di Montecassino, *Storia dei Normanni*, ed. Vincenzo de Bartholomeis (Roma, 1935). Reference may also be made to: Aimé de Montecassino, *Ystoire de li Normant*, ed. O. Delarc (Rouen, 1892).

[2] It may have been used by Peter the Deacon when making a recension of the chronicle of Leo of Ostia in the second quarter of the twelfth century.

[3] F. Chalandon, *Domination normande*, I, p. xxxix.

[4] *La Geste de Robert Guiscard*, ed. M. Mathieu (Palermo, 1961).

[5] Ed. E. Pontieri (Muratori, *Rerum Italicarum Scriptores*, new edition, vol. V, pt i (1928).

[6] Here to be cited from the edition with a translation by R. Hill (1962). See also the edition by H. Hagenmeyer (Heidelberg, 1890).

Geoffrey Malaterra has been much discussed, but such connexions as may exist between them are slight.[1] Nor is there any significant interdependence to be detected between these southern narratives taken as a whole and the comparable work of William of Poitiers and the *Carmen*. All these writers make use of legendary material, and of poetic conventions common to the age in which the earliest *chanson de geste* appear.[2] But, speaking generally, it may be said that the eleventh century narratives written about the Normans in the south were substantially independent of those which had been produced in the north. The point is, moreover, of some importance. For if it should be found that there is uniformity of sentiment or opinion in the various treatises about Norman acts in widely separated lands, then it will clearly be of the highest interest that such unanimity should have been independently reached.

It must be reiterated, however, that these writers were partisans. Their works were addressed in the first instance to the Normans themselves, and while for that reason they are of particular value in revealing Norman aims and emotions, they need to be checked by other testimony so far as external events are concerned. Fortunately this too is available. The Anglo-Saxon annals in their various recensions are for example reasonably full for the period 1050–1100,[3] and reference can likewise be made to the annals from southern Italy such as those of Monte Cassino and Benevento,[4] and more particularly those of Bari both in their anonymous version, and in the recension which is described, as by 'Lupus Protospatarius'.[5] Again, while many of the problems of Anglo-Norman relations are considered in the anonymous *Life* of Edward the Confessor that was completed shortly after the Norman conquest of England,[6] the earlier phases of the Norman intrusion into Italy are illustrated in the chronicles of Adémar of Chabannes[7] and Rodulf Glaber.[8] It is moreover particularly fortunate that before the end of the eleventh century, many of the acts of the Normans in Italy were recorded by Leo, later cardinal of Ostia when still a monk of Monte Cassino in one of the best chronicles of the age.[9]

---

[1] Chalandon, *op. cit.*, I, pp. xxxi–xl; Pontieri, *op. cit.*, pp. x–xix.
[2] See M. Mathieu, *op. cit.*, pp. 46–50.
[3] Cf. *English Historical Documents*, II, pp. 116–76.
[4] *Mon. Germ. Hist.*, *Scriptores*, III, pp. 173; XXX, pp. 1385–1429.
[5] *Ibid.*, V, pp. 51 and 53.   [6] Ed. F. Barlow (1962).
[7] Ed. J. Chavanon (1897).   [8] Ed. M. Prou (1886).
[9] *Chron. Mon. Casinensis* (*Mon. Germ. Hist. Scriptores*, VII, pp. 574 *et seq.*). It is usually considered that the first recension written by Leo himself was completed before the end of the

Finally, the anonymous Norman author of the *Gesta Francorum*, describing the deeds of Bohemund, was only one of several writers who gave eye-witness accounts of the First Crusade.

The narrative sources for Norman history at this period could, of course, be supplemented to a greater or less extent by record evidence. The wealth of charter testimony for Anglo-Norman history in this age can be gauged by the collections that have been made of the deeds of the dukes of Normandy and the kings of England between 1050 and 1100,[1] and there are a vast number of private charters of the same period to be discovered in the cartularies of the religious houses of Normandy and England.[2] In similar fashion the charters of the Norman rulers in Italy and Sicily, and of many of the Norman magnates who surrounded them, are to be found in the collections which have been formed of deeds relating, for instance, to the monastery of La Cava, to Brindisi, to Aversa, and most particularly to Bari.[3] But here it is above all the papal documents which must attract attention. Apart from the numerous 'lives' of eleventh-century popes[4] which are extant and in print, there are a very large number of papal letters and 'bulls' available for study through the medium of the great 'calendars' of these texts which have been made by scholars such as Philip Jaffé[5] and Paul Kehr.[6] And it is indeed a happy circumstance that the 'Register' of Pope Gregory VII[7] has survived as a unique eleventh-century example of such an

---

eleventh century. The second recension was very probably made by Peter the Deacon who certainly composed the very inferior continuation of Leo's chronicle. See further Chalandon, *op. cit.*, vol. I, pp. xxxiv, xxxv. A warm appreciation of the work of Leo of Ostia is given by E. A. Lowe in *The Beneventan Script* (1914), pp. 13, 14.

[1] *Receuil des Actes de Ducs de Normandie*, ed. M. Fauroux (1961); H. W. C. Davis, *Regesta Regum Anglo Normannorum*, vol. I (1913).

[2] For a summary list of some of these see Douglas, *William the Conqueror*, pp. 430–4.

[3] See for instance, *Codice Diplomatico Brindisiano*, vol. I (1940) ed. Annibale de Leo; *Codice diplomatico normanno di Aversa* ed. A. Gallo, 1926; and above all *Codice Diplomatico Barese*, 18 vols. (1897–1950). The *Codex Diplomaticus Cavensis*, 8 vols. (1873–93) only reached the second quarter of the eleventh century, but several important charters relating to the Norman age will be found, in the Appendix to P. Guillaume, *Essai historique sur l'abbaye de Cava* (1877). For Sicily see in the first instance the works of C. A. Garufi, and R. Starrabba listed below.

[4] For these see in particular J. M. Watterich, *Pontificum Romanorum vitae*, vol. I (1862).

[5] P. Jaffé, *Regesta Pontificum Romanorum* (1851). This was re-issued in an augmented form in 1885, and it is here cited as 'Jaffé-Loewenfeld' from that edition. For the period 1050–1100 over sixteen hundred items are listed.

[6] P. H. Kehr, *Regesta Pontificum Romannorum*. Kehr classified his documents not (like Jaffé) according to time but under the regions or institutions to which they particularly refer. For this study the relevant volume is *Italia Pontificia*, vol. VIII: *Regnum Normannorum-Campania* (1935).

[7] Here cited from the edition by P. Jaffé with the title of *Monumenta Gregoriana* (1865).

official collection.[1] The bulls of Pope Urban II are also of particular value.[2]

The bare citation of selected items may at least indicate that the contemporary testimony relating to Norman history between 1050 and 1100 is abundant, and as the twelfth century advanced it was to be rapidly supplemented by narratives which could further serve to check the earlier evidence. The great history of Ordericus Vitalis[3] was completed by 1141, and in it the two great streams of earlier Norman historiography seem to meet, since Ordericus used as sources, for instance, not only William of Poitiers but also Geoffrey Malaterra, and if he approached history from the Norman standpoint he never forgot his own early upbringing in England. At the same time, much work was being produced in England itself by men such as William of Malmesbury[4] and Eadmer[5] whose narratives have a special bearing on Norman enterprise during the previous generations. In the south as well the same process was taking place. The Norman achievement in the Mediterranean is, speaking generally, only sparsely illustrated in the Arabic and Greek sources, but there is one notable exception. About 1140 Anna Comnena, the Byzantine princess, as an old woman produced her notable work on the history of the eastern empire in the time of her father the Emperor Alexis I, namely the *Alexiad*.[6] Though this lively narrative has not always escaped criticism, Anna Comnena had certainly much information to impart about the Normans of the eleventh century,[7] and as a corrective to the earlier panegyrists her words are of particular value since she wrote about the Normans not as a friend but as an enemy.

A man interested in the causes and consequences of the Norman achievement between 1050 and 1100 and conscious of its importance, has assuredly no reason to complain of lack of material for his study. Undoubtedly, the testimony is often difficult to interpret, but its very bulk may perhaps serve as an excuse for a comparative investigation of the common characteristics exhibited in all the enterprises under-

---

[1] On the character and importance of this famous register see R. L. Poole, *Papal Chancery* (1915), pp. 122–7.

[2] These may be conveniently consulted in *Pat. Lat.*, vol. CLI.

[3] Ed. A. Le Prévost and L. Delisle, 5 vols. (Paris 1838–55).

[4] In particular his *Gesta Regum* (ed. W. Stubbs) 2 vols. (1887).

[5] *Historia Novorum* ed. M. Rule (1884); *Vita Anselmi* ed. R. W. Southern (1962).

[6] Ed. B. Leib; *Collection Budé*, 3 vols. (Paris, 1937–45). Also in translation, in *The Alexiad of the Princess Anna Comnena*, translated by E. A. S. Dawes (London 1928; re-issued 1967).

[7] Cf. Runciman, *Crusades*, I, pp. 327, 328.

taken with such surprising success by the Normans at this time. Such an inquiry might also help to explain the highly individual and powerful impact which the Normans made on the politics of the whole of Christendom, and the distinct influence they exercised on the later development of all the countries they conquered.

Chapter 2

WHO WERE THE NORMANS?

I

No province in Europe is better known in England than Normandy.
Directly facing the English coast from Kent to Dorset, from Folkestone
to Poole, its development has for long been closely associated with that
of England, its countryside is similar in appearance to our own, and its
cities such as Rouen and Caen, Bayeux, Dieppe and Cherbourg, are
familiar names north of the Channel. Yet this very familiarity with
modern Normandy might easily convey a false impression of the province from which the eleventh-century Normans came. This region of
northern France does not derive its unity from geographical circumstances, and medieval Normandy could be better described as a creation of history than of nature. Even today the land frontiers of Normandy are inconspicuous. The Bresle and the Epte on the east, the
Sélune and the Couesnon on the west, even the Avre on the south, do
not provide well marked boundaries; nor is there any physical uniformity in the area which they enclose. The open countryside of orchards
and cornfields characteristic of eastern Normandy could be contrasted
with the more rugged landscape of the *Bocage normand*, and the great
river of the Seine linking Rouen to Paris, and Le Havre to the centre of
France, cuts into two a province which Nature seems to have conspired
to divide.

It was perhaps the Roman administrators who first determined that
the north-facing coastal sweep from Eu to Barfleur might form the sea-
frontier of a single province. Certainly they here established within
Gaul the province of Lugdunensis Secunda – the second Lyonnaise –
and this, later to be the province of Neustria in the Carolingian Empire,
was to survive in the ecclesiastical province of Rouen with its six dependent bishoprics of Bayeux, Avranches and Évreux, Sées, Lisieux and
Coutances. From Roman times, therefore, this region had been held
together for centuries as an administrative, a governmental and an
ecclesiastical unity, when about the beginning of the tenth century it

22

began to be given a more individual character under the influence of men from overseas. Carolingian Neustria had suffered cruelly from the Viking raids on western Christendom, and it was to receive settlers from the North, by way of the Seine and the Loire, as a result of the out-pouring from the Scandinavian lands which took place at that time. The distinct history of medieval Normandy is thus often held to have begun with these events, and in particular on the occasion when one of these Vikings leaders named Rolf was established as a ruler in Neustria by the Emperor Charles III.

Rolf[1] (whose name was later Gallicized as Rollo) came originally from Norway, and after a long career of depredation, particularly in Ireland, he entered France by the estuary of the Loire. He fought his way north-eastward until in 911 he was defeated in a pitched battle out-side the walls of Chartres by the troops of the reigning Emperor Charles III. Thereupon, Rolf accepted baptism from the archbishop of Rouen in token of submission, and before 918 he and his followers had been granted lands by the emperor in the valley of the Lower Seine. The original grants were confined to an area centred upon Rouen and bounded by the Epte and Avre, the Bresle, the Dives and the sea. Only in the time of Rolf's son, William 'Longsword', was the rule of the family extended beyond the Orne, and in 933 as far as the Couesnon. By this time, however, the new Viking dynasty was firmly established in Gaul, and it was to hold the Norman future in its hands. All the same, it is pertinent to inquire what these events really implied, and how far this Scandinavian settlement determined the character and social structure of the country which was later to be Normandy.

There is considerable evidence to suggest that changes took place in Neustria at this time, and in such a manner as to affect the eleventh century future.[2] Later chroniclers such as Dudo of St Quentin and William of Jumièges assert that a considerable depopulation then occurred.[3] Much exaggeration may here be suspected but when all allowances have been made there can still be no doubt that Neustria suffered much damage at this time, and new bands of invaders con-tinued to come into the province during the central decades of the tenth century. Certainly, too, the ecclesiastical life of the province was

[1] On him see Douglas in *Eng. Hist. Rev.*, LVII (1942), pp. 417–43.
[2] M. de Bouard, 'De la Neustrie carolingien a la Normandie féodale' (*Bull. Inst. Hist. Research.*, XXVII, pp. 1–14).
[3] Dudo of St Quentin, ed. J. Lair, p. 166; William of Jumièges, ed. Marx., pp. 8, 66.

then so disrupted that the episcopal succession was impaired. No less than five bishops of Coutances were forced to reside in Rouen, and the region, once so famous for its monasteries, was for a space completely denuded of religious houses. Evidently the immediate consequences of the Scandinavian raids on Neustria were often violent, and the damage they inflicted was not easily repaired.

The new ruling dynasty itself seems at first to have relinquished somewhat reluctantly the traditions of its Viking past and Rolf perhaps reverted to paganism before his death; and a pagan reaction took place in western Normandy after the murder of Rolf's son, William Longsword, in 942. Subsequently a chronicler from Rheims could refer to Rolf's grandson, Duke Richard I as *piratarum dux*, a 'pirate chief', and as late as 1013 William the Conqueror's grandfather, Duke Richard II of Normandy, styled 'the Good', could welcome at Rouen a Viking host which had recently ravaged Brittany. The puzzling dichotomy that runs through so much of Norman history in the eleventh century was here in fact displayed. It was perhaps surprising that Duke Richard II should have received the pagan raiders in Rouen, but it is scarcely less significant that during their sojourn by the Seine one of their leaders named Olaf was converted to Christianity and baptised by Robert, the worldly archbishop of Rouen who was himself brother to the reigning Duke[1] Olaf, who later succeeded to the kingdom of Norway, and was in due course to become the patron saint of the Scandinavian world.

The Scandinavian factor in the making of eleventh-century Normandy is not to be ignored. But it was never predominant, and it would be easy to over-emphasize the break which the events of the tenth century made with the past. A Viking dynasty had in truth been set up in this region of Gaul, but the extent of its dominion had been determined by the limits of the old Roman province which had survived as the ecclesiastical province of Rouen. In such a way were the frontiers of ducal Normandy established. Correspondingly, its rulers, converted to Christianity, and recognized by the imperial power, were from the first to claim administrative and fiscal rights, which had previously pertained to counts in the Carolingian empire. Again, the place-names of Normandy suggest that the peasant population had not been radically changed in character by any large-scale migration from Scandinavia, and it has been shown that on many large estates in the province, continuity of tenure proceeded without substantial interruption throughout

[1] Richer of Rheims, ed. Waitz, 1877, p. 180; William of Jumièges, pp. 85, 96.

the tenth century.[1] It is, in short, unlikely that men from the north ever constituted more than a minority of the inhabitants of the province which was soon to be called Normandy.

Of course, a new ruling class from Scandinavia had been established, but these men themselves rapidly became absorbed in the surrounding Latin and Christian culture of France. In the words of an early chronicler: 'they received the Christian faith and forsaking the language of their fathers they accustomed themselves to Latin speech'.[2] And we know that by 1025 Scandinavian speech had already become obsolete in Rouen though it still persisted in Bayeux.[3] At the same time trade and ideas crossed over the little rivers which formed the boundaries of Normandy, and up and down the great waterway of the Seine. The process could in fact be widely illustrated, but the conclusion to which the evidence points is clear. When full allowance is made for the intensely individual character of the Normans in the eleventh century, it remains true that the conquests which they made between 1050 and 1100 were made by men who were French in their language, in the rudiments of their culture and in most of their political ideas.

They were themselves conscious of this, and even prone to exaggerate its significance. The extent to which the Norman rulers of Neustria early aspired to be the champions of Latin Christendom was celebrated by them in epic verse before the end of the tenth century; and just as at a later date, the Norman Richard of Capua could style himself 'Prince of the French and the Lombards', so also was William the Conqueror as ruler of Normandy and England wont to address his continental subjects as *Franci*.[4] This, indeed, was to become part of the Norman convention; and when in 1096 Bohemund, son of Robert Guiscard, appealed to his fellow Normans in Italy to join the Crusade, he was made by a contemporary to say;

> Are we not Franks? Did not our fathers come from France and have we not made ourselves masters here by force of arms? It would be a disgrace

[1] See in particular, L. Musset, 'Les Domaines de l'époque franque et les destinée du régime domainiale de IXe à XI siécle' (*Bull. Soc. des Antiquaires de Normandie*, XLIX, pp. 7–97).

[2] Adémar of Chabannes, ed. Chavanon, p. 148.

[3] Dudo of St Quentin, ed. Lair, p. 221.

[4] *Regesta*, I, *passim*; Cahen, *Régime féodale*, p. 36; cf. Douglas in *French Studies*, XIV, p. 110. The matter is sufficiently significant to be given precise illustration. The style constantly used by the Norman princes of Capua, that is to say Richard I (1058–1078), and Jordan I (1078–1093), who had supplanted the Lombard dynasty, is '*Francorum* et Langobardorum princeps'. This is strictly analogous with the normal address of William the Conqueror as King 'omnibus fidelibus suis *Francis* et Anglis'.

if our brothers and kinsfolk went without us to martyrdom, and to Paradise.[1]

The distinction between the Vikings of the tenth century and the Normans of the eleventh could hardly be set out more clearly, and the rhetoric of the reporter certainly reflected the truth. The individual character of medieval Normandy can be properly ascribed to the absorption of Scandinavian invaders into a region of Gaul, and for this reason the Normans cannot be equated with the inhabitants of any other of the French provinces. On the other hand the Normans, as they appeared to Europe between 1050 and 1100, are for all their ruthless violence to be sharply distinguished from the 'Northmen' who at an earlier date had brought a pagan terror to the West.

This transformation must be taken into account in assessing the Norman impact upon the lands they conquered, and its consequences may perhaps be detected in earlier estimates that were made of the Norman character. The Normans, says one of these, are 'a restless people'. 'They are a turbulent race' says another, 'and unless restrained by firm rule they are always ready for mischief'.[2] But the most notable description comes from the eleventh-century Italian narrative of Geoffrey Malaterra:

> The Normans – he remarks – are a cunning and revengeful people; eloquence and dissimulation appear to be their hereditary qualities; they can stoop to flatter; but unless they are curbed by the restraint of law they indulge the licentiousness of nature and passion. Their princes affect the praise of popular munificence; the people blend the extremes of avarice and prodigality, and in their eager thirst of wealth and dominion, they despise whatever they possess and hope whatever they desire. Arms and horses, the luxury of dress, the exercises of hunting and hawking, are the delight of the Normans; but on pressing occasions they can endure with incredible patience the inclemency of every climate and the toil and abstinence of a military life.[3]

To this sufficient description need only be added the amplification of Ordericus Vitalis who concludes:

> When under the rule of a strong master the Normans are a most valiant people, excelling all others in the skill with which they meet difficulties and strive to conquer every enemy. But in all other circumstances they rend each other, and bring ruin upon themselves.[4]

[1] Robert the Monk, II, c. 2.   [2] Ord. Vit., III, pp. 230, 474.
[3] Malaterra, I, c. 3, as paraphrased by Edward Gibbon, *Decline and Fall*, ed. Bury, VI, p. 179.   [4] Ord. Vit., III, p. 230.

It was true: and the statement emphasizes how fortunate
Normans during the period of their greatest achievements to
the direction of men who, with all their vices, possessed such e
capacities for leadership as were to be exhibited, for instance,
William the Conqueror, Robert Guiscard, Roger, count of Sicily, or
Bohemund of Taranto. Certainly, plunder remained a constant, and a
deplorable feature of Norman conquests whether they were undertaken
in England or Italy or Sicily or Syria. But no one who considers the
progress of these conquests, the propaganda which was used to justify
them, or the results which they entailed, can possibly acquiesce in a
theory that the Norman political achievement can be explained simply
by reference to a lust for plunder. Once again, the distinction between
the Vikings of the eighth century, and the Normans of the eleventh is
emphasized.

The character of Normandy in the brief period of Norman expansion
had in fact been conditioned by developments in the province during
the tenth century, and these were not to be concluded until the eleventh
century was well advanced.[1] Norman power for instance was to derive
in large measure from a notable feudal aristocracy, and from a reformed
and vigorous Church. The former provided the sinews of Norman
strength, and the latter determined much of Norman policy. But both
these movements had in 1050 only lately taken effect in the duchy. Of
the great feudal families which between 1070 and 1100 were to attain
power in Italy and Sicily, and to provide a new aristocracy for England,
few, indeed, can be traced back before the first quarter of the eleventh
century. And it was the same with the reforming movement in the
Norman Church. The earliest evidence that the Norman episcopate had
been reconstituted after its disintegration comes from a charter of 990,
and though certain monasteries had been established earlier, the great
monastic revival in the duchy took place after that date. The results
of both these developments, the secular and the ecclesiastical, were,
however, to be rapidly disclosed. Between 1020 and 1050 a wholesale
and violent re-distribution of landed property in the duchy provided
Normandy with a warrior aristocracy whose acts were sensibly to
affect the history of Europe for a hundred years. And an ecclesiastical
province which in 1065 could be represented by men of such
contrasted distinction as Odo, bishop of Bayeux, Geoffrey, bishop of
Coutances, Herluin, abbot of Le Bec, Lanfranc the future archbishop of

[1] Douglas, 'Rise of Normandy' (*Proc. Brit. Acad.*), XXXIII (1947), pp. 113–30.

Canterbury and the young St Anselm was most certainly not to be ignored.

The accession of strength which derived from these developments was enhanced by the fact that they were closely connected. The Norman episcopate for example was largely representative of the greater Norman families and the Norman aristocracy in its turn provided the chief patrons of the new Norman monasteries. Over all was the controlling authority of the ducal dynasty which was in due course to reach a climax during the Norman reign of Duke William II, the future conqueror of England.[1] Here too, however, it is necessary not to antedate what occurred. William was a direct descendant of Rolf the Viking after seven generations. But he was a bastard son of Duke Robert I, and he succeeded precariously to his inheritance in 1035 when a child of some six years old after his young father had died on pilgrimage to Jerusalem. William's own boyhood was in fact spent in lethal peril in a bloodstained court, while Normandy was threatened with progressive anarchy. In 1047 he narrowly escaped destruction from a rebellion in the west of the duchy which was suppressed after the battle of Val-ès-Dunes near Caen, but between 1047 and 1054 William had none the less to wage with little intermission a war for survival against his enemies within the Duchy, and his foes outside it such as the count of Anjou and the king of France. Indeed, he cannot have felt fully secure until after the invading troops of the French king had been defeated in 1054 at Mortemer; and in 1060 death removed both Geoffrey Martel of Anjou, and King Henry I of France who had been the duke's chief rivals in Gaul.

Ever since 1047, in fact, the prestige and the power of Duke William had been steadily growing. A strong party in the duchy was beginning to attach itself to his personal fortunes, and the results of his own constructive statesmanship were now to appear. William was beginning to identify the interests of the new aristocracy with his own, and he was starting to intervene constructively in the affairs of the Norman Church. A remarkable concentration of political power was thus achieved. By 1050 the consolidation of a dynasty, the reform of the Church, and the formation of a notable secular aristocracy were being fused together by a political genius to provide the overmastering strength of a unique province during the greatest period of Norman achievement.

The wide expansion of Norman power between 1050 and 1100 thus

[1] Douglas, *William the Conqueror*, pp. 53–159.

took place at the same time as the Norman character was becoming finally formed, and at the same time also as the Norman duchy was itself undergoing cultural change and political development. That fact may indeed go some way to account for some of the variations of Norman action in the areas which were chosen for its operation. The first Anglo-Norman contacts were made when Normandy was very different from the province which confronted England in 1066. Similarly, the earliest Norman adventurers in Italy during the period 1015–1035 will be found in many respects to resemble their Viking ancestors more closely than the Normans of the succeeding generation. The earlier development of Normandy (which was barely completed in 1050) also goes far to explain why it was that England, Italy and Sicily were to be the chief zones of Norman enterprise in the eleventh century.

II

The great expeditions from Scandinavia in the tenth and early eleventh century had forged between Normandy and England a political link from which neither could escape. In Gaul they established the Viking dynasty: in England they planted those settlements in Lincolnshire, the northern Midlands and East Anglia, which made the Danelaw (as it was called) a distinct social unity within England. The Danelaw might in fact be termed the English Normandy, whilst Normandy (though never so thoroughly colonized) might be described as the French Danelaw. For the same reason, the kings of the English during this period, faced with the problem of maintaining authority over their reluctant Scandinavian subjects, could never be indifferent to the policy across the Channel of the successors of Rolf the Viking. The mutual interests of the two dynasties were to be recognized early. In 991 a pact between them was ratified at Rouen under papal sponsorship. And in 1002 there took place the momentous marriage between Ethelred II, king of the English, and Emma, daughter of Duke Richard I of Normandy.[1] This dynastic alliance was only important so far as it symbolized political realities but these it reflected with remarkable fidelity. It deserves some emphasis that the son of Ethelred and Emma, King Edward the Confessor, who died in 1066, and William the Conqueror who became king of the English in the same year, had a common ancestor in Richard the Fearless, duke of Normandy.

[1] A.S. Chron., 'C', s.a. 1002.

The dynastic web which was beginning to be formed early in the eleventh century was soon to be given fresh significance. In 1013 Sweyn Forkbeard, king of Denmark, launched his last great invasion of England and so successful was he that Ethelred together with Emma and their two sons Edward and Alfred were forced to fly from England to take refuge at the Norman Court of Emma's brother. It was thus from Normandy that Ethelred later returned to England to fight his last and unavailing war against Sweyn's son, Cnut the Great. He died in 1016 and before the end of that year Cnut was established as king in England. When therefore, within a few months of his accession, Emma astutely married Cnut, the event concerned Normandy scarcely less than England. Emma was to remain strongly Scandinavian in sympathy until her death in 1052, and her influence on affairs was never negligible. Herself the consort for a time of the lord of a great Scandinavian empire, she was later to see reigning in England first Harthacnut, her son by Cnut, and then Edward, her son by Ethelred. By her career and through her connexions she formed a link between many of the personalities involved in the Anglo-Norman crisis of the eleventh century.[1]

Many of the special features of that crisis were already beginning to be disclosed. Cnut died in 1035 and was succeeded by his short-lived sons Harold and Harthacnut. Then in 1042 Edward the Confessor, son of Ethelred, who was still in Normandy managed to secure the English succession, and the Norman dynasty inevitably felt itself to some extent committed to his cause. Even at this date, moreover, there were beginning to appear those bitter personal animosities which imparted an element of personal tragedy to so much of Anglo-Norman history in this age. Edward owed his succession in England largely to the efforts of Godwine, the powerful earl of Wessex, and as the price of his support the king had been compelled to marry Edith the earl's daughter. But only six years before Godwine had been involved in one of the most spectacular crimes of the age: a murder which most closely affected the new king in England. In 1036 Alfred, Edward's younger brother, had come to England, and while in this country he had been seized, blinded, and brutally killed. The crime if not instigated by Godwine was undoubtedly connived at by him,[2] and it would seem that Edward the Confessor always regarded as his brother's murderer the earl on whom

---

[1] On everything connected with Emma, see A. Campbell's edition of *Encomium Emmae* (1949).
[2] A. S. Chron., 'C', s.a. 1036; Campbell, *op. cit.*, p. 63.

he was so often forced to be dependent.[1] In these circumstances it is understandable that the first ten years of the reign of Edward the Confessor should have been coloured by personal hatreds and marked by political tensions.

It was inevitable too that these should be reflected in Anglo-Norman relations. The pro-Norman sentiments of Edward the Confessor may have been exaggerated by some modern historians, but he was always fully conscious of the advantages he might gain from his earlier contacts with Normandy, especially during the earlier years of his reign when he was beset by problems of great danger and difficulty. He had supplanted the Danish dynasty which had deposed his father, and he was always threatened by an invasion from Scandinavia.[2] Scarcely less formidable were Edward's difficulties in dealing with his own magnates. Powerful comital dynasties were forming in England. Godwine, earl of Wessex (who survived until 1053) and his sons Harold and Tosti (who perished in 1066) were to play a large part in English history. And in the Midlands, Leofric was to be succeeded as earl of Mercia in 1057 by his son Ælfgar, whilst his grandsons, Edwin and Morcar, were to be prominent in the drama of 1066. From 1042 onwards it was perhaps only the endless rivalries between these families which prevented them from overwhelming the monarchy itself.

In these circumstances it was natural that Edward should seek support from the Normans, but his policy on introducing Normans into his kingdom was not wholly original, since not a few Normans had followed his mother, Emma, into England after 1002.[3] It will moreover be recalled, that the duke and his greater followers in Normandy were, between 1042 and 1066, too fully occupied in maintaining their position at home to be able to pay much attention to England. As a consequence, Edward's early courts, like those of his immediate predecessors remained strongly Scandinavian in composition, and few of the laymen who came to England from France in these years were of the first rank. In the Church, however, the situation was different. Important bishoprics in England were given to men from overseas, and particularly to Normans. One of these, Robert, abbot of Jumièges, was made bishop of London about 1044, and speedily became very influential in the councils of the king.[4] In 1051 he was promoted to the metropolitan see of

[1] Douglas, *op. cit.*, pp. 412–13.
[2] A.S. Chron., 'D' and 'E' for 1047 and 1048.
[3] R. L. G. Ritchie, *The Normans in England before Edward the Confessor* (Exeter, 1948).
[4] *Vita Edwardi*, ed. Barlow, pp. 17–23.

Canterbury, and this appointment precipitated the great crisis of the Confessor's reign. In that year, and probably for that reason, Godwine earl of Wessex, feeling that his own influence was diminishing, launched an open rebellion. Siward and Leofric, however, came to the king's support, and civil war was thus narrowly averted. But Godwine and his sons were forced into exile, leaving the king for the first time in unrestricted control of his kingdom.[1]

If the conditions prevailing in England at the end of 1051 had been allowed to continue it is even possible that the developing connexion between England and Normandy might have crystallized peaceably into a political union between them. For about this time Edward the Confessor, who was childless, and would evidently remain so, seems to have nominated William duke of Normandy as his heir. It is unlikely that, as has often been supposed, the duke came over in person to receive the grant. More probably the promise was conveyed to him by Robert of Jumièges who between mid-Lent and June 1051 passed through Normandy on the way to Rome to receive from the pope his *pallium* as archbishop of Canterbury.[2] Whether this is so or not, is perhaps immaterial since the royal victory in England was speedily followed by a reaction. Godwine and his sons effected their return to England by force and had the king at their mercy. The Norman party in England was suppressed and most of its leaders driven from the country.[3]

Among these was Robert of Jumièges, who was now replaced as archbishop of Canterbury by a protegé of Earl Godwine, named Stigand, who was bishop of Winchester. As a result the primate of England was from 1052, until after the advent of the Normans, to be a man who was unrecognized as a legitimate metropolitan either at Rome or throughout much of western Christendom. This was to have a considerable bearing upon later Norman propaganda, but in 1052 it made little difference to the English situation. For the rest of Edward's reign the family of Godwine was dominant in England. Ever conscious of its own interests this family was naturally utterly hostile to the Normans, and ever wary also of the reviving Scandinavian claims to the throne of England. Soon too its ambitions were to be yet further enhanced. In 1053 Godwine was succeeded as earl of Wessex by his son Harold, and after the mysterious death four years later of Edward the

---

[1] A.S. Chron., 'C', 'D' and 'E' for this year.
[2] Douglas in *Eng. Hist. Rev.*, LXVIII (1953), pp. 526–45.
[3] A.S. Chron., 'D' and 'E' for 1052.

Atheling, the grandson of Ethelred II, who might on grounds of heredity be considered the Confessor's heir,[1] this same Harold, already the most powerful man in England, must have begun to think of himself as the future king. Thus already by 1057 all the parties most concerned in the approaching crisis were moving into position. Already the fundamental questions were being posed. They could only be answered by war.

The fates of Normandy and England were now inextricably intertwined, and it only remains to add that the realm to which Norman policy was being inexorably directed was one of the most interesting kingdoms in western Europe. Some of the changes which for good or ill were to be wrought by the Normans on the social and cultural life of England will hereafter be noted, but already in the middle of the eleventh century, Anglo-Saxon England was rich in an extensive trade and her political structure was in many ways noteworthy. The operation of the local courts of shire and hundred, and the connexion of these with the monarchy reflected administrative progress, and so, if judged by the standards of the time, did the fiscal system by which the royal taxes were collected. Furthermore there were at least some representative people in Edward the Confessor's England who seem to have been conscious of an overriding English unity which sectional interests should not be allowed to disturb or destroy. When for instance in 1051 the forces of the king and Earl Godwine confronted each other in Gloucestershire, it is said that all in the royal host were ready to attack the rebel earl if the king wished it, but

> Some of them thought it would be a piece of great folly if they joined battle because in the two hosts there was most of what was noblest in England, and they considered it would be opening a way for our enemies to enter the country and cause great ruin among ourselves.[2]

These isolated statements cannot be ignored. On the other hand, such sentiments found little expression in the political history of England in the time of Edward the Confessor. England was continually vexed by the struggles among the earls, whilst the intense social individualism of the Danelaw was always liable to be reflected in the support of invaders from overseas. In fact it would be easy to overestimate the degree of political unity in pre-conquest England. There were pronounced weaknesses in the Old English state, and these were to be exploited by the

[1] A.S. Chron., 'D', s.a. 1057, and see below, Genealogy 6.
[2] *Ibid.*

Normans. But here was a country in which civil war was 'hateful' to at least some of its inhabitants and where the monarchy enjoyed high prestige, though in varying degrees, throughout the land. It was against such a political structure, and against such loyalties that Norman power was soon to be stretched across the Channel. For this reason the Norman impact upon England, already inevitable in 1050, was, when it came, of a special nature, and it was to entail complex and sometimes surprising results.

III

The other great area of Norman enterprise during the latter half of the eleventh century had likewise been indicated by the previous history of Normandy. But there the conditions were wholly different. The conquests of the Normans in southern Italy and in Sicily were achieved not in a realm unified by ancient traditions but in a region in which past history had created a bewildering number of competing states and contending authorities.[1] The eastern emperor, for instance, claimed from Constantinople to be supreme in the peninsular south of Rome or more precisely south of a line which might be drawn roughly from Termoli to Terracina. But within this area there were Lombard principalities such as Benevento, Capua and Salerno, while city states based upon the sea were established under 'dukes' at Naples, Gaeta and Amalfi. Finally, the whole region was subject to the continuing aspirations of the western emperor from north of the Alps, and to the claims of the see of Rome to hegemony over the whole Church. And over all hung the Saracen threat which was centred in Sicily, now under Moslem rule.

In this confusion, the strongest power in southern Italy during the first quarter of the eleventh century was undoubtedly the eastern empire,[2] whose authority was exercised from Bari by officials who were usually styled *catepans*, and who provided a stable administration based on the old imperial principles. The influence of Constantinople and of the Hellenic east was thus inevitably very powerful throughout all the southern part of the peninsular. In Calabria, and in the region round

---

[1] Chalandon, *Domination normande*, I, pp. 1–41; Jamison in *Papers of the British School at Rome*, VI, pp. 211–20.

[2] Cf. J. Gay, *L'Italie, méridionale et l'empire byzantine*, pp. 366–431. Even at the end of the eleventh century The 'Emperor' for a writer such as William of Apulia is always the Eastern Emperor: the emperors north of the Alps were for him 'Kings of the Germans'.

Otranto, Greek speech and Greek administration was accepted as normal, and these provinces could be regarded as integral parts of the Greek world. Elsewhere, too, Greek culture had spread. In southern Apulia it was dominant, and much of that province was directly under the control of the Greek capital of Bari. Even the Lombard principalities, where resistance to Byzantium was strong, were not unaffected, and throughout southern Italy, and particularly in the mercantile city states, Greek influence was strengthened by trade. Part of the achievement of the eastern emperors in the half century before 1025 had been to make the Adriatic reasonably safe for Christian shipping, and ports such as Bari, Brindisi and Otranto, and to a lesser extent those of Amalfi and Naples had access to the eastern shores of that sea where they could make contact with the *Via Egnatia* which ran from Durazzo to Constantinople itself.

The Byzantine preponderance in southern Italy was however challenged at this time from two quarters. The Greek and Latin traditions in this area were delicately balanced. Outside Calabria, Otranto and southern Apulia, the whole country tended to look to Rome for inspiration, and Roman influence could always be expressed most effectively in an ecclesiastical form. Constantinople might exercise authority over the metropolitan sees of Reggio and Otranto, and there had been a multiplication of Greek monasteries in Calabria. But the Latin rite was dominant through most of Apulia, in the Lombard principalities, and at Naples, Gaeta and Amalfi. Here was, in fact, what might be called the southern bastion of the Latin Church, and its importance was enhanced by the fact that it contained two of the most revered shrines of Latin Christendom: Monte Cassino the home of Benedictine monachism, and Monte Gargano to which pilgrims came from all over the West to do homage to St Michael. Finally, in close proximity was Rome itself. At the beginning of the eleventh century the papacy had not yet emerged from the political decadence into which it had been plunged, but it could call to loyalties far wider and deeper than those involved in the rivalries between the south Italian states. Rome – and those who spoke for Rome – had never ceased to claim authority over the whole Church.

The other challenge to Byzantium during the first quarter of the eleventh century came from Islam. The failure of the Macedonian emperors to retake Sicily was here of capital importance. As a consequence Byzantium found itself faced in the peninsula with an alien and hostile power that not only held Sicily, but also exercised a large measure of control over the Tyrrhenian Sea. At this time Sardinia and Corsica were also in Moslem hands, as were numerous harbours, such as Fréjus, on the coast of Provence. Hardly surprisingly therefore southern Italy was constantly subject to Moslem raids which impaired the authority of the Eastern Empire, gave opportunity to its rivals, and opened the possibility that some other power might intervene to claim in this area the function of the protector of Christendom. It was precisely these circumstances which were to impart permanent importance to the Norman intervention in the Mediterranean lands.

IV

During the first quarter of the eleventh century however, all this had still to be disclosed. What was immediately apparent, and widely known in Normandy through the tales of pilgrims and other travellers, was that the political instability of southern Italy offered a great opportunity to armed and unscrupulous adventurers. It is, therefore, perhaps not necessary to look much further for an explanation of the earliest arrivals of the Normans in Italy. Over-population at home has also been suggested as a contributory cause, but the case of the famous family of Tancred of Hauteville, which is usually here cited as evidence, is perhaps capable of other explanations. Tancred, who was a minor landowner in the Cotentin had at least twelve legitimate sons besides a number of daughters;[1] and a small squire of such philoprogenitive tastes might, in any age or place, have found it difficult to provide for all his offspring at home. Normandy may well have been over-populated at the beginning of the eleventh century[2] and Norman expansion was certainly stimulated by economic pressures. But an equally compelling cause of the coming of the first Normans to Italy can be found in the earlier political and social history of the duchy. There are good reasons for believing that many of the Normans who first came to Italy belonged to families which had suffered in the fierce struggles which marked the rise at this time of the new feudal aristocracy in Normandy, and the great redistribution of landed wealth which this entailed. Many of them, also, and perhaps for the same reason, left the duchy out of fear for the duke and in his despite.

[1] Chalandon, *op. cit.*, I, pp. 81, 82 and see below, Genealogy 2.
[2] Amatus, I, cc. 1 and 2.

Everything connected with the earliest intrusion of the Normans into Italian politics is obscure,[1] but it is reasonably certain that it occurred during a revolt against the Byzantine government of Apulia which broke out in 1009 under the leadership of Meles, a Lombard notable of Bari, and which was not suppressed until 1018. After some initial successes, Meles, it seems, was forced to fly from Bari. He took refuge with Guaimar IV the Lombard prince of Salerno, and in due course found himself at Capua.[2] According to Leo of Ostia[3] it was while Meles was in that city that:

> there came to Capua about forty Normans. These had fled from the anger of the Count of Normandy, and they were now with many of their fellows moving about the countryside in the hope that they might find someone who would be ready to employ them. For they were sturdy men and well set up and also most skilled in the use of arms. The names of their leaders were *Gilbertus Butericus, Rodulfus Todinensis, Goismannus* and *Stigandus*.

Leo wrote about the end of the eleventh century, and he was in close touch with earlier material available at the monastery of Monte Cassino. His account may therefore command considerable confidence.

It can moreover be confirmed in large measure by the testimony of two writers who, although they lived outside Italy, were contemporary with these events and had opportunity for getting to know about them. These were Adémar of Chabannes and Rodulf Glaber.[4] The statement of Adémar runs as follows:

> When Normandy was ruled by Richard, the son of Richard, count of Rouen (i.e. Duke Richard II of Normandy, 996–1026) a large number of Normans under the leadership of Rodulf came armed to Rome, and afterwards with the encouragement of Pope Benedict (i.e. Benedict VIII, 1012–1034) they attacked Apulia, and laid everything waste.[5]

[1] In what here follows I am particularly indebted to the remarkable article of Einar Joranson 'The Inception of the Career of the Normans in Italy', *Speculum*, XXIII (1948), pp. 353–96.

[2] Chalandon, *op. cit.*, I, pp. 42–57.

[3] *Chron. Mon. Casinensis*, bk I, c. 37 (*Mon. Germ. Hist. SS.*, VII, p. 652, note 'a'). This is usually considered as being from the first recension of this chronicle which was written by Leo himself, with reference to earlier materials and during the last decade of the eleventh century.

[4] Adémar finished his history before 1034, and Glaber apparently before 1044. They were both therefore alive when the revolt of Meles occurred, though one lived in Aquitaine and the other in Burgundy. Glaber is a most untrustworthy writer, but in this matter he may have received information from Odilo abbot of Cluny who made a pilgrimage to Monte Cassino in or about 1023.

[5] Ed. Chevanon, p. 178.

It is admirably concise, and Rodulf Glaber who is far more verbose is clearly alluding to the same incident when he says:

> A certain Norman named Rodulf, a man of bravery and prowess, who had incurred the displeasure of Count Richard ... came to Rome to state his case before Pope Benedict. The Pope struck by his noble and martial bearing complained to him of the invasion of the Roman empire by the Greeks ... Rodulf then offered to make war on the Greeks provided he had the support of the Italians ... The Pope therefore addressed himself to the magnates of the region of Benevento bidding them put themselves under Rodulf's orders ... This being done Rodulf made war on the Greeks. He killed many of them and took much booty.[1]

This Rodulf is probably the same as the Rodulf *Todinensis* in Leo's account, and he is usually believed to be Rodulf II of Tosny, head of an important family in central Normandy.[2] In any case the men he led must surely have been represented among the Normans who according to Leo came to Capua (in the region of Benevento) and whom Meles took into his service. In May 1017 he led them into Apulia where his rebellion (perhaps by reason of their support) now met with such success that almost all Apulia passed into his hands.[3] But the central government at Constantinople was at last ready to act. An organized force was mobilized against the rebels, and inflicted a bloody defeat upon them at Canne in June, 1018.[4]

Such is the bare narrative of these events which can be derived from contemporary or nearly contemporary chronicles. But two traditions, widely current both in Normandy and Italy at a later date, associate the advent of the Normans in the peninsular with the return of Norman pilgrims from Jerusalem. The former of these traditions[5] records with varying details that a group of such pilgrims when on their way home arrived at Salerno while the city was being besieged by the Saracens whom they put to flight. On their return to Normandy they were

[1] Ed. Prou, pp. 52–3.

[2] See below, pp. 123, 124. Some confirmation of this identification is perhaps to be obtained from a Sens chronicle (*Rec. Hist. Franc.*, X, pp. 25, 26) which describes the exploits of a Count Rodulf who started on a pilgrimage to Jerusalem but when returning through Apulia was persuaded to stop and fight against the Greeks. It is added that this Rodulf had a son who fought in Spain. As a matter of fact Rodulf of Tosny did have a son named Roger who fought in Spain and, in due course brought back relics of Ste Foy from Conques in Rouergue to Chatillon (Conches) in Normandy. See further on this in Douglas, *French Studies*, XIV, pp. 110, 111.

[3] Ann. Benevent., s.a. 1017.   [4] Chalandon, *op. cit.*, I, 57.

[5] Reported in Amatus of Monte Cassino, I, cc. 17–20. Repeated in the second redaction of Leo of Ostia (by Peter the Deacon), and given with variation by Ordericus Vitalis (II, pp. 53, 54).

accompanied by emissaries from Salerno who persuaded many other disaffected Normans in the duchy to come and seek their fortunes in Italy. The other tradition[1] states more simply that Norman pilgrims returning from Jerusalem went to visit the shrine of St Michael at Monte Gargano, and there they met Meles who was in exile. Meles promised the Normans rich rewards if they would help him against the Greeks, and so they departed to Normandy and brought back many other Normans to join them in the venture.

In view of the character later to be assumed by Norman enterprise, these traditions linking the advent of the Normans in Italy to a pilgrimage deserve close attention. Many of the details given in them, particularly in respect of dates and the names of persons, certainly require correction, but the stories may well contain elements of truth,[2] and they have frequently been accepted as history.[3] On the other hand, they should certainly be received with caution.[4] Whatever truth may lurk behind the belief that these men were pilgrims who performed prodigies of valour against the pagans, the fact remains that the Normans who first came to Italy are better to be regarded as armed adventurers seeking their fortunes in a distracted land and living by violence and pillage. They found a patron in Meles, and perhaps also in Guaimar IV, the Lombard prince of Salerno, and thus they entered into war with the Greeks. In so doing, moreover, they appear to have gained the approval of Pope Benedict VIII who, apprehensive of Byzantine encroachments on the papal patrimony, sought to use them against the eastern empire. But when all is said, it must be added that the warlike achievements of the Normans in this early period in Italy were certainly exaggerated by their descendants, and the defeat of Meles at Canne in 1018 put an end for the time being to their concerted activity. During the next decade the Normans were to exercise little influence on Italian affairs.

In 1027, however, the perpetual rivalries among the south Italian states gave a fresh opportunity to those Normans who remained in the peninsula. In February the death of Guaimar IV led to a disputed succession at Salerno, whilst later in the year Pandulf III, the Lombard ruler of Capua, attacked Sergius IV of Naples and drove him into exile. Sergius, it would seem, thereupon called on Rannulf, one of those Normans who with his brothers is alleged to have been present

---

[1] Will. Apul., I, vv. 10–45.
[2] Chalandon, *op. cit.*, I, 42–52; Gay, *op. cit.*, 399–413.
[3] Cf. *Cambridge Medieval History*, V, pp. 167–72.
[4] Cf. Einar Joranson, *op. cit.*, *loc. cit.*

at the meeting with Meles at Monte Gargano, and with his aid won his way back to Naples in 1029.[1] The results were to be far-reaching. Rannulf had of course served for pay, but in return for his support (or in order to retain it) Sergius in 1030 gave to Rannulf and his followers the hill fortress of Aversa with its dependencies, and this was to prove the foundation of the first Norman state to be established in Italy. Its beginnings were indeed precarious, but its development was ensured by the subsequent actions of Rannulf himself. Aversa, manned by a contingent of expert and ruthless warriors, was, as a fortress, geographically well placed to exercise an influence both on Naples and Capua, and even on Salerno and Benevento; and Rannulf, whose services were ever in demand, showed himself adroit in exploiting the situation. He deserted the duke of Naples to join the prince of Capua, and later he forsook the prince on Capua to support the prince of Salerno.[2] So successful, and so lucrative, were these repeated betrayals that when in 1040 the territories of Capua and Salerno were united by the action of the Emperor Conrad II who was then campaigning in Italy, Rannulf found himself dominant in fact, though not in title, in the new conjoint principality. He died in 1045 as count of Aversa and duke of Gaeta; and his nephew Richard was, after an interval, to be recognized as prince of Capua.[3]

Rannulf was perhaps the first Norman in Italy to rise above mere brigandage in the sense that he displayed that blend of martial skill and unscrupulous diplomacy which was to be characteristic of so much Norman action at this time. Certainly his career as it was reported in Normandy, suggested that there were glittering prizes to be won in Italy by those with stout hearts and sharp swords; and it is known that many such came to Aversa from the duchy during these years.[4] Much more important, however, was the concentration of another group of Normans further to the south. It was during this period that the numerous and famous sons of Tancred of Hauteville-le-Guichard, began to arrive in Italy.

[1] Chalandon, *op. cit.*, I, pp. 73–8.

[2] Leo of Ostia (last recension), II, c. 56; Amatus, I, cc. 41, 42; Chalandon, *op. cit.*, I, pp. 70–87, 112–15.

[3] The succession of the *comté* of Aversa went at first to other nephews of Rannulf. Richard became count of Aversa about 1049; he was recognized as prince of Capua in June 1058. He became duke of Gaeta in 1063. He married Fredesendis, a sister, or half-sister of Robert Guiscard. See below, Genealogy 5.

[4] The names of some of those who came to Italy at various times are given by Ordericus Vitalis (Ord. Vit., II, p. 54).

Not less than twelve sons of this minor landowner came to Italy, and it is no exaggeration to say that by their acts they were substantially to modify the future of the whole Mediterranean world. With their associates they began to settle in the neighbourhood of Melfi, and many of them rapidly became rich and powerful, offering their services as warriors wherever it might be profitable, and for the rest living like brigands off the countryside. Thus the two eldest of them, William Bras de Fer and Dreux first entered the service of the Lombards, and then in 1038 served the eastern emperor in Sicily. They seized territory for themselves on the mainland, and with such success that by 1043 William was acknowledged as the most powerful man in Apulia. After his death his brother Dreux was in 1047 recognized as count by the Emperor Henry III who further enlarged his possessions. Dreux was murdered by the Lombards in 1051, and much of his power was inherited by his brother Humphrey who survived until 1057.[1]

But the most important of the sons of Tancred of Hauteville were those by his second wife, Fredesendis, and of these the most notable was Robert, styled Guiscard or 'the wily'. This man, wrote Anna Comnena[2] who hated him, was of a tyrannous temper, in mind most cunning, and brave in action. Tall in stature and well proportioned, 'his complexion was ruddy, his hair flaxen, his shoulders were broad, and his eyes all but emitted sparks of Fire'. For the rest, his shouting was loud enough to terrify armies, and 'he was by nature indomitable and ready to submit to nobody in the world'. He arrived in Italy in 1047, and the start of his career in the peninsular was sordidly inconspicuous, as with a few followers he haunted the hills hiding in caves, and issuing out to attack travellers and rob them of their horses and weapons. He looted the inhabitants of Calabria without discrimination, and on occasion he stretched his depredations northwards in order to dispute the profits of pillage with his elder half-brothers.[3] His growing power was indicated by his marriage about 1050 with Aubrée, the relative of a Norman holding a substantial estate at Buonalbergo near Benevento,[4] and by her he was to have a son who was baptised Mark,[5] but who on account of his size when in his mother's womb was to receive the nickname of the

---

[1] Will. Apul., II, vv. 20–40, 75–81, 364–70; Ann. Bari., s.a. 1046, 1057. See Genealogy 2.

[2] *Alexiad* I, c. 10.

[3] Amatus III, c. 7; Malaterra, I, c. 16; Will Apul., II, vv. 320–43; Anna Comnena, *Alexiad*, I, cc. 10, 11.

[4] Amatus, III, c. 11. Cf. M. Mathieu, *op. cit.*, p. 342. Her tomb is in the church at Venosa with an interesting inscription. (Bertaux, *L'art dans l'Italie meridionale*, p. 321).

[5] Malaterra, I, c. 33.

giant Bohemund, which he later made famous throughout Christendom. The marriage also marked the beginnings of Robert Guiscard's own successes as a conqueror. From this time forwards we are told he 'devoured land', and the sequel was to show that the metaphor was not inapt.

The coming of Robert Guiscard to Italy in 1047 signalized the opening of an epoch, and some nine years later he was joined by his youngest brother Roger. Already this young man was showing the varied qualities which were to make his own career so remarkable. According to his admiring biographer, he was at this time:

> a handsome youth tall and well built. He was very ready of speech, but his gay and open manner was controlled by calculating prudence. Brave and valiant himself he was fired by the ambitions proper to his years, and he sought by means of lavish gifts and favours to collect a party of adherents who would be devoted to furthering his fortunes.[1]

He was in fact in every way suited to follow the lead of his formidable elder brother, and together these two, Robert Guiscard and Roger, were, with Richard of Capua, to dominate the Norman conquests of Italy and Sicily during the latter half of the eleventh century. Thus, already in 1050, some of the conditions of those conquests had been indicated. The Norman settlement of Aversa would expand into the Norman principality of Capua; the Norman settlement at Melfi would grow into a Norman duchy of Apulia.[2] Later, and as a consequence, Norman power would stretch into Moslem Sicily.

A great political movement was, in fact, about to begin, and one which, if judged by results, may bear comparison even with that which the Normans were to accomplish in the north where by force of arms they would change the destinies of an ancient kingdom. The magnitude of the transformation which the Normans were to bring about in southern Italy and Sicily can in fact be easily summarized. In 1050, all this wide area, divided by the sea, was under the dominion of many rulers of differing traditions and varying powers. It was disputed between two religions and two systems of Christian ecclesiastical government. Three languages were spoken and three systems of law were operative. Yet within half a century this whole region was to come under Norman dominance, and within seventy years it was to form a single Norman kingdom. Whatever judgment may be passed on the gain and

[1] Malaterra, I, c. 19.
[2] Jamison, *op. cit.*, pp. 222–4.

loss which was involved, on the sufferings which were entailed, and the methods which were employed, this must surely rank as a major political achievement. And it was effected by men from the same restricted province of Gaul, who during these same years, were achieving and consolidating the conquest of England.

Chapter 3

NORMAN CONQUESTS, 1050–1100

I

By 1050 the stage had been set for Norman action both in the north and in the south of Europe. In southern Italy, the Normans had become deeply involved in the rivalries between the established powers, and were ready to exploit these conditions in a manner that would affect the whole Mediterranean world. In the north, too, a special situation had been created, and Anglo-Norman relations were moving towards a crisis which would affect not only Normandy and England but also France and the Scandinavian lands. Thus it was that when on 5 January 1066, Edward the Confessor, king of the English, died childless at Westminster the succession question became immediately a matter of the utmost importance not only to the Normans but to a large part of northern Europe.

By modern notions of heredity, the legitimate heir to the English throne was Edgar the Atheling (or Prince), the great nephew of the late king, but he was only a boy and had lived most of his life in exile in Hungary. At this stage therefore his claims seem hardly to have been considered. The new king, it would seem, must be sought in one of three places. The first was Scandinavia. Within living memory England had formed part of the northern Empire of Cnut the Great, and in 1066 many of the inhabitants of England were Scandinavian in blood or in sympathy. It was therefore with a certain logic that Harold Hardraada, king of Norway, the most famous warrior of the northern world,[1] should now seek the English throne. Second among the claimants, was Harold, son of Godwine, who since 1053 had ruled his father's earldom of Wessex. For many years he had been the most powerful man in England, and since 1057 he had entertained hopes of the royal succession. Finally there was William, duke of Normandy, who had presided over the consolidation of his own remarkable duchy, and who in 1063 had

[1] He had already fought unsuccessfully in Sicily, which the Normans were to conquer, and had paused by Antioch where Bohemund was to rule.

44

added Maine to his dominions. He asserted – probably with truth – that he had received from Edward the Confessor the promise of the English succession and he certainly hoped to obtain the English throne. Consequently both he and Harold Hardraada felt it as a personal challenge when, on the very day of Edward's funeral, Harold, son of Godwine, had himself crowned king of the English in the presence of a small group of magnates and of London citizens.

The dramatic story of 1066[1] has been made so familiar in England that there is no need in this place to do more than recall a few of its episodes. The position of Harold as king in England was essentially precarious, and it was made the more so in that he had quarrelled with his brother Tosti, earl of Northumbria, who had been driven into exile. Moreover, some two years earlier, when Harold was in Normandy he had taken his famous oath to Duke William which was widely held to commit him to the duke's cause. Nor could he be sure even of support in England outside his own earldom of Wessex. It was therefore with impaired resources that in August 1066 he prepared to receive attacks both from Norway and from Normandy. Since a large Norman fleet had already assembled at the mouth of the Dives, he decided that the Norman danger was the more imminent, and he therefore took up his position with a land and sea force on the south coast of England.

Early in September however two events occurred which transformed the situation. Harold found that he could no longer provide for his troops who had to live off the countryside, and so

> the men were allowed to go home – and the ships were sent to London, and many of them perished on the way there.[2]

Soon, too, William on the other side of the Channel changed his base. Unlike Harold he had been notably successful in supplying his force, but he may have decided that the Dives offered insufficient protection from the equinoctial gales which were just starting, or he may have thought that there was more chance of a favourable wind in the Straits of Dover. At all events, the Norman fleet was now moved hastily up the Channel in some confusion, and by 12 September it was at St Valéry in the mouth of the Somme.[3] There William impatiently waited for the wind that might carry him to England.

[1] Freeman, *Norman Conquest*, vols. II and III; Stenton, *Anglo-Saxon England*, ch. xvi; Douglas *William the Conqueror*, ch. 8.

[2] A.S. Chron., 'E', s.a. 1066.

[3] See now J. Laporte, 'Les Operations navales en Manche et Mer du Nord pendant l'année 1066' (*Annales de Normandie*, XVII (1967), pp. 2–36).

It was this delay that enabled the King of Norway to strike first. On 18 September a Scandinavian host led by Harold Hardraada was landed at the mouth of the Humber. There it was joined not only by Tosti who came down from Scotland, but also by many supporters of the Norwegian king in the north of England. An army from the Midland shires led by Edwin, earl of Mercia, was ready to oppose the invading host, and on 20 September there took place at Gate Fulford outside York, the first of the three great and bloody battles of 1066. The invaders were completely victorious, and the next day York, the northern capital, surrendered rejoicing to the king of Norway.

The problem for Harold Godwineson, still in the south, was whether he could cope with the invasion of the north of England, and return to the south before the wind enabled William to sail from St Valéry. He attempted the feat, and his conduct of the ensuing campaign is conclusive proof of his capacity as a soldier. Taking with him a corps of elite troops which he reinforced with such local levies as he could collect, he reached the neighbourhood of York within five days, and surprised the invading army at Stamford Bridge just outside the city. By nightfall on 25 September he had gained one of the most complete victories of the Middle Ages. Among those that were killed were Tosti and Harold Hardraada, and their army was dispersed. Even this success could not however allow for the Channel wind. Two days after Stamford Bridge, while Harold was still in Yorkshire, the wind veered in William's favour. The duke immediately put to sea, and on the morning of 28 September he reached the English coast near Pevensey. There, unopposed, he landed his whole force which has been estimated as consisting of some 7000 men, including perhaps 1000 trained horsemen (many with their mounts) and a substantial contingent of archers. Chance had undoubtedly played into his hands, but he had none the less seized a very hazardous opportunity, and he had carried out one of the most influential amphibious operations known to history.[1]

Harold on his part did not delay in meeting the new threat. By 5 October he was in London where for a week he waited in vain for reinforcements from the Midlands. Then, without further delay he moved south to meet William, reaching the ridge of the Downs some seven miles from Hastings with the advance part of his force during the night of 13 October. It was here that he made what was probably his

<hr />

[1] Will. Poit., p. 160; *Carmen*, vv. 50–75; Bayeux Tapestry, plates 37–42; Douglas, *op. cit.*, Appendix 'D'; J. Beeler, *Warfare in England*, pp. 12–14.

most serious strategic mistake. William, precariously established in hostile territory, had everything to gain from an early engagement, and indeed did his best to provoke one by ravaging the countryside. Harold, on the other hand, would surely have profited by waiting until he could mobilize the superior manpower at his disposal. As it was, his impetuous rush into Sussex was to cost him dear. On the morning of 14 October he was still marshalling his men in close order on the top of the hill when about 9 a.m. William came upon him 'unexpectedly'. It was the Norman duke who had achieved surprise.[1]

No military engagement has been debated at greater length than the battle of Hastings,[2] but while many of the details are still in dispute, the authorities seem to be agreed at least on the main course of the action. William opened the battle by moving his infantry forward so that by discharging their missiles they might soften up the defence. They failed however in this, and the duke thereupon sent in his horsemen in the hope that with their weight and by their swords they might achieve a swift success. But though fierce hand-to-hand fighting now ensued, this attack also failed, and the horsemen were turned down the hill in great confusion. Here perhaps was Harold's last great opportunity. If he had ordered a general advance he might have turned the disordered retreat of the enemy into a rout. But he neither took this course, nor could he control his defence upon the hill. As a result some of his troops, thinking that victory was in sight, started in haphazard pursuit, whereupon the mounted knights wheeled and cut to pieces the isolated groups that followed them. William was, thus, given the chance of restoring order in his army, and he seized it. He sent his weary horsemen once again upon the hill and now he gave them support from his archers who were ordered to rain down their arrows on the heads of the enemy. This time the charge of the mounted knights carried all before it. Harold himself was killed and the defenders were overwhelmed. The Norman victory was complete.

William had won what was to prove the most decisive battle ever fought on English soil, but on the morrow of his victory, his position must still have seemed hazardous. He therefore moved cautiously eastward taking Romney and Dover, and then advanced slowly to Canterbury which surrendered on his approach. Meanwhile he had

---

[1] A.S. Chron., 'D', s.a. 1066; Flor Worc., s.a. 1066; Will. Poit., 185.

[2] There are many admirable descriptions of the battle. The classical account is W. Spatz, *Die Schlacht von Hastings* (1896). Reference must be made also to J. F. C. Fuller, *Decisive Battles of the Western World*, I (1955), pp. 360–85.

received the important submission of Winchester, and he now determined after a short delay to isolate London. Having moved to the south bank of the Thames, he fired Southwark and, then passed through north Hampshire and Berkshire which he devastated, and finally crossed the Thames at Wallingford arriving at last at Berkhampstead.[1] His object had been to demonstrate his freedom of movement, and the success of his plan was now apparent. Already at Wallingford, Archbishop Stigand had made his submission, and to Berkhampstead there came:

> Archbishop Aldred (of York), and Edgar the Atheling and Earl Edwin and Earl Morcar and all the chief men from London. And they submitted . . . and they gave hostages . . . and he promised that he would be a good lord to them.[2]

They urged him moreover to be crowned forthwith 'since the English were accustomed to have a King for their lord', and to this the Norman magnates also assented.

It was therefore with the support of the leading men of Normandy and of England that William entered London and came at last to his crowning. The coronation[3] was celebrated on Christmas Day 1066 by Archbishop Aldred of York in place of the schismatic Stigand, and it took place in the Confessor's church at Westminster. The solemn ritual was that which had for long past been used in the coronation of the kings of the English, but the crown that was placed on his head was of Byzantine workmanship, and the new monarch was presented for acceptance to the people both in English and in French. Here indeed was the culminating event in the spectacular life of William the Conqueror, and it also marked a turning point in the history of England and in that of medieval Europe.

II

Thus had England been made to receive her first Norman king. 'And if anyone wishes to know what sort of a man he was, or what dignity he had or of how many lands he was lord – then we will write of him even as we, who have looked upon him, have perceived him to be.'

[1] For William's military acts between 14 October and 25 December 1066 see Beeler, *op. cit.*, pp. 25–33.
[2] A.S. Chron., 'D', s.a. 1066; Will. Poit., pp. 216–18. There has been controversy whether Great or Little Berkhampstead is in question.
[3] Douglas, *op. cit.*, ch. 10.

This King William of whom we speak was a very wise man, and very powerful and more worshipful and stronger than any predecessor of his had been. He was gentle to the good men who loved God and stern beyond measure to those people who resisted his will . . . Also he was very dignified . . . Amongst other things the good security he made in this country is not to be forgotten – so that any honest man could travel over his kingdom without injury with his bosom full of gold; and no man dared kill another . . . and if any man had intercourse with a woman against her will he was forthwith castrated . . . Certainly in his time there was much oppression . . . He was sunk in greed and utterly given up to avarice . . . These things we have written of him both good and bad that men may imitate his good points and entirely avoid the bad.[1]

This vivid account is the more interesting because it was written by one of William's English subjects. But it is necessary to remember that after his coronation, William was the royal ruler of a con-joint realm consisting of England and Normandy together with the Norman dependencies of Brittany and Maine; and for the rest of his life he was to be hazardously engaged in defending what he had won. For it was precisely this political union between Normandy and England which so altered the balance of power in north-western Europe as to provoke a concerted opposition from many quarters. Thus William's defence of his realm and the suppression of risings in England was always connected with the persisting threat of attack from Scandinavia or Scotland, from Anjou or Paris. And the protection of his northern frontier beyond Yorkshire could never be dissociated from the hostility that was manifest in France and in Flanders and in the Baltic lands. It was, moreover, characteristic of this situation that after 1072, the attacks, directed from so many quarters against the newly established Norman dominion, should have been co-ordinated by King Philip I of France whose object throughout was to break the Anglo-Norman connexion.[2]

The European implications of the Norman conquest of England were displayed from the beginning of William's reign as king. At first he might seem to have been exclusively concerned with the subjugation of his new kingdom. Thus early in 1068 he went westward to enforce the submission of Exeter and Bristol, and later in the year he moved north to York by way of Warwick and Nottingham returning through Lincoln, Cambridge and Huntingdon, where he left trusted lieutenants established in newly built castles.[3] But though these events, together

[1] A.S. Chron., 'E', s.a. 1087. [2] Douglas, *op. cit.*, ch. 9.
[3] Ord. Vit., II, pp. 181–5.

with the fighting in Devon and the revolt of Hereward in the Fens two years later, might seem to be of purely English significance, the true character of the composite threat to the Anglo-Norman realm was already being revealed. The cause of Edgar Atheling was taken up both by Malcolm III, king of Scotland and by Philip I, king of France; and the great rising of the north, that occurred in 1069–70, was assisted not only by the Scottish king but also by a large Scandinavian fleet which was in fact to operate off the English coast for four years. And contemporaneously with the rebellion in Yorkshire occurred the revolt of Maine which began in 1069 and culminated in 1073 with the defection of Le Mans.

The interconnexion of all these events can be seen in William's reaction to them. The northern rising was suppressed, with terrible brutality, after a campaign which took William into Teesdale, and then back by a hazardous winter march over the Pennines to Chester; and before the end of 1071 Hereward had surrendered at Ely. But far more serious to William than the Fenland revolt was the loss of Maine and the continuing menace from Scotland; and William's resulting campaigns were so rapid that they can almost be considered as a single operation. It was in the autumn of 1072 that he launched his great expedition by sea and land against Scotland – an expedition which carried him and his Norman knights to the gateway to the Highlands, and brought King Malcolm to terms at Abernethy. By November William was back at Durham, and a few weeks later he was across the Channel once more. His reconquest of Maine was in fact probably completed by March 1073 when the king held his court at Bonneville-sur-Touques.[1]

William's grasp of a defence which needed to be conducted against odds on many fronts may be seen also in the period 1075–80 when he was by no means so successful. In 1075 a revolt of the earls of Hereford and Norfolk was suppressed in England, and Waltheof, son of Earl Siward of Northumbria, who had been associated with it, was in due course executed. But this rebellion too had immediate reactions outside England. The rebels appealed as a matter of course to Scandinavia, and the east coast of England had to be put in a state of defence. Moreover, the war soon spread to Brittany. Ralph of Gael, the earl of Norfolk, was a great Breton lord, and after his defeat in England he took refuge at

---

[1] Ritchie, *Normans in Scotland*, pp. 30–8; Simeon of Durham (*Opera* 1, 106); Douglas, *op. cit.*, p. 229.

Dol where he was joined not only by many of his fellow magnates of Brittany, but also by troops from Anjou. Such was the alliance which King Philip I of France had done so much to foster and the French king, who had already established Edgar Atheling at Montreuil, lost no time in supporting William's enemies in the west. The sequel was logical. By October 1076 William was besieging Dol, and the French king came promptly to its rescue. Early in November he relieved the city and drove William with heavy loss from its walls.[1]

The enemies of the Norman king had now gained the initiative, and in 1078 they were joined by William's discontented son Robert. As a consequence, William was again defeated in January 1079 outside Gerberoi near Gournay, and no sooner had the news of this reverse reached the north, than Malcolm of Scotland invaded England. The northern frontier of the Anglo-Norman realm was thus in its turn placed in danger, and no effective reply was made until 1081 when Robert, now reconciled to his father, led against Malcolm the successful expedition which ended with the foundation of Newcastle. The Anglo-Norman state always depended for its survival on withstanding an inter-related menace that threatened it from every side.[2]

It was thus entirely characteristic of the conditions which had been created by the Norman conquest of England that during the last twenty months of his life, King William should not only have been menaced by a combined invasion of England from Scandinavia and Flanders – from Cnut, king of Denmark and Count Robert – but that he should have also been compelled to conduct his final campaign in defence of the south-eastern frontier of Normandy. In the late autumn of 1085 this impending invasion brought him hurriedly across the Channel with a large force, and it was in connexion with this crisis that he initiated the Domesday Survey and convoked a famous assembly of his feudal magnates at Salisbury.[3] It is true that, in the event, the threatened invasions of England did not take place, but even so the defence of the Anglo-Norman kingdom could not be relaxed. In the spring of 1087 William was back in Normandy; and that summer the French king invaded the duchy whilst William counter-attacked in the Vexin. He was to receive his lethal injury at Mantes, and he died on 9 September 1087 in a suburb of his own Norman capital of Rouen.

[1] A.S. Chron., 'E', s.a. 1075, 1076; Davis, *Regesta*, i, Nos. 78–82; *Annales S. Aubin*, ed. Halphen, p. 88.
[2] Simeon of Durham, *Opera*, I, 106, 114; *Hist. Mon. Abingdon*, II, pp. 9, 10; Ritchie, *op. cit.*, pp. 50, 51.　　　　　[3] Douglas, *Domesday Monachorum*, pp. 32, 33.

The social and political changes which were effected in England after the Norman Conquest were thus achieved against a background of continuous defensive war; and after the death of the Conqueror, the primary object of the French king in disrupting the union between Normandy and England was for a time attained. For the duchy passed to Robert, the Conqueror's eldest son, whilst his second surviving son William, nicknamed 'Rufus', became king of the English. The immediate results of this division were in every way unfortunate. Robert was unable either to control Normandy or to raise a successful rebellion in his own favour in England, and neither of the brothers were able to withstand the encroachments of King Philip. Only in the north was any Norman progress made during these years. There, however, as a result of successful campaigns in 1090 and 1091, the northern frontier of the kingdom was to some extent stabilized at last. It was now agreed that the debatable provinces of Cumbria and Lothian should be divided, the king of Scotland receiving, on terms, all Lothian from the Forth to the Tweed, whilst Rufus annexed to his own kingdom all Cumbria up to the Solway. At the same time Carlisle was built and garrisoned as a northern bastion of the Norman kingdom of England. The strangely oblique frontier between England and Scotland that was indicated in these arrangements made by the second Norman king of the English has with certain modifications persisted to this day.[1]

It was the most permanent contribution of William Rufus to the realm he ruled. He was himself wholly lacking in his father's statesmanship, and his wars with his brother entailed no constructive result.[2] Not until 1096 were there any indications of a return to better conditions. But in that year, as will be seen, Robert decided to go on Crusade, and needing money he gave Normandy in pledge to his wealthier brother in return for a loan. Henceforth Robert's contributions to the Norman achievement were to be made in Mediterranean lands and largely in company with his compatriots from Italy. On his return, with greatly enhanced prestige, he was unable to impede the succession of his younger brother Henry to the English throne after the death of Rufus. In 1106 indeed Henry felt himself strong enough to invade Normandy, and by his victory over Robert at Tinchebrai[3] he reunited England and Normandy. The relative importance of the two chief

[1] A. L. Poole, *Domesday Book to Magna Carta*, 107, 108; G. W. S. Barrow, *The Border* (Durham, 1962).
[2] C. W. David, *Robert Curthose*, esp. ch. III.
[3] *Ibid.*, pp. 91, 173–6 and Appendix 'F'.

parts of the Anglo-Norman kingdom had evidently altered, but the political unity of that realm established by William the Conqueror, and so consistently defended by him for twenty years, had been restored.

III

Northern Europe had thus been made to accept the new distribution of political power consequent upon the Norman conquest of England, and during the same decades the Normans were effecting a transformation of equal or greater magnitude in the south. The manner in which the Norman adventurers first arrived in Italy has already been noted, but after 1050 the character of the Norman impact on the south began to change. In place of mere brigandage there emerged designs of political conquest, and at the same time the men who were to be primarily responsible for those conquests began to rise to positions of power. The Norman cause in Italy thus began to be bound up with the careers of Richard of Aversa, and Robert Guiscard, and it was under their leadership that the decisive transition in the Norman advance was made. Between 1050 and 1060 the settlements of Aversa and at Melfi were transformed into the Norman principality of Capua and into the Norman duchy of Apulia.

By the middle of the eleventh century the Normans had most certainly become a power to be reckoned with by all the established authorities in Italy. The Lombard states had suffered great damage, and the eastern empire had cause to feel itself menaced. The papacy, too, was naturally disturbed at the distress in the devastated districts south of Rome, and Leo IX, who became Pope in 1049, was further concerned with the Norman threat to Benevento which had recently become a papal town. In these conditions a coalition against the Normans in Italy began to form. The emperor's representative was an official named Argyrus, the son of the former Lombard rebel, Meles of Bari, and he promised the papacy his support. Thus it was in circumstances that seemed particularly propitious that, in 1053, Leo IX determined to use force on a large scale to expel the Normans finally from Italy. Proclaiming his cause as holy, he collected a considerable army composed of Lombard and Italian troops together with a formidable contingent of German mercenaries from Swabia. This army the pope led in person to Benevento.[1]

[1] Will. Apul., II, vv. 70–4; on Leo's mixed motives, see Chalandon, *op. cit.*, I, pp. 122–357.

The Normans on their part were quick to respond, and the coopera-
tion which was at once achieved between the rivals Richard of Aversa,
Humfrey, son of Tancred, and Robert Guiscard is in every way notable.
Argyrus was penned in the south,[1] and the three Norman leaders,
acting it would seem under the direction of Humfrey, combined their
followers into a single striking force which met the papal army at
Civitate some thirty miles north of Foggia on 23 June 1053.[2]

On the right was Richard, count of Aversa, who attacked the Lombards
with squadrons of picked horsemen. Humfrey led the centre against the
Swabians, whilst the left wing was under the command of his brother
Robert (Guiscard). And it was Robert's duty to stand in reserve with his
troops from Calabria, ready to go to the assistance of his fellows should
they be in danger.[3]

The battle began when Richard's trained horsemen charged against
Leo's Italian troops. These were a miscellaneous band with little
military experience, and they were immediately put to flight. But the
resistance of the Swabians was much more formidable, and it continued
even after Robert Guiscard, according to his orders, came to Humfrey's assistance. What finally determined the issue was that Richard
of Aversa was able at this juncture to call back his horsemen who were
pursuing the Italians, and hurl them against the Swabians who were
overwhelmed. Thus the papal army was defeated with terrible carnage,
and the battlefield was littered with the bodies of those who had gone
to war at the command of the Vicar of Christ. Leo, himself, made
prisoner by the Normans, was brought by them in honourable captivity
to Benevento.[4]

The years that followed were crucial in the Norman conquest of
Italy. Between 1054 and 1057 the Normans of Aversa made rapid
progress northwards towards Gaeta and Aquino, and it was in June
1058 that at last Richard of Aversa captured Capua itself and overthrew
the Lombard dynasty. In the extreme south, Robert Guiscard was
slowly extending his conquests in Calabria, and after the death of

[1] Ann. Benevent., s.a. 1053 (2nd recension).
[2] The place is now uninhabited: it is on the banks of the river Fortore between S. Paolo
di Civitate and Serracapriola.
[3] Will. Apul., II, vv. 185–92.
[4] The campaign and the battle are described in Will. Apul., II, vv. 80–256; Leo of Ostia,
II, cc. 81–4; Amatus, III, cc. 37–41. The Lives of Leo IX which refer to it may be conveniently
consulted in Pat. Lat., vol. CXLII, and in Waterrich, Vitae Pont., I, pp. 93–177. These lives
must however be used with caution. (See H. Tritz, in Studi Gregoriani, ed. Borino, IV, 191–
304.)

Humfrey, son of Tancred, in 1057 he took the lead in the Norman advance in Apulia.[1] Further to the west his chief opponent was now Gisulf II of Salerno, but in 1058 this man consented to treat with Robert Guiscard, and, in token of the pact between them Guiscard repudiated his Norman wife Aubrée, and married Sigelgaita, Gisulf's sister.[2] She was to show herself a woman of commanding influence, and her exploits particularly on the battlefield, were eventually to pass into legend. But the immediate result of her marriage was that the hostile attentions of her terrible husband were turned away from the Lombards and against the Greeks.

It was, however, in connexion with the relations between the Normans and the papacy that the years 1053 to 1059 were chiefly important. Leo IX and his immediate successors, never changed in their bitter hostility to the Normans, but a fundamental alteration in papal policy was none the less being prepared at Rome. At this time the relations of the papacy both with the imperial power in Germany and with the ecclesiastical authorities at Constantinople were becoming increasingly strained. A strong party at Rome was therefore urging that the papacy would be well advised to enlist in its service the Normans who were now the strongest power in Italy, who had already despoiled the western empire, and who were the declared enemies of the Greeks. Thus was prepared the incongruous alliance between the papacy and the Normans, and in 1059 it took definite shape. At a synod held at Melfi in August of that year Pope Nicholas II received Richard and Robert Guiscard as his own vassals: Richard as prince of Capua, and Robert with the ominous title of

> Duke of Apulia and Calabria by the Grace of God and of St Peter; and, with their help in the future, Duke of Sicily.

In return Robert Guiscard (and apparently also Richard of Capua) swore to protect the person and the status of Pope Nicholas and

> to support the Holy Roman Church everywhere and against all men in holding and acquiring the possession of St Peter.[3]

[1] Leo of Ostia, III, c. 15; Amatus, IV, cc. 2-8. Malaterra, I, cc. 16, 17, 18, 19. Gay, *L'Empire byzantine*, p. 505. Assaults on Bisigniano, Cosenza, Gallipoli and Otranto are recorded at this time, and the whole gulf of Taranto was threatened. The imperial authorities, doubtless owing to the troubles they were facing from the Turks and the Petchenegs, seem to have been strangely inactive in Italy during these years.

[2] Will. Apul., II, vv. 416-32; Malaterra, I, 30; Amatus, IV, c. 21. See Genealogy 3.

[3] Will. Apul., II, vv. 384-405. There are two versions of Robert's oath (Delarc, *op. cit.*, pp. 324-6). That here followed is given in *Liber Censuum de L'Eglise romaine*, ed. P. Fabre and L. Duchesne (1910), p. 424.

The full implication of this momentous alliance upon the politics of Christendom at large will be considered in a wider context,[1] but its immediate impact upon the position of the Normans in Italy was fundamental. The pope had solemnly bestowed on the Normans rights which belonged not to the papacy but to others. And though much fighting would still be necessary before the Normans could fully secure those rights, their status in Italy had now been recognized by the highest ecclesiastical authority in Christendom.

Not surprisingly therefore the Norman advance was now accelerated. Richard prince of Capua whose connexions with Popes Nicholas II and Alexander II were particularly close, steadily extended his power, and the progress of Robert Guiscard was even more notable. It is no part of the present study to describe the details of his ruthless and inexorable advance.[2] The resistance to him in Calabria continued, but he gradually overcame it, and the slow subjugation of the province to the Normans can be marked by the submission about this time of Reggio Gerace Squillace and Rossano. Again, in the south of Apulia, the region of Otranto came a little later firmly into Guiscard's hands, whilst all the Normans in Italy, with the exception of the vassals of the prince of Capua, had been subjected to him. Thus though he was later to face several formidable rebellions, he was able in 1067 to prepare for the largest single operation that had as yet been undertaken by the Normans in Italy.

This was nothing less than a direct attack on the city of Bari which was the head of the Byzantine administration in Apulia.[3] As early as August 1068 Guiscard was beginning to lay siege to the city by sea and land, and the struggle was to be prolonged since the defenders could expect only limited help from the government at Constantinople which was now fully occupied with the menace from the Turks. So, after a siege which had continued intermittently for over two years and eight months, Bari at last surrendered to the Normans. Robert Guiscard entered the city in triumph on 16 April 1071, and the rule of the eastern emperor in southern Italy, which had endured for over five centuries, was brought to an end at last. Not without reason was Robert Guiscard in his charters[4] to date the years of his reign as duke of Apulia from the capture of Bari.

[1] See below, pp. 130–4. [2] Gay, *op. cit.*, 541–3.
[3] For the siege and capture of Bari, see Ann. Bar., s.a. 1068–71; Will. Apul., II, vv. 486–570, III, vv. 110–160; Amatus, V., c. 27; Malaterra, II, c. 40.
[4] *Cod. Dipl. Barese*, I, nos. 27, 28; V, nos. 2 and 3.

IV

Meanwhile an equally important development was beginning in Moslem Sicily. Sicily at this time was disputed between three rival emirs who not only fought among themselves but who all acted in virtual independence of the Zirid sultan of Mehdia in north Africa to whom they were nominally subject.[1] The rich island thus offered itself as a tempting prize to the Normans, and more particularly to Roger, the youngest brother of Robert Guiscard. This Roger had arrived in Italy in 1056, and he had been uneasily associated with Guiscard in the attacks on Reggio and Squillace. Then he established himself at Mileto. But already his covetous eyes were looking southwards, and he appears early to have entered into relations with Ibn at Timnah, the emir of Syracuse. At all events, in the autumn of 1060, and again very early in 1061, Roger crossed the Straits and tried to capture Messina. These attempts failed, but in April 1061 Robert Guiscard came to his help, and Messina fell into their hands. The brothers thereupon renewed their alliance with Ibn at Timnah, and with him they defeated a rival Saracen force near Castrogiovanni.[2] Relations between Robert and Roger were however becoming strained, and the expedition was abandoned. None the less, early in 1062, Roger was back in Sicily, and he now established himself in the hill city of Troina. But Ibn at Timnah was killed shortly afterwards, and Roger found himself hard-pressed. Nevertheless in 1063 he was able to sally out of his mountain stronghold, and to inflict a major defeat on the chief of his Moslem opponents at Cerami near Nicosia.[3]

Roger could now regard himself as firmly established at Troina, and he was coming to dominate the southern end of the Val Demone. But his hold on Messina was precarious and he was unable to extend his authority either to the west or the south. His best hope lay in the dissensions among the Moslem emirs, and in their common hostility to the Arab troops which had been sent to Sicily from Africa to sustain the interests of their overlord. It was in fact these quarrels alone that enabled Roger in 1068 to move from Troina towards Palermo. He defeated the Africans at Miselmeri in the immediate neighbourhood of the great

---

[1] Chalandon, *op. cit.*, I, 191. The Moslem emirates seem to have been centred upon (i) Mazzara and Trapani; (ii) Agrigento and Castrogiovanni; and (iii) Syracuse and Catania.
[2] Malaterra, II, cc. 1–3; Cf. D. P. Waley, in *Papers of the British School at Rome* (1954), pp. 118–25; R. S. Lopes in Setton and Baldwin, *Crusades*, I, 52–69.
[3] Malaterra, II, cc. 33, 34 and see below pp. 103, 104.

city,[1] but the Moslem metropolis successfully withstood him, and Norman progress in Sicily was thus stayed for another three years. Not until 1071 did the Sicilian venture of the Normans move at last to its climax.

In that year Roger had joined Robert Guiscard at the siege of Bari, and within a few months of the fall of that city, they set sail together for Sicily with a fleet of fifty-eight ships manned by Calabrian, Apulian and Greek sailors. This time they carried all before them. Announcing themselves as friends of the Moslems of Catania they were received into that port which they promptly occupied. Then they moved against Palermo. It was August, but Roger led the bulk of the force across the island by way of Troina through the intense summer heat, whilst Robert Guiscard moved around the north coast by sea with the remainder of the troops. Once arrived in front of Palermo they repeated the tactics which had served them so well at Bari, setting up a blockade by sea and land. A Moslem fleet, which had been sent from north Africa to relieve the city, managed to land some provisions in the harbour, but these were not sufficient for the besieged, and the defence became sensibly weakened through increasing famine.[2]

On 7 January 1072 therefore, the Normans were able to begin the assault. Roger with most of the Norman troops attacked the Moslem citadel at the top of the hill where now stands the Porta Nuova and the cathedral. He forced an entrance, and fierce hand-to-hand fighting ensued. Meanwhile Robert Guiscard moved swiftly round to the coast, and made an unopposed entry into the lower city near the present Villa Giulia and the Piazza della Kalza. He pushed rapidly up the hill and thus took the invaders in the rear. The move was decisive, and though the citadel itself was to hold out for a few days longer, its surrender was inevitable. On 10 January 1072 the great Moslem metropolis passed into Norman hands.[3] The effect on Norman policy and on Norman prestige was immense. In the spring of 1072 Palermo was, with the single exception of Constantinople, the largest and richest city in the world under Christian government. And Palermo was now ruled by the Normans.

V

The battle of Civitate (1053), the synod of Melfi (1059), the fall of Bari (1071) and the capture of Palermo (1072) are the cardinal events

[1] Malaterra,, II, c. 41.   [2] *Ibid.* II, c. 45; Will. Apul., III, vv. 185–98, 235.
[3] Amatus, VI, cc. 18–19; Will. Apul., III, vv. 199–330.

in the Norman conquest of southern Italy and Sicily. What followed was in the nature of a consolidation of their gains. Even so, the Norman rulers still had formidable difficulties to overcome. Richard of Capua was confronted with the hostile Lombard duchy of Naples, while Count Roger at Mileto had to face continuous opposition from the Greeks in such cities as Gerace, Rossano and Cozenza. Even Robert Guiscard could not feel wholly secure. In 1072, his possession of Bari, Brindisi and Otranto gave him effective control of southern Apulia, but his authority over the coastal towns to the north was not undisputed,[1] and the Norman conquest of Apulia was only to be completed gradually between 1072 and 1085.

Indeed, during the years immediately following the capture of Bari, the Norman fortunes in Italy moved towards a new crisis. The initial success of the Normans in the peninsular had been won (as will be recalled) first through the unity among the Normans (as in 1053), and secondly through the papal support which was given them after 1059. Now both these conditions were to be changed. Gregory VII who became pope in 1073 could not view with equanimity the ever-increasing power of the Normans, or the uses to which it was put. Moreover, also in 1073, Robert Guiscard had wrested Amalfi from Gisulf II of Salerno, and the Norman duke was thus beginning to threaten the papal patrimony. In these circumstances the pope attempted to divide the Normans in Italy. In 1074 he secured the alliance of Richard of Capua against the duke of Apulia, and in the same year he pronounced the first of the three sentences of excommunication he was to launch against Robert Guiscard.[2]

The position of Robert Guiscard was now critical since he had reason to suspect the loyalty of some of his own vassals in Italy and the pope was trying to build up a formidable coalition against him.[3] Characteristically, he reacted vigorously. In the autumn of 1074 he was engaged against the rebels in Calabria while his brother Roger attacked Richard of Capua. And then two events occurred which relieved the Norman situation. The pope became more deeply implicated in German politics, and at the same time Desiderius, the influential abbot of Monte Cassino, brought about a reconciliation between the Norman rulers of Capua and Apulia. The results were soon to be disclosed. In October 1076

---

[1] Gay, *op. cit.*, pp. 542, 543. Norman administration had not yet been set up in Bitonto even in 1078.
[2] Jaffé, *Monumenta Gregoriana*, p. 36 (Reg. I, 21a), p. 108 (Reg. I, no. 86).
[3] *Ibid.*, p. 65 (Reg. I, no. 46), p. 199 (Reg. II, no. 75).

Robert Guiscard, now with the support of Richard of Capua, attacked Gisulf in Salerno, blockading the city by sea and land. The siege continued for many weeks and the inhabitants were reduced to terrible straits. But at last on 13 December the gates were opened and the Normans entered Salerno. Only the citadel still remained in Gisulf's possession, and that fell at last to Robert Guiscard in May 1077.[1]

Salerno was, after Bari, the most important city in southern Italy to be captured by the Normans. Not only was it a stronghold of Lombard power but it was the centre of a widespread sea-borne traffic, and it would soon be the home of a cultural revival. Robert Guiscard was himself fully conscious of the implications of his victory, and he may even have considered transferring his administration from Bari to Salerno. In truth he had now good reasons for satisfaction, for with the death of Richard of Capua in 1078 he was left as the strongest power in southern Italy. Even the pope had to recognize the changed situation. In June 1080 he made a settlement with Robert Guiscard at Ceprano which was in reality a Norman triumph. Three times in six years Robert Guiscard had been excommunicated in respect of his seizure of Amalfi, Salerno and the march of Fermo. Now, he was confirmed in these conquests which were to be held independently of any overlord. In return he renewed (to his own advantage) the oath of fealty to the papacy which he had originally taken in 1059.[2]

This final establishment of Robert Guiscard in Italy was made, moreover, at a time when his ambitions were being further stretched. In 1074 he had sent his daughter, Helena, to be betrothed to Constantine, the son of the Eastern Emperor Michael VII,[3] and it would appear that, from this time forwards, he was actually beginning to contemplate seizing the imperial dignity for himself. In 1078 Michael was deposed, and shortly afterwards died, and the marriage contract with Helena was repudiated. Guiscard, thereupon, produced a Greek impostor whom he declared to be the deposed Emperor Michael, and he prepared to invade the eastern empire. As long as he was engaged in Italy he could not however put his plans into effect. But after 1080 this was changed. At Ceprano, Gregory VII actually recognized the pseudo-Michael, and it was with papal support, and under a papal banner,

[1] Amatus, VIII, cc. 13–29; Will. Apul., III, vv. 425–45. Ann. Benevent., s.a. 1077.
[2] The text of Robert Guiscard's oath at Ceprano is given in Jaffé, *Monumenta Gregoriana*, p. 426.
[3] Chalandon, *op. cit.*, I, pp. 259–63. Imperial titles were then given to both the young people and also to Robert Guiscard.

that in May 1081, Robert Guiscard, together with his son Bohemund, set sail from Otranto with a considerable force. Having safely crossed the Adriatic, they seized the island of Corfu, and moved forward to attack Durazzo.[1]

This was the beginning of a general war that was to entail widespread and disastrous consequences. At first the expedition suffered a severe check when in July a Venetian fleet came down the Adriatic to disperse the Norman ships and to give such relief to the defenders of the city that they were enabled to repel all attacks throughout the summer. Then in October a relieving army arrived under the command of the Emperor Alexis I. This was beaten off by the Normans, and the siege continued throughout the winter. On 21 February 1082[2] the Normans were at last able to effect an entrance into Durazzo, and Robert Guiscard seemed to have all Illyria at his mercy. But events in Italy were to check him. The Emperor Henry IV had now entered Italy from Germany, and all the enemies of the pope and of the Norman duke of Apulia were ready to support him. Robert Guiscard was compelled hastily to return, in response to the papal pleas, and also to deal with his own rebellious vassals in Apulia. His son Bohemund was, however, left to carry on the campaign against Alexis, and so successful was he in his progress eastward that he began to threaten Constantinople itself.[3] None the less, he was defeated in 1083 by the imperial troops at Larissa, and one by one the Norman gains in the Balkans were lost.[4] The steady advance of Norman might which had wrested Bari from the Greeks, and Palermo from the Saracens, had failed at last before Byzantium.

But in Italy events now moved forward inexorably to a terrible conclusion. The Emperor Henry IV, after a long siege, entered Rome on 21 March 1084, and Robert Guiscard, who had now quelled the rebellion among his own vassals, moved north to the pope's assistance. Henry IV retreated before his advance so that when Robert Guiscard with a large force of Calabrian and Saracen mercenaries reached Rome in May, he had the city at his mercy. On 28 May he forced an entrance

---

[1] For the expedition against Durazzo see Will. Apul. IV, vv. 75–505; Anna Comnena, *Alexiad*, IV, cc. 2–7; Malaterra, III, cc. 26–8.

[2] Ann. Bari, s.a. 1082; Lupus, s.a. 1082. For the chronology of the Durazzo campaign I follow Mlle Mathieu in her edition of William of Apulia. A different version is given in Buckler, *Anna Comnena*, p. 413.

[3] Yeatman, *Bohemund*. In May 1082 Bohemund invaded Epirus and captured Janina. During the summer of 1082 he dominated Albania and Thessaly.

[4] Yeatman, *op. cit.*

through the Flaminian Gate, and fought his way across a flaming city to the Castello Sant'Angelo where the pope had taken refuge. Three days later a rising by some Roman citizens proved the occasion for renewed arson and destruction, and thereafter the city was given over to wholesale robbery, rape and murder. The loss of life must have been great, and many of the leading citizens were sent in slavery to Calabria.[1]

Such was the appalling climax in Italy of the alliance between the papacy and the Normans which had been established at Melfi in 1059, and restated at Ceprano in 1080. And in the year following the destruction of Rome, both Gregory VII and Robert Guiscard passed from the scene. The great pope, driven from his ravaged capital, died on 25 May 1085 at Salerno: the great Norman, at the outset of yet another campaign, died on the island of Cephallonia on 17 July of the same year.[2] Less than eight weeks thus separated their passing which occurred (as will be recalled) only some two years before William the Conqueror, the architect of the other Norman conquest, died outside the walls of Rouen.

VI

The preoccupations of Robert Guiscard during the last ten years of his life, first with the papacy and then with the eastern empire, meant that the Norman cause in Sicily fell more and more under the control of his younger brother Roger. Even so, Roger's independence at this date should not be exaggerated for it was only by Guiscard's favour that he could get reinforcements from Italy. And these were sorely needed since in 1072 even after the capture of Palermo, the Norman hold on Sicily still remained precarious. The Normans held all the northern coast from Messina to Palermo, and a zone stretching from the hill city of Troina southwards towards Castrogiovanni. They had also Mazzara in the west and Catania in the east. But at each end of the Norman territory, the Moslems held Trapani in the west and Taormina on the east, whilst all the rest of the island was directly under their rule. Roger could, however, hope to exploit the rivalries between the various emirs, and his possession of the great Moslem metropolis gave him great prestige.

At first, therefore, he was concerned to consolidate his position, and

---

[1] Bonitho, *Epist. ad Amicum* (Jaffé, *Monumenta Gregoriana*, pp. 679, 680; Malaterra, III, cc. 37, 38, and see below p. 63).

[2] Jaffé-Loewenfeld, p. 649; Will. Apul., V, vv. 295–330.

in the period 1072–1074 the construction of the Norman castles at Paterno, Mazzara and Calascibetta was probably begun. Moreover, in 1075 Roger concluded with Tamin, sultan of Mehdia, an important treaty which resulted in the withdrawal of those Moslem troops from Africa who had fought so vigorously against the Normans in Sicily.[1] It was a notable diplomatic success, but Roger was soon to meet the most resolute of all his Moslem opponents, Ibn-el-Werd ('Benarvet') emir of Syracuse. The war between him and Roger was in fact to plunge Sicily into turmoil for some ten years, and it had many vicissitudes. Thus between 1077 and 1079 the Normans captured Trapani and Taormina, but both these cities together with Catania were to change hands several times in the years which followed. In this period, also, Roger was frequently recalled to the mainland to assist his elder brother, and this gave Ibn-el-Werd the chance not only to gain ground in Sicily but even to carry the war across the Straits of Messina. During the autumn of 1084 he ravaged Calabria, bearing off the nuns of Reggio to decorate the harems of Syracuse.[2]

Roger could now however mount a major offensive. Before the end of 1084 he had begun to build a new fleet, and in May 1085 his ships sailed down the east coast of Sicily past Taormina to blockade Ibn-el Werd in Syracuse. At the same time Roger's bastard son, Jordan, moved across country with a strong contingent of troops to attack the city from the land. The siege of Syracuse, which was thus begun, lasted for several months, but, at last in October the great port fell into the hands of the Normans. It was a decisive victory. Taormina and Catania were now in Roger's firm possession; he controlled the whole *massif* of Etna; and in 1087 Catrogiovanni, the ancient Enna, which had for so long resisted him, surrendered. The triumph might seem to be complete, but there was in fact more to come. In 1090 Roger took his victorious fleet with troops over the sea to Malta, and there he was welcomed as lord both of that island and of Gozo.[3] In the same year he subjugated the region round Noto, the only Sicilian district that still held out against him. By 1091 Roger 'the Great Count' was effectively master of Sicily.

The 'Great Count' must assuredly rank high among the Norman conquerors, and he was able also to take advantage of the dissensions which developed on the mainland of Italy after the death of Robert

[1] Mas Latrie, *Traités de Paix et de Commerce* (1866), pp. 28, 29.
[2] Malaterra, IV, c. 1; Amari, *Musulmanni in Sicilia*, III, pp. 151–67; Chalandon, *op. cit.*, I, p. 338.
[3] Malaterra, IV, cc. 2, 5, 6, 7, 15, 16.

Guiscard in 1085. On his death-bed Robert Guiscard had designated Roger 'Borsa', his son by the Lombard Sigelgaita, as his successor both as duke of Apulia and as overlord of Sicily.[1] The motives behind this arrangement are not very clear, but they may have been designed to attract to the Norman régime the surviving Lombard elements in northern Apulia and the Abruzzi. But Roger Borsa had none of his father's brutal strength, and his advance disinherited his elder half-brother Bohemund who had already won fame as a commander in the field, and would certainly not now acquiesce in the status of a penniless soldier of fortune. It is not surprising therefore that a critical situation developed in southern Italy, or that the Norman duchy of Apulia began to show signs of disintegration between 1085 and 1100.

Roger Borsa's succession had doubtless been promoted by his formidable mother Sigelgaita, and some charters actually suggest that she may have been in some sense recognized as joint ruler in Apulia with her son.[2] Their position was however soon to be challenged. Bohemund at once seized for himself the cities of Oria, Otranto and Taranto, and in 1090 he was actually in possession of Bari itself.[3] Any further acquisitions by him in Italy were however stayed by Count Roger. The 'Great Count', having completed his conquest of Sicily and added Malta to his dominions, was now free to return to his Calabrian possessions, and from there to push his power northward. Neither Roger Borsa nor Bohemund would be allowed to stand in his path, and the death of Jordan I of Capua in 1090 gave him a new opportunity which he was not slow to seize. Before his death in 1101, Roger the 'Great Count' had in fact come to dominate the whole political situation in southern Italy, and the consequences for the future were already indicated. The eventual dominance of Norman Sicily over Norman Italy was clearly foreshadowed by the end of the eleventh century, as well as the creation of a single Norman state in the south with its capital at Palermo.

VII

The political balance in southern Italy between 1085 and 1100 also set the stage for yet another Norman conquest. When in the early summer of 1096 the first contingent of Crusaders arrived from the north, they found the three Norman leaders all together engaged in a joint attack on Amalfi which was then in revolt. Naturally they called

---

[1] Will. Apul., IV, vv. 186; V, vv. 345-50.
[2] Cf. *Cod. Dipl. Barese*, I, pp. 56-9, 61-5.   [3] *Ibid.*, V, pp. 26-8, 55-7.

I   William the Conqueror from one of his seals

II   Robert Guiscard

III Norman horsemen and archers at Hastings

on the Normans to join them and this appeal was diversely received. Roger Borsa was sympathetic but personally unmoved, while Roger, the 'Great Count', had no intention of allowing any of his own vassals to leave for the east. With Bohemund however the case was different, and he lost no time in taking the Crusader's oath. His motives were doubtless complex, but with all his cunning there was a strain of romantic rashness in him, and he may have been genuinely moved by the impulse to rescue the Holy Places. But he had also his private ambitions to satisfy. His recent advances in Apulia had been checked by his uncle from Sicily, and his earlier campaigns in Greece and Thrace may have led him to hope for conquests in the east. In this respect his aspirations were evidently shared by the remarkable company which formed around him, and which resembled one of those Norman groups that in the previous generation had fought their way to power in Italy.[1]

Whether Bohemund had formed any precise designs on Antioch before he left Italy is doubtful. Nor were his intentions made clear when he passed through Constantinople in May 1097. But his former hostility to the empire must have been anxiously recalled by the imperial authorities, and his appearance was certainly striking. The impression he was to make on the young Byzantine princess, Anna Comnena, was so enduring that in old age she could still write about him in terms of fascinated horror:

> He was so tall in stature that he stood above the tallest . . . He was thin in loin and flank; broad shouldered and full chested; muscular in every limb; and neither lean nor corpulent but excellently proportioned . . . His hands were full of action, his step firm, his head well enough set, though if you looked close you saw that he stooped a little. His body was very white all over, though in his face the white was mingled with red. His hair was blond . . . and cut short to the ears. He was closely shaven. His blue-grey eyes gave him dignity but they could flash with anger . . . A certain charm hung about this man but was partly marred by a general air of the horrible. For in the whole of his body the entire man showed himself implacable and savage both in his size and glance, and even his laughter sounded to others like snorting. He was so made in mind and body that both courage and passion reared their crests within . . . and both inclined to war.[2]

Such a man was destined to command, and by the time the Crusade reached Antioch late in 1097 Bohemund, who had taken a prominent

---

[1] Jamison, *Essays . . . M. K. Pope*, pp. 195–206.
[2] *Alexiad*, XIII, c. 10. Based upon the translation by E. A. S. Dawes.

part in the victory of Dorylaeum earlier in the year, was firmly established among the leaders. It is clear too that he had now determined to seize Antioch for himself.

All his plans were therefore directed to that end, and he was assisted throughout by the prestige which he deservedly won as a soldier. It was Bohemund who, in February 1098, repelled the attacking force of Ridwan of Aleppo at a time when the Christians, besieging Antioch, were lamentably distressed by hunger and privation. It was Bohemund again who, aided by treachery from within the walls, led the successful assault which resulted in the capture of Antioch by the Crusaders on 3 June. Finally it was Bohemund who commanded and controlled the whole crusading army when it sallied out of Antioch on 28 June 1098, to defeat the relieving force of Kerbogha, emir of Mosul, in what was the greatest single military success won by the Christians during the First Crusade.[1]

Proud legends were soon to gather round the 'Great Battle of Antioch' where the Christian victory had, as it seemed, been presaged by the discovery of the Holy Lance, and ensured by the visible intervention of warrior saints. But for Bohemund it was important in ensuring the fulfilment of his territorial ambitions. By this time the majority of the crusading leaders were ready to acquiesce in his taking personal possession of the city he had done so much to win and defend, the more especially as they felt they had been betrayed by the eastern emperor and had no desire to protect his rights. So the only serious opposition came from Raymond of Toulouse, and he was forced by his own troops to proceed southwards to Jerusalem leaving the Norman in possession of the city. The red banner of Bohemund floated over Antioch.[2]

All that he now needed was a legitimate title, and there is little doubt that at this juncture Bohemund was guided by the example of his father. Even as in 1059 Robert Guiscard had obtained a sanction for his authority by becoming a nominal vassal of the pope, so now in 1100 did Bohemund receive investiture as Prince of Antioch at the hands of Daimbert, archbishop of Pisa, the papal legate.[3] Of course, the new principality would have now to be defended not only against

---

[1] *Gesta Francorum*, VI, c. 17; VII, c. 20. Cf. Runciman, *Crusades*, I, pp. 213–65.

[2] *Gesta Francorum*, X, cc. 33, 34. For Bohemund's red standard, see Fulcher, XVII, c. 6.

[3] C. Cahen, *Syrie du Nord*, pp. 223, 224; Yeatman, *Bohemund*, p. 229. In Italy before 1096 Bohemund had styled himself simply 'Bohemund son of Robert Guiscard the Duke', and it was with a similar style that he issued in 1098 at Antioch his charter for the Genoese. But by 1100 Bohemund was 'Prince' and he was 'Prince of Antioch'. (*Cod. Dipl. Barese*, I, pp. 56–9; 61–5; V, pp. 38–42. Hagenmeyer, *Kreuzzugsbriefe*, pp. 156, 310.

the Turks but against the eastern empire, and as will appear,[1] the acts of Bohemund were to entail lamentable results on the politics of Christendom. But what was evident to all in 1100 was that a new Norman state had been founded in the East. And it was to endure. Though Bohemund's later career was to be chequered, he was succeeded by his nephew Tancred and then by no fewer than six successors bearing the nickname he had made so famous. Indeed, the Norman dynasty at Antioch was to outlast the Norman dynasty in England, and even the Norman dynasty in Sicily.

VIII

By 1100 the Norman conquests had reached a term. Bohemund had been invested with the principality of Antioch, and on 5 August of that year Henry I was crowned king of the English. Syria had thus been given a Norman dynasty, and northern Europe would soon have to reckon once more with the Anglo-Norman realm that had been founded by William the Conqueror. In Italy a similar consolidation had taken place. The principality of Capua had been stretched northwards into the Campagna, and the duchy of Apulia, uneasily held together by Roger Borsa, extended from the frontiers of Naples across Italy to the Adriatic coast, and then away down south past Bari and Brindisi to Otranto. Moreover, Roger, the 'Great Count', was now supreme over all Sicily. He was also effectively master of Calabria, and his administration was laying the foundations of the kingdom which, under his great son Roger II, would include all southern Italy as well as Sicily. In this way the Norman conquests during the latter half of the eleventh century had set up the strongest Latin state in the East. And they had established in the north and in the south of Europe two states which in their several ways, through their culture and their administration, would set an example of effective government to the men of the Middle Ages.

[1] See below, pp. 80, 81, 163–8.

Chapter 4

COMPARISONS AND CONTRASTS

I

The most summary account of the Norman conquests between 1050 and 1100 invites comparison between them, and prompts the question whether there were common causes for their success. But at first sight it might seem that the differences between them were more notable than any similarities. The Norman impact upon England began, as has been seen, with a formal treaty and a dynastic alliance; it was to reach its climax with a carefully organized expedition led by a Norman duke; and it was to result in the conquest of an ancient kingdom whose political unity it preserved and strengthened. By contrast, the Norman impact upon Italy and Sicily began with isolated acts of brigandage; it operated upon a large number of independent and contending states; it created, at first, a few disparate Norman lordships; and, at the last, it imposed political unity over a wide area which had previously been divided and distraught.

These distinctions go some way to account for the fact that, while in each case the Norman conquests were to be achieved only at the cost of terrible devastation, the sufferings of England in this respect, though severe, were to be shorter and less grievous than those endured by southern Italy. Between 1020 and 1066 England was to endure many misfortunes but none of these were inflicted by Norman hands, and when the Normans came in 1066, they were under firm leadership. In Italy, on the other hand, the Normans who arrived during the earlier half of the eleventh century were mostly men who had left the duchy from fear of the duke and their depredations were at first uncontrolled by authority and unrestrained by morals. They came from Normandy at a time when the political character of the duchy was itself in process of formation, and they might be compared more readily with the companions of Rolf the Viking than with the men who accompanied William the Conqueror to England in 1066.

There is abundant evidence of the wanton devastation caused by the

68

early adventurers who came from Normandy to Italy. They showed themselves as savage marauders devoid both of mercy and scruple, and their brigandage was ruthless and indiscriminate. They turned Aversa and Melfi into depots for the storage of loot, and a particularly repulsive feature of their depredations was their systematic destruction of the crops so that hunger and pestilence often passed in their wake through the stricken countryside. Thus in 1058 (we are told) three disasters fell upon Calabria, namely famine, plague and the pitiless sword of the Normans.[1] Again, in 1062 the Normans caused widespread famine in northern Sicily, and in 1076 Count Roger was to devastate the whole region of Noto in the south. The annalist of Benevento bitterly lamented the cruelty of the Normans, and in 1053 the men of Apulia complained to Leo IX that their country had been 'ruined' by this savage race.[2] Early in 1054 the pope himself described their acts to the Emperor Constantine IX in yet more forcible terms. They are utterly without restraint, he declared, and worse than the Saracens in the atrocities they inflict upon their fellow Christians, sparing neither the women whom they rape nor the old men whom they put to the sword.[3] Even children were not safe from them. It was not for nothing that Richard of Capua earned the nickname of the Wolf of the Abruzzi, and at a later date, Anna Comnena gave a lurid description of the cruelties of Robert Guiscard during his early career in Calabria.[4]

It is true that these accounts were given by enemies of the Normans. But they can be confirmed in many respects by evidence from those who were the Normans' friends. John, abbot of Fécamp, for instance, declared to the pope in 1053 that such was the hatred which the invaders had inspired in Italy that no Norman could freely travel through the country even if he was on pilgrimage,[5] and in like manner Amatus, William of Apulia and Geoffrey Malaterra all gave plentiful examples of Norman violence and lack of scruple. The testimony of Malaterra is here particularly noteworthy. Of Robert Guiscard, he remarks, that his lust for plunder was particularly fierce in the hey-day of his youth. And then the author turns to Roger 'the Great Count' who is of course the hero of his book. Roger, he remarks, lived without restraint off the countryside when he was a young man in Calabria, and 'finding poverty unpleasant' he was content to be sustained by robberies

[1] Malaterra, I, c. 27.   [2] Ann. Benev., s.a. 1042, 1053; Will. Apul., II, vv. 70-4.
[3] A translated text of the letter is in Delarc. op. cit., 248-50.
[4] Alexiad, I, c. 11. Cf. Amatus III, cc. 6-11; Malaterra I, cc. 16, 17.
[5] Pat. Lat., CXLIII, col. 79.

conducted by his armed followers.[1] The oppressive violence of the Normans in these regions became less indiscriminate with the rise to power of their leaders, and it is noteworthy that neither the capture of Bari in 1071 nor that of Palermo in 1072 was marked by unrestrained pillage and slaughter. None the less, almost down to the end of the eleventh century the bishops of Apulia and Calabria found it necessary to proclaim the Truce of God in their dioceses.[2]

Finally, the sack of Rome in May 1084 must rank among the major crimes of war. All the authorities agree that the two great fires which swept through a great part of the city were deliberately started on Norman orders, and the human suffering which this entailed needs no emphasis. The destruction of the monuments of antiquity must also have been very great, and scarcely less damage was done to ancient Christian shrines such as that of S. Clemente. Rome suffered more from the Normans in the eleventh century than from the Vandals in the fifth, and some quarters, notably those on the Aventine and Celian hills, still show traces of the Norman devastation. For long years after the event Rome was to present a sorry spectacle to the world: when Hildebart, archbishop of Tours, visited the city some sixteen years later he was moved to compose a long sermon in verse, and he could declare that 'the statues and palaces have fallen; the citizens have sunk into servitude; and Rome scarcely remembers Rome'. Perhaps the heaviest indictment that can be brought against the Normans in Italy is that as allies of a pope they sacked the capital of Christendom.[3]

The deplorable story of Norman devastation in Italy suggests a contrast with England. During the period when the most widespread depredations were being made in the south, England was immune from Norman attack, and at a later date Norman violence in England was of a different character. Even so, the distress caused to England by Norman arms between 1066 and 1072 should not be minimized. The slaughter at Hastings was grievous, and William's subsequent campaigns were ruthless. London was isolated in 1066 as a result of a brutal march, and though William was careful to spare Exeter after its surrender in 1068, the suppression of later English risings by the king's lieutenants such as Odo, bishop of Bayeux, was often formidable. Outstanding in its savagery was, however, William's own treatment of the

[1] Malaterra, I, cc. 19–23, 25.
[2] Lupus, s.a. 1089.
[3] Jaffé, *Monumenta Gregoriana*, 679, 680; Gregorovius, *Rome in the Middle Ages*, IV, pt. i, pp. 242–54.

north of England in 1069–70. The harrying of the north which then occurred was regarded by contemporaries as exceptionally cruel. The Anglo-Saxon annals tersely remark that all Yorkshire was 'utterly ravaged and laid waste', but in truth the devastation spread as far as Cheshire and Staffordshire. A deliberate attempt was further made to destroy the livelihood of the inhabitants. Famine and plague inevitably followed. A northern chronicler speaks of the rotting corpses which littered the high roads of Yorkshire, and another writer tells how refugees in the last stages of destitution arrived in pitiful groups as far south as Evesham.[1] In the record of Norman destruction, the devastation of Yorkshire by William the Conqueror may be set alongside the sack of Rome by Robert Guiscard.

There, however, the comparison ends. Even as Norman violence began in England later than in Italy, so also did it end sooner; William's reign after 1071 is in this respect to be contrasted with the five years that followed Hastings. The earlier devastations, horrible as they were, were part of a defined military policy, and after the military necessity had passed, they were not indiscriminately continued. The grimmest feature of this later period was the dispossession of the native nobility, and though this was indeed tragic, its replacement by a highly competitive aristocracy, imported from overseas, was effected without general anarchy, and with at least an overt respect for legal precedent.[2] The Conqueror's rule over England was harsh, but it never degenerated into purposeless anarchy, and though his taxes were savage, the good order he maintained proved some protection for the humbler among his subjects, and was praised by one of them for that reason.[3] William the Conqueror, avaricious himself, was able and determined to check the rapacity of his followers. He was in fact in control of the situation as were none of his contemporaries in the south.

Even here, however, some distinctions must be made. In southern Italy neither Richard of Capua nor Robert Guiscard in their early days could assert supremacy, as of right, over the other Norman leaders who at first claimed to be equal with each other.[4] In Sicily, by contrast, Robert Guiscard and his brother Roger had no rivals of their own race

---

[1] Ord. Vit., II, p. 196; Simeon of Durham. *Opera*, ii, 188; *Chronicon de Evesham*, ed. W. D. Macray, pp. 90, 91.

[2] Douglas, *William the Conqueror*, ch. 11. And see below, pp. 173, 174.

[3] A.S. Chron., 'E', s.a. 1086 (equals 1087).

[4] This is brought out very clearly in the negotiations between William Bras de Fer, and Pandulf III of Capua (Amatus, III, cc. 28, 29).

in the land they conquered, and they could thus at their own discretion invest their followers with land and dictate the terms on which it was to be held.[1] In this matter, they were in a position similar to that occupied by the Conqueror in England but in the closing years of the eleventh century the contrast between England and the south was, in general, pronounced. After the death of the Conqueror conditions in England worsened, but even so many of the results of his work persisted. In the conflict between his sons William Rufus and Robert, England suffered no misfortunes comparable to those which befell southern Italy after the death of Robert Guiscard; and nothing in the civil war which broke out in Kent in 1088 can be compared with the situation which St Anselm found outside Capua ten years later when the fighting was complicated by the presence of large numbers of Saracen mercenaries.[2]

Any assessment of the Norman achievement must take full account of its cost, both to Italy and to England – of the suffering it entailed, and the devastation it brought about. But ruthless destruction has accompanied war in every century, and in this respect the Normans were not unique even among their contemporaries. The cruelties perpetrated by the earls in England during the three decades preceding the Norman Conquest were as revolting as anything that took place later, and according to Simeon of Durham, no military operation of the period – not even the 'harrying of the north' – was marked by greater atrocities than those committed by Malcolm III, king of Scotland, in his raids on Teesdale and Cumberland.[3] Again, the bestial cruelties inflicted on their opponents in Calabria by the men of Gerace in 1086 were utterly revolting,[4] and nothing in the career of Robert Guiscard was more repulsive than the treatment meted out to the citizens of Amalfi by his enemy Prince Gisulf II of Salerno.[5]

Neither the Norman conquests nor their enduring results are, however, to be explained simply by reference to men whose dominant passion was a love of cruelty, or whose ambitions were confined to wanton pillage. The successes of the Normans in this period derived in the first instance from the fact that everywhere they showed themselves to be among the foremost warriors of the age. They were skilled in

[1] See below, pp. 175–8.
[2] Eadmer, *Vita Anselmi*, ed. Southern, pp. 111, 112; Douglas, *Domesday Monachorum*, 32, 33.
[3] Simeon of Durham, *Hist. Regum. (Opera Omnia*, II, pp. 191, 192).
[4] Malaterra, II, c. 24.
[5] *Ibid.*, III, c. 3; Amatus, VIII, cc. 3–7.

battle, and able, also, as at Civitate and Hastings and Antioch, to submit themselves profitably to disciplined leadership. Their exploits were undoubtedly to be magnified by later writers of their own race, but in the eleventh century, the Normans in Britain, in Italy, in Sicily and in Syria, proved more than a match for any troops that could be brought against them. And the Norman conquests between 1050 and 1100 were largely due to the fact that they everywhere adopted with success their own particular methods in the waging of war.

II

Reference is often made to the good fortune that attended the Normans, and to a limited extent this is justified. The opportune deaths of King Henry I of France and Geoffrey Count of Anjou in 1060, the invasion of England by Harold Hardraada in 1066, and perhaps also the behaviour of the Channel wind during September of that year – all these things assisted William the Conqueror. Correspondingly the rivalries between the various states of southern Italy, the decline of Byzantium after the death of Basil II in 1025, and the civil wars among the Moslem rulers of Sicily all helped the progress of the Normans in the south. Similarly at a later date the civil war which followed the death of Malik Shah, sultan of Baghdad in 1092, and the death of his brother, Tutush in 1095, may have facilitated the establishment of the Norman principality of Antioch, four years later.[1] But opportunities need to be seized, and the long series of Norman victories during these few decades in so many countries is not to be explained by fortuitous chance. These victories themselves offer conclusive testimony of the eminence of the Normans as warriors.

Their distinction as fighting men was early demonstrated in Italy by the constant demands which were made for their services; and these they met with a complete lack of scruple. Guaimar IV of Salerno used them against the Saracens, and Meles employed them against the eastern empire. After the battle of Canne in 1018 many of them offered their services to the Greeks with whom they had recently fought, and subsequently a considerable body of Normans went across the straits to Messina under Byzantine leadership in a fruitless attempt to regain Sicily from the Moslems. Even during Robert Guiscard's early years in

[1] H. A. R. Gibb, ed., *Damascus Chronicle*, pp. 21, 22; *Gesta Francorum*, ed. R. Hill, pp. xxvi, xxvii.

Italy many Normans remained in the service of the Greeks, and there were Normans fighting on both sides during the crucial siege of Bari in 1071. These were of course men of minor importance, but in the early days the same temper was shown by the leaders themselves. The changing alliances of Rannulf of Aversa between 1030 and 1045 are evidence of this, and while the two eldest sons of Tancred of Hauteville served the Greeks in Sicily about 1038, Roger, the youngest of those remarkable brothers, was about 1060 in alliance with Ibn at Timnah, emir of Syracuse.[1] Clearly, the armed support of the Normans was something that was rated at the highest value.

The characteristic Norman warrior of this period was a heavily armed combatant who fought on horseback; nor is there any reason to suppose that either his fighting qualities or his equipment were essentially different in England, Italy or Sicily. The Norman warrior depicted in the Bayeux Tapestry with his conical helmet, and his kite shaped shield, with his sword, and (though only for the wealthy) with his hauberk of metal rings, was doubtless in the latter half of the eleventh century to be found not only in Sussex but also in Apulia and Sicily. Evidence of this is admittedly scanty for no inspired stitchwork, alas, was fashioned to commemorate the deeds of Robert Guiscard. But the mounted troops who fought under Bohemund in 1107 were fortunately described by Anna Comnena, and she noted that:

> their chief weapon of defence is a coat of mail, ring plaited into ring, and the iron fabric is so excellent that it repels arrows and keeps the wearer's flesh unhurt. An additional weapon of defence is a shield which is not round, but a long shield very broad at the top and running out to a point, hollowed out slightly in the inner side but externally smooth and gleaming with a brilliant boss of brass.[2]

Anna Comnena wrote about 1145 towards the close of a long life and doubtless the brass boss on the shield is an addition of the mid-twelfth century. Apart from that, the picture which emerges from her description is strikingly like that given in the Bayeux Tapestry which certainly she had never seen.

In one further respect, moreover, it is here possible to make a more specific comparison. The importance of mounted troops to the success of William's expedition to England is well known, and the exploits of the Norman horsemen at Hastings have been fully commemorated in the Bayeux Tapestry.[3] But in the East too the special skill of the Normans

[1] Malaterra, I, c. 7, II, c. 3. [2] Alexiad, XIII, c. 8. [3] Plate III.

as horsemen was well known and, by the first quarter of the twelfth century, the charge of the Normans had become both feared and 'famous'. It was held to be almost 'irresistible', and its impact was such as 'might make a hole in the walls of Babylon'.[1] It is hardly surprising, therefore, that Turkish tactics during the First Crusade were to be largely directed towards minimizing the effect of this formidable charge, and, as will be seen, it was a feature of the generalship of Bohemund that he initiated counter measures to make effective the onslaught of his mounted knights.

Anna Comnena did not always distinguish clearly between Normans and other 'Franks', but the justice of her remarks is demonstrated since most of the Norman victories in the West between 1050 and 1100 were won by horsemen over infantry. Here, indeed, it is possible to make a direct comparison between two of the earliest and most important of those victories, namely the battle of Civitate in 1053, and the battle of Hastings thirteen years later. Both these battles are described at some length by early writers, the former by William of Apulia and the biographers of Leo IX, the latter by William of Poitiers and the author of the *Carmen*.[2] And all these writers stress that in each case the final Norman success was won by warriors fighting on horseback against resolute foot-soldiers. At Hastings, the repeated charges of the Norman knights against Harold's infantry massed on the summit of their hill are well known. But at Civitate very similar tactics had produced a like result. There too the Norman attack was repeatedly and vigorously made on horseback. The chief resistance came from the pope's Swabian mercenaries, who fought on foot in very close order, 'like a wall', forming themselves, at the last, into 'squares' before they were finally overwhelmed.[3] The parallel with the action of Harold's men at Hastings is at once apparent. These, too, were massed in the closest formation shield to shield, and it was long before they were overcome by the Norman horsemen.

The mounted charges which were so successfully made by the Normans at Civitate and at Hastings were certainly designed to produce a collective shock on the enemy. But they tended to become an

[1] Alexiad, V, c. 4; XIII, c. 8.
[2] Will. Apul., II, vv. 180–226; Will. Poit., 186–205; *Carmen*, XV, 410 et seq.; Watterich, *Vitae Pont.*, I, 95–177; Amatus, II, c. 37.
[3] Facta tamen de se quasi muro in modo corone mortem expectantes. (Cf. Gregorovius, *op. cit.*, IV, pt i, p. 84.) The parallel with Hastings (Will. Poit., p. 186, *Cuncti pedites densius conglobati*) is indeed remarkable.

aggregate of individual attacks. For this reason it must have been difficult for any commander to regroup his horsemen after failure in such a
charge, so that they could make a second attempt. Control in the field
was difficult. None the less, Richard of Aversa was able at Civitate to
call off the pursuit of his mounted men against the routed Italians, and
to regroup them for a fresh assault on the Swabians, whilst at the crisis
of the battle of Hastings William the Conqueror succeeded, albeit with
difficulty, in rallying his discomfited knights, and sending them once
again up the hill for their final attack.[1] Such discipline could not have
been imposed during battles, which must have been extremely confused, unless the Norman horsemen had been previously trained (together with their mounts) to act to some extent in concert. In this
context it would be interesting to know, for instance, what were the
peace-time duties of Gilbert du Pin who was not only the vassal but the
princeps militiae of Roger of Beaumont,[2] and the 'inherent cohesion' of
the mounted contingents of the Norman lords at Hastings has been
noted.[3]

There is, indeed, evidence which has been held to suggest that at
Hastings such discipline was confronted with a test of particular
severity and survived it. According to both William of Poitiers and the
author of the *Carmen*, the Norman horsemen at the height of the battle
successfully resorted, under orders, to the device of a feigned flight in
order to tempt their opponents to pursuit, and thereafter to turn and
destroy them.[4] This manoeuvre is so difficult to perform, in the midst
of savage conflict, that several modern commentators have refused to
believe that it ever took place, alleging that the account was inserted
to cover what was in fact a disorganized retreat.[5] This may have been
so, but the tactical device was frequently used in contemporary engage-
ments. It was employed by the Normans in 1053 near Arques, and
again by the imperial troops at Larissa in 1082,[6] and when the Crusaders reached Syria in 1099 they found it to be a commonplace of
Moslem tactics.[7] Moreover, not only was the device often employed, it

[1] Will. Poit., pp. 190–3.   [2] Ord. Vit., III, p. 342.
[3] Stenton, *Anglo-Saxon England*, p. 385.
[4] Will. Poit., p. 194; *Carmen*, vv. 420–30.
[5] E.g. A. H. Burne (*Battlefields of England*, 19–45); C. H. Lemmon in *The Norman Conquest*,
ed. C. T. Chevalier, p. 109; J. Beeler, *Warfare in England*, p. 21.
[6] Will. Jumièges, p. 120; *Alexiad*, V, c. 6.
[7] Sir H. A. R. Gibbs (ed. *Damascus Chronicle*, p. 40) remarks: 'The Arab cavalry maintained
their traditional tactics of advancing and wheeling in simulated flight – then when the enemy
started in pursuit wheeling round again at a prearranged point and charging upon them'.

was also one to which (as it seems) the Normans were particularly addicted. It was apparently used by them in an engagement outside Messina in 1060.[1] It is said to have been employed by Robert of Flanders (who had Norman allies) at the battle of Cassel in 1071,[2] and it was used by the Turks against the Normans at Artah in 1105.[3] There is thus, perhaps, reason for not discarding too readily the early statements that the device was successfully used in 1066 at Hastings. If so, it was an outstanding example of the discipline and efficiency of Norman mounted troops at this time.

III

There can be no doubt that the military successes of the Normans during these decades owed very much to the fighting qualities of their specially armed horsemen. It would, however, be easy to exaggerate the number of these. It is extremely doubtful that, as was later stated, three thousand mounted men sustained the Norman cause at Civitate[4] and if William's army at Hastings can be estimated at about 7,000 men only a small proportion of whom were fully armed or on horseback. Indeed, during the latter part of his English reign when conditions were far more favourable to him, the total number of knights whose services the Conqueror might expect to receive as a result of all the enfeoffments made in England between 1070 and 1087 was probably no more than 5,000, and it could never be anticipated that all these would be present at the same time. The number of mounted knights available in Italy and Sicily must have been smaller than this. Roger's landing in Sicily early in 1061 was made with about 160 knights, and the total number of knights who came with their mounts in two relays across the Straits later in the year to take Messina was about 450. It was asserted that in a subsequent campaign Roger had 700 knights, but it is doubtful whether before 1091 he could ever put into the field more than 1,000 mounted men with very varied equipment at any one time.[5]

In these circumstances, the Normans certainly depended largely upon supporting troops, most of whom fought on foot. These were recruited in various ways. Just as the Normans in Italy had served many masters for pay, so also did they themselves use mercenary

---

[1] Amatus, V, c. 12–16; Malaterra, II, c. i–9; Waley, *op. cit.*, p. 123.
[2] Cf. Fliche, *Philippe I*, pp. 252–61.
[3] Runciman, *Crusades*, II, p. 52.   [4] Will. Apul., II, vv. 137, 138.
[5] Waley, *op. cit.*, pp. 122–3; Douglas, *op. cit.*, pp. 276–8.

troops, plentifully and profitably, in all the countries where their conquests were achieved. The importance of mercenaries in Anglo-Norman warfare is for instance particularly well attested.[1] For his great expedition of 1066 the Conqueror recruited mercenaries from all over western Europe, and after his coronation the number of such troops was increased by the addition of many Englishmen who came to take his pay. In 1068 he dismissed many of these stipendiary soldiers, but he engaged more for his war in the north in 1069–70. The treasure he is alleged to have taken from English monasteries in the latter year was doubtless used to pay for the many English soldiers who followed him to Scotland in 1072 and to Maine in 1073; and about 1078 he employed the money gained by confiscating the estates of Norman rebels to increase the number of his own mercenaries. The exceptionally heavy tax which he exacted from England early in 1084 must have been employed to finance the very large force he brought back from Normandy in the next year, but even so riots broke out because of the levies needed to sustain it.

In Italy and Sicily, likewise, the Normans made wide use of mercenaries recruited from the lands they sought to conquer. The Calabrians who came with Robert Guiscard to Civitate must have been serving him for pay; and mercenaries from southern Italy were being hired to support the expeditions which he and Roger took to Sicily in 1060, 1061 and 1072.[2] Stipendiary troops from Apulia assisted the Norman capture of Bari in 1071, and soldiers from Calabria are known to have accompanied Robert Guiscard and Bohemund when they crossed the Adriatic ten years later.[3] Even more noteworthy were the circumstances of Guiscard's march against Rome in 1084. Early in 1083 we are told he had levied an exceptionally heavy tribute on Bari, and he collected a large tax from all over Apulia and Calabria to pay for the soldiers he was to lead against Henry IV in the following year.[4] It was certainly a very mixed army which went to the sack of Rome in 1084, but there were Saracens in it,[5] and Moslem troops were constantly in the pay of Roger, the 'Great Count'. Evidently the Normans everywhere employed mercenaries during this period, and the fact goes some way to

[1] J. O. Prestwich, 'War and Finance in the Anglo-Norman state (R. Hist. Soc., *Trans.*, Ser. 5, IV (1954), pp. 19–44).
[2] Malaterra, II, c. 45; Waley, *op. cit.*
[3] *Alexiad*, I, c. 14; Will. Apul., IV, vv. 120–30. For other instances see Malaterra, I, c. 16; Will. Apul., III, vv. 235.
[4] Ann. Bari, s.a. 1083; Lupus, s.a. 1083; Malaterra, III, c. 35.
[5] Landulf, *Historia Mediolanensis*, III, c. 33.

explain (though not to excuse) their heavy taxation of the peoples subjected to them.

The auxiliary troops used by the Normans were not only secured as mercenaries. They were also recruited by means of the military arrangements which the Normans found already existing in the countries they conquered. In their early wars against the Greeks in Apulia the Normans received assistance from the organized militia of the Lombard cities,[1] and it is in every way probable that Robert Guiscard at a later date utilized the institutions which the Greeks in Italy had operated for local defence. Again after 1066, the Normans made full use of the military institutions of Saxon England. Whatever may have been the precise character of the Anglo-Saxon *fyrd*, or the obligations to serve in it, there is no doubt that the Norman kings of England utilized the levies which they summoned from the shires and hundreds of England.[2] Such levies were, for instance, called out to suppress the rebellion of the earls in 1075, and William Rufus owed to the militia of the south-eastern shires much of the success he achieved at the beginning of his reign against his brother Robert and his uncle Odo, bishop of Bayeux.[3]

The vast majority of the auxiliary troops recruited by the Normans fought as infantry,[4] and the use made by the Normans of foot-soldiers in their conquests deserves some emphasis. As early as 1051 the Conqueror, when duke of Normandy, had discovered their value while besieging Domfront and Alençon, whilst after 1066 foot-soldiers, recruited from England, were effective in capturing Norwich in 1075, and both Tonbridge and Rochester in 1088.[5] In the south, too, the same conditions prevailed. The capture of Bari in 1071, of Durazzo in 1082, and of Rome in 1084 must have been achieved not only by dismounted knights but also by recruited foot-soldiers, whilst Roger, the 'Great Count', is known to have used Saracen infantry to besiege Cosenza in 1091, Castrovillari in 1094, Amalfi in 1096, and Capua in 1098.[6] The seizure of cities and fortresses was an essential concomitant of

---

[1] Chalandon, *op. cit.*, I, p. 37.

[2] Hollister, *Military Obligations of Norman England*, pp. 216 et seq.

[3] A. S. Chron., 'E', s.a. 1075; 1088. Cf. Beeler, *op. cit.*, p. 62.

[4] The stipendiary knights who served the Norman magnates in England were probably unenfeoffed men from Normandy, but despite some opinions to the contrary it appears to be extremely unlikely that many of the Anglo-Saxon fyrd fought on horseback (cf. Beeler, *op. cit.*, pp. 310–3).

[5] A.S. Chron., 'E', s.a. 1088; Will Malms., *Gesta Regum.*, II, 362; Flor Worc., s.a. 1088.

[6] Malaterra, IV, c. 18, 22, 24; Eadmer, *Vita Anselmi*, ed. Southern, p. 111.

Norman progress, and this could not be achieved except by warriors fighting on foot.

The role of infantry in seige warfare is self-evident. It became however a pressing problem for the Norman leaders to determine how, in a pitched battle, they could best combine the services of foot-soldiers with the charge of the mounted knights. In this matter indeed a certain progression can perhaps be detected in the development of Norman tactics between 1050 and 1100. At Civitate, it would appear that the Calabrian foot-soldiers who came with Robert Guiscard played only a minor part in the engagement.[1] At Hastings, on the other hand, William made great use of his infantry. At the beginning of the battle they went forward in front of the squadrons of knights, first the archers and slingers and then the more heavily armed foot-soldiers. Their purpose was to harrass individually the men established on the hill, before the knights made their assault. As has been seen, the issue was long in doubt. But before the end of the battle William evidently made a real and successful effort to co-ordinate the action of his archers with the attack of his mounted knights, and this was in fact to make a major contribution to his victory.

Finally, Bohemund, in very different conditions, developed this co-operation still further. In the First Crusade he found himself faced with a new type of opposition in that the Turks relied for their defence upon mobility rather than mass. Not only, therefore, had they to be manoeuvred into position before the mounted charge of the knights could be delivered, but the flanks of the charging horsemen had to be protected from the mounted archers who constituted the most effective part of the Turkish armies. In these circumstances Bohemund firstly attempted to counteract the enveloping tactics of the Turks by the formation of a special reserve of knights of which he was wont himself to take personal command; and secondly he devised a new role for the numerous foot-soldiers at his disposal. He had noted the general services that these had performed at Doryleum in July 1097, and he now determined that in the future these foot-soldiers should supplement the effort of his knights in a controlled and definite manner. And at the 'Great Battle' outside Antioch on 28 June 1098 the results were to be seen. Then the foot-soldiers emerged from the beleaguered city in front of the knights (as at Hastings), but now their purpose was not so much to assault the enemy, as to protect the Norman horsemen from flank

[1] Will. Apul., II, vv. 180 et seq.

IV   San Giovanni dei Lepprosi, Palermo

V   Melbourne Church, Derbyshire

attack until these should be ready to deliver the 'irresistible' charge.[1] And in the event it was this charge thus prepared that routed the army of Kerbogha, and ensured the establishment of the Norman principality of Antioch. In the history of Norman warfare during the latter half of the eleventh century, the battle of Civitate (18 June 1053), the battle of Hastings (14 October 1066) and the Great Battle of Antioch (28 June 1098) form a logical as well as a chronological sequence.

IV

Equally remarkable was the co-ordination which was everywhere effected by the Normans between the land and sea forces at their disposal. Once the Normans in the south had determined to extend their operations into Sicily, they were immediately faced with the problem of sea transport. But they had no ships of their own, and at first no ship-wrights, or technicians who could construct ships for their use. They were thus dependent upon such ships as they could acquire in the Apulian and Calabrian ports such as Otranto, Brindisi and Reggio which they had captured. The Byzantine rulers had in the past compelled such towns to provide ships for their defence, and these arrangements the Normans continued. But they also hired both ships and sailors, and thus acquired the miscellaneous collection of vessels which carried the first Norman expeditions across the Straits of Messina to Sicily in 1060 and 1061.[2]

It was not long, however, before the Normans began to build ships for themselves. There perhaps existed a Norman navy in the time of Duke Robert I,[3] but it was the invasion of England by his son that inspired the feverish outburst of ship building which is so graphically displayed in the Bayeux Tapestry. The number of vessels which transported the Conqueror's army across the Channel on the night of 27–28 September 1066 has been variously estimated, but it was probably not far short of 700. These must however have been of various types and sizes. But the clinker-built ships depicted in the Tapestry with their graceful lines and their billowing sails were clearly the product of a major effort of ship construction. Nor was it long before

---

[1] *Gesta Francorum*, ed. Hill, pp. 18–21, 54–5, 67–71. Smail, *Crusading Warfare*, 168–78; Fuller, *Armaments and History*, pp. 71–2.

[2] On the early use of ships by the Normans in Italy see throughout D. P. Waley in *Papers of the British School at Rome*, XXII (1954), pp. 118–25.

[3] Cf. J. Laporte in *Annales de Normandie*, XVII (1967), p. 7.

the Normans in the south were likewise to start building ships. It is probable that ships were built for the Norman attack on Trapani in 1076, and Robert Guiscard certainly built ships of his own for his invasion of the Eastern Empire in 1081.[1] Similarly, in 1085, Roger, the 'Great Count', caused ships to be built in Calabria for his onslaught on Syracuse in the next year, and doubtless these vessels formed part of the expedition which he took to Malta in 1090.[2]

None the less, the Normans continued to rely very heavily upon the ships which they commandeered and upon the sailors whom they pressed into their service. The sailors who after 1066 served the Conqueror and his son so well must have been English, and as late as 1096 a grandson of Tancred of Hauteville spent a large sum of money in hiring Italian ships which by the efforts of 200 oarsmen transferred across the Adriatic, 1,500 soldiers and 90 horses.[3] For his great expedition against the East in 1081 Robert Guiscard is known to have collected ships and sailors not only from Italian cities such as Brindisi and Otranto, but also from Illyrian ports such as Ragusa, whilst Roger in his turn continued to use ships from Reggio and from Sicilian cities such as Messina, Catania and Syracuse.[4] The fact perhaps deserves emphasis. The Norman realm of King Roger II of Sicily was to create and utilize one of the most powerful navies of the Middle Ages. But this was a development of the twelfth century, and whilst Robert Guiscard and Roger, his brother, deserve full credit for its inception, only limited progress was made in their time. During the latter half of the eleventh century the Normans continued everywhere to depend very directly upon ships made by others and upon sailors recruited from the conquered lands.

None the less, the use they made of the fleets they collected was very notable. The landings effected by the Normans near Messina in 1060 and 1061 are of interest in that then for the first time the Normans are to be found transporting war horses by sea.[5] This is a difficult art which the Normans may have learnt from the Italian sailors whom the Greeks had earlier employed for that purpose, and the Normans were certainly to profit by any instruction they may have received. The

[1] Malaterra, III, c. 11; Will. Apul., IV, vv. 122, 123.

[2] Malaterra, IV, c. 2.

[3] *Alexiad*, III, c. 8, and see Bréhier, *Monde byzantine*: *Institutions*, p. 422.

[4] Will. Apul., IV, vv. 122–40; Malaterra, IV, c. 2.

[5] Waley, *op. cit.*, 120–2. Perhaps in 1066 William profited in this respect from the instruction he received from those men from Apulia and Calabria, who are recorded by the *Carmen* as having joined his expedition against England.

straits of Messina are narrow, and though not always calm, they are sheltered, but the Norman passage of the English Channel was over an exposed stretch of more than twenty miles, and the crossing from Otranto to Corfu is nearly sixty miles in extent. But the horses which crossed in William's little ships in 1066 are engagingly shown in the Bayeux Tapestry, and Robert Guiscard is expressly stated to have brought horses with him across the Adriatic in 1081.[1] The matter was, indeed, of importance. The Normans at this period depended directly for their success in battle upon the charge of their mounted knights, but for this to be effective trained horses were necessary, and in both England and in Sicily these had perforce to be brought in ships. It does not, therefore, seem too much to suggest that the successful transportation of horses by sea made a real contribution to the Norman victories on land.

Certainly, the Norman conquests during this period were everywhere facilitated by the co-ordination effected between the land and sea forces of the Normans. The Conqueror's campaign which culminated at Hastings would have been impossible without the fleet he built, and it was his command of the Narrow Seas which, later in 1066, enabled him to receive in England the reinforcements he sorely needed.[2] Again, it was a co-ordinated blockade by sea and land which brought about the capture of Bari in 1071, and immediately after the fall of the city the fleet not only transported the Norman troops to Catania but participated in a combined operation against Palermo, Robert Guiscard proceeding with the ships along the north coast while Roger advanced overland from Catania with the bulk of the troops.[3] This campaign in the autumn of 1071 may be closely compared with that undertaken in 1072 by William the Conqueror against Scotland. In 1071 he had commandeered ships for the defence of his English realm, and in 1072, he

> led a naval force and a land force to Scotland, and blockaded that country with ships, and went himself with his land forces over the Forth.[4]

The parallel with the Sicilian strategy of the previous year is exact.

The employment of ships for purposes of transport and blockade continued to be practised everywhere by the Normans during the eleventh century. In 1077, for example, Salerno fell to Robert Guiscard

---

[1] Anna Comnena, *Alexiad*, III, c. 12.
[2] A.S. Chron., s.a. 1066; Fuller, *Decisive Battles*, I, p. 382.
[3] See above, p. 58.   [4] A.S. Chron., 'E', s.a. 1072.

after a siege in which both ships and troops took part, and the same methods were employed (though this time unsuccessfully) by Richard of Capua against Naples.[1] Meanwhile, ships of Robert Guiscard had been raiding the Dalmatian coast, and in 1081 his fleet brought the Norman expeditionary force to Corfu.[2] It was perhaps fortunate for the Normans that the Byzantine navy was at this time in decline,[3] for it was only with difficulty that they withstood the Venetians in the Adriatic. Venetian ships not only defeated those of the Normans outside Durazzo in 1081, but continued their vigorous resistance to the Normans at sea throughout 1084 only to be themselves defeated later in that year and in 1085.[4] Meanwhile, the amphibious operations of the Normans continued. In 1086 Syracuse fell as the result of a long siege by sea and land. In 1088 in a smaller engagement William Rufus used ships to capture Pevensey from his enemies,[5] and in 1090 Count Roger took his great expedition over the sea to Malta. The successful use by the Normans of ships to support their land forces was thus demonstrated in the north in 1066, 1071, 1072 and 1088, and in the south in 1071, 1077, 1081, 1086 and 1090. It is small wonder that one of the first acts of Bohemund when in precarious possession of Antioch in 1099 was to secure the co-operation of the Genoese fleet.[6]

V

Despite the obvious differences which existed between them, all the Norman conquests between 1050 and 1100 were achieved in the first instance by an *élite* of mounted and well-armed warriors acting in co-operation with foot-soldiers, and supported when necessary by fleets of ships. It was in fact this co-ordinated action between horsemen and foot-soldiers, between land and sea forces, which was the distinguishing mark of Norman military operations during the latter half of the

[1] Will. Apul., III, vv. 412–42; Amatus, VIII, cc. 18, 24, 25, 33.

[2] Chalandon, *op. cit.*, pp. 268, 269.

[3] Bréhier, *Monde Byzantine: Institutions*, pp. 419–29; Runciman, *Byzantine Civilisation*, p. 168. It was perhaps fortunate for the Normans that the ships which took William across the Channel never had to fight a naval action. What happened to the Saxon ships in the autumn of 1066 is a mystery. Did they refuse to fight for Harold? At all events the ships of the Normans everywhere seem to have been used generally for transport and blockade, and only rarely in this period did they fight at sea.

[4] Cf. M. Mathieu, *Guillaume de Pouille*, p. 332.

[5] A.S. Chron., 'E', s.a. 1087 (equals 1088). Flor. Worc., s.a. 1088.

[6] See the charter of Bohemund to the Genoese dated 14 July 1098 and the subsequent pact (Hagenmeyer, *Kreuzzugsbriefe*, nos. XIII and XIV; Rohricht, *Regesta*, no. 12).

eleventh century. But the efficacy of this depended directly upon one further consideration: the establishment on every critical occasion of a unified command. In this the Normans of this age were outstandingly successful. Robert Guiscard never failed in co-ordinating the operations of his knights with those of his Calabrian and Apulian mercenaries, or, when occasion served, in reinforcing both with the ships he had mobilized for war. Similarly, at Hastings during a battle that was prolonged and confused, William the Conqueror exercised a remarkable degree of control over all his troops: the mounted knights, the foot-soldiers, and the archers. Moreover, both he and William Rufus during the years that followed always managed to weld into a single coherent force the feudal knights whom the Normans had established in England, and the infantry of the Anglo-Saxon militia. In like manner, Count Roger not only enfeoffed his feudal tenants with land in Sicily, but combined their military service with that of his Saracen mercenaries. Finally, it was Bohemund's greatest distinction as a tactician to make full use of his infantry in support of his mounted knights.

These were, of course, all outstanding men, but many other of the Norman leaders also showed the same high capacity. The spectacular career of Richard I, prince of Capua, was due to military dexterity as well as to brute force, and William Rufus was justly regarded by his contemporaries as a commander of great ability. Jordan, the bastard son of Count Roger, could play his individual part in the complicated combined operation which led to the fall of Syracuse in 1086, whilst Tancred was to prove an admirable supporter of Bohemund. In Italy, the Norman advance was assisted by the efforts of such men as William of Grandmesnil, and William, a son of Tancred of Hauteville, who was the first count of the 'Principate'.[1] Similarly, the Norman conquest of England owed much to William Fitz-Osbern, earl of Hereford, who died at the battle of Cassel in 1071, Roger II of Montgomery, who became earl of Shrewsbury, and Robert, count of Mortain, the Conqueror's half-brother. Nor was it merely the secular Norman magnates who displayed military ability. Robert of Grandmesnil, when abbot of S. Euphemia in Calabria, competently defended Vicalvi in the cause of Robert Guiscard, whilst Odo, bishop of Bayeux, and Geoffrey, bishop

[1] See Genealogy 2. The career of William de Principatu is discussed with a wealth of learning by Professor L. R. Ménager in *Quellen und Forschungen* XXXIX (1959), pp. 67–73. The *comté* of the Principate was situated to the south of Naples. See also below p. 75.

of Coutances, successfully conducted in England punitive expeditions of some magnitude.[1]

The high quality of Norman leadership and its co-operative character assisted the Normans in solving one of their greatest military problems at this time. Victories might be won by the exploitation of new tactical techniques, but afterwards it was necessary to control large areas of conquered territory with only a limited number of troops. The method adopted to deal with this situation was, everywhere, the erection of fortified strong-points, each under the command of a responsible Norman magnate. The importance of the castle in the Norman conquest of England has been widely recognized.[2] 'Motte and bailey' castles such as had been depicted in the Bayeux Tapestry at Dol and Rennes were widely constructed in England between 1067 and 1070. A stronghold of this type had immediately been erected at Hastings and the submission of Exeter was marked by the beginning of Rougemont castle. In 1068 as William moved towards the north, castles were erected as has been seen at Warwick, Nottingham and York, whilst on his return march they were built at Lincoln, Huntingdon and Cambridge.[3] The castle – usually a wooden erection placed on an entrenched earthen mound, but sometimes, as at Colchester, Dover, Richmond and Chepstow, reconstructed at an early date in stone – was thus introduced widespread into England by the Normans as a military device. And early commentators are emphatic in asserting that such castles made a substantial contribution to the Conqueror's success.

A similar pattern of progress may be discerned, though perhaps less clearly, in the south. There in distinction to England, the Normans found many fortresses already in existence. But they speedily made special use of castles for themselves. The earliest Norman settlements in Italy, it will be recalled, were in the hill strongholds of Aversa and Melfi, and before 1055 Robert Guiscard was erecting castles in Calabria such as 'Scribla' in the Val di Crati, at Rossano, and in the neighbourhood of Cozenza, both at San Marco Argentano, and at Scalea.[4] When Roger came to Italy in the next year, Robert Guiscard at once set him up in a stronghold at Mileto, and the two brothers forthwith followed

---

[1] Ord. Vit., ii, 193, 262, 263. Cf. Chalandon, *op. cit.*, i, 232.

[2] See J. Beeler in *Speculum*, XXXI (1956), pp. 581–601, and more particularly in his *Warfare in England*, pp. 49–57, and Appendix 'A'.

[3] Ord. Vit., ii, pp. 181–5.

[4] Malaterra, I, c. 12, 16, 24. Amatus, IV, c. 24, 25. Leo of Ostia, III, c. 15.

the same practice in Sicily. As early as 1060–1 castles were built by them at San Marco di Alunsio in the Val Demone, and at Petralia Soprana near Cefalù,[1] whilst the hill stronghold of Troina remained Roger's base for several years. But the Sicilian parallel to what occurred in England between 1067 and 1070 can best be sought in Roger's actions after the fall of Palermo. For between 1071 and 1074 he attempted with some success to consolidate his rule over the northern part of the island by erecting castles at Mazzara, Calascibetta and elsewhere.[2] Finally, though the conditions in Syria were of course very different, the successors of Bohemund at a later date may have learnt from earlier Norman practice. At all events Norman castles were set up at Antioch and Latakia, whilst (as at York and Norwich) strongholds were erected to control the frontier towns of Artah, Atharib and Zardana. Again, within forty miles of Latakia itself, work was begun before 1140 on the great castle of Sahyun.[3]

It is reasonable also to suppose that the earlier erection of castles by the Normans in the West had proceeded according to definite plans adopted by such rulers as William the Conqueror and Count Roger.[4] Certainly, both in the north and south of Europe, the sites of the castles built by the Normans in their time seem to have been very carefully chosen both for themselves and in relation to each other. They probably formed part of a co-ordinated military strategy, and they were normally placed in the charge of powerful and trusted Norman magnates. William Fitz-Osbern was thus for a time castellan of York, and Henry of Beaumont at Warwick. The castle at Exeter was entrusted to Baldwin, son of Gilbert, count of Brionne, and that of Hastings came into the custody of Robert, count of Eu.[5] In Italy and Sicily the same policy was adopted. Robert Guiscard placed his brother Roger at Mileto, and Count Roger in his turn confided his Sicilian castles to the most important of the followers he enfeoffed.

[1] Malaterra, II, c. 17, 38.

[2] Above p. 63. It should be noted that many of the castles of Frederick II both in Italy and in Sicily were developed from existing erections which were doubtless made by Robert Guiscard and Count Roger. The castles of Bari and Trani in Apulia come to mind, and in Sicily those of Trapani, Lentini, Termini and Milazzo. See G. Masson, *Frederick II*, pp. 176, 182.

[3] Cahen, *Syrie du Nord*, pp. 327–30; Smail, *op. cit.*, pp. 60–62, 212.

[4] This has been disputed, but for the case of England, see Beeler, *op. cit.*, pp. 51–5, which should however be read in connexion with the review by H. A. Brown in *Eng. Hist. Rev.*, LXIII (1968), pp. 818–20.

[5] Douglas, *William the Conqueror*, pp. 216, 217. The estimate there given that 'at least eighty-four' castles were built by the Normans in England before 1100 is however a serious understatement.

The possession of such strongholds by powerful members of a violent aristocracy inevitably enhanced the dangers of feudal rebellion, and this was demonstrated on several occasions during this period. A short civil war occurred in England after the death of William the Conqueror, and when Robert Guiscard died in 1084, his sons and his brother, with their followers, fell-a-fighting over his inheritance. Guiscard had himself been compelled to face feudal opposition in Apulia in 1074, 1078 and 1082, whilst rebellions broke out in England in 1074 and 1102. But as will appear the Norman magnates usually found it to their advantage to co-operate with their rulers, and this gave a special importance to the early castles which the Normans built and manned. They served as links in a co-ordinated chain of defence, as well as centres of local administration through which the Norman will could be imposed over wide areas of territory. In short, at least until after 1100, the Norman castle placed in the charge of a trusted lieutenant of the Norman ruler served everywhere as an effective instrument whereby the Norman conquest might be consolidated.

In all the varied warfare conducted by the Normans during the latter half of the eleventh century certain common characteristics may thus be discerned. The differences between the wars which created the Norman states of Capua, Apulia and Antioch, and which resulted in the Norman conquests of England and Sicily are obvious. But the similarities between them have also to be recognized. In all of them, the Normans, while dealing with distinct problems in widely separated lands, used similar military expedients to gain their ends. Neither the Norman conquests of this age nor the connexions between them can in fact be explained without reference to the military techniques which the Normans made their own, and which they everywhere exploited with such outstanding success.

Chapter 5

THE HOLY WAR

I

The Norman achievement during the latter half of the eleventh century did not depend solely upon Norman military strength. It derived also from special factors in Norman policy, which must be related to wider movements in European thought and sentiment that the Normans themselves did much to promote. Chief among these must be ranked the growing enthusiasm for the waging of war on behalf of religion. The concept of the Holy War[1] which coloured so much of the political activity of Europe during these years owed a great deal to the Normans. It contributed to their successes, and it was to be distorted by their acts. It also imparted a unifying principle to most of the enterprises they undertook. No explanation of what the Normans accomplished between 1050 and 1100 can thus afford to ignore their close association with the development of this idea.

A religious element has existed in most if not all of the great struggles of human history, and the invocation of Divine assistance in battle has not been confined to any one period or to any single faith.[2] None the less, the notion of the Holy War was given a particular expression in Christendom during the latter half of the eleventh century, and the Normans not only helped to propagate that notion, but were themselves profoundly influenced by it. Indeed, there are few contrasts in history

---

[1] The topic of the Holy War must be approached with great circumspection, and assuredly with no preconceived feelings of romantic sentiment or of indiscriminate cynicism. The will to fight appears as a constant in human history, and is likely so to remain. If this be so, then the wars most capable of justification are surely those which are waged for the highest motives. On the other hand, devotion can be simulated as well as felt, and propaganda is here given special opportunities to condone atrocities or to prolong hostilities on such pleas as 'unconditional surrender' or 'a fight to a finish'. Granted a just cause, the object of war should surely be to impose the will of the victor on the vanquished with the least possible damage to either, since destruction should here be a means to an end and not the end itself. But few wagers of 'holy' or 'ideological' wars have been disposed to accept any such limitations to their scope. Genocide may be their ultimate horror.

[2] The practice goes back to the beginning of recorded history – and to Homer. For modern preaching of the Holy War, see above, p. 15.

more striking than that which is here suggested. Not long previously the Normans had been justly regarded as among those enemies of Christendom against whom a Holy War might properly be waged. The defeat of Rolf the Viking before the walls of Chartres could be hailed as a Christian victory, and as late as 1053 an army blessed and led by a pope was to take the field in Italy against the Normans. Yet before the eleventh century had closed the Normans were outstanding among the self-styled 'Soldiers of Christ', and the wide conquests which they made were to be facilitated by that claim.

By promoting and exploiting the notion of the Holy War, the Normans became actively associated with a movement in European political thought which, already of long duration, only reached its climax during the decades when the Norman conquests were made. Modern scholars have demonstrated how gradual was the process by which, in the political theology of western Christendom, the condemnation of war came to be overshadowed by a belief that in particular circumstances it might be permitted, and even blessed.[1] That complex and protracted movement is often considered directly in relation to the Crusades. But in truth it had already produced many of its most characteristic results – and not least through the efforts of the Normans – before ever the First Crusade was planned or launched. The matter had of course always been regarded as one of great delicacy. 'Blessed are the peace-makers', and the sanctification of war might seem difficult for those who had been enjoined to love their enemies.

Thus, though certain of the Fathers and particularly St Augustine, appear to have recognized that there might be occasions when war could be condoned (though not sanctified),[2] most responsible prelates in the West during the earlier Middle Ages were more concerned to denounce war, to limit its occasions and to restrict its scope. Such institutions as the Truce of God, which forbade fighting on certain days of the week, or seasons of the year, are evidence of this effort, and heavy penances were often imposed upon those who killed, or even wounded, their adversaries in battle.[3] A man fighting under orders, or in response

---

[1] The standard authority is here C. Erdmann, *Die Enstehung des Kreuzzuggedankens* (Stuttgart, 1935). See also P. Alphandéry, *Le Chrétienté et l'idée de Croisade* (Paris, 1954).

[2] Erdmann, *op. cit.*, pp. 5–14.

[3] Mr J. J. Saunders (*Aspects of the Crusades*, p. 17) cites a recommendation by St Basil that a soldier who has killed his enemy in battle should abstain from Holy Communion for three years. At the other end of the period there may be noted the penances alleged to have been imposed in 1070 by a papal legate on those Normans who had killed or wounded their enemies at the battle of Hastings (Douglas, *English Historical Documents*, II, no. 81). If this

to secular loyalities religiously ratified by oath, might well find himself under risk of dying with his salvation imperilled. Before the ninth century, indeed, the dominant, though not the unequivocal teaching of the western Church was probably to condemn war as essentially evil. Its necessity was only admitted in very exceptional circumstances, and even then only with extreme reluctance.

Nevertheless, belief that wars might be waged on behalf of God, and with His approval appears early in the history of the Church. It is manifest, for instance, in the developing stories of Constantine the Great whose victory at the Milvian Bridge in 312 was presaged by the Sign of the Cross in the sky; and more particularly was it carried to the city on the Bosphorus which perpetuated his name, and which Constantine dedicated to the Blessed Trinity and to the Mother of God.[1] Constantinople from the fourth century to the eleventh was not merely the new Rome; it was the Christian capital; and successive emperors in the East continuously asserted themselves as the armed champions of Christendom. The emperor's hand, it was claimed, enforced the will of Christ; ikons were carried before his armies; and men were constantly reminded that the long wars waged over the centuries against Persians and Arabs were directed against enemies of the Faith.[2] Much of the legislation, and many of the wars, of Justinian were infused with this spirit, and the theory found spectacular expression in the seventh century during the campaigns of Heraclius which were to recover the True Cross. Similarly, in the tenth century, the wide extension of Byzantine power by the Macedonian emperors was accomplished at the expense of enemies whose hostility to Christendom was loudly proclaimed, and the religious connotations of the wars which between 961 and 975 restored to Christendom, Crete, Aleppo, Antioch, and much of Syria, were recognized by both parties to the struggle. It does not thus seem unreasonable to conclude that in 1050 the concept of the Holy War had for centuries been part of the political consciousness of Byzantium.[3]

In the West, however, the notion had made slower progress. The

penitential is authentic, it is highly remarkable since the Norman expedition to England had been blessed by the pope.

[1] N. Baynes, 'Constantine the Great and the Christian Church' (*Proc. Brit. Acad.*, XV, esp. pp. 396–404 – a fascinating discussion).

[2] N. Baynes and Moss, *Byzantium*, pp. xxi, 10–12, 102. There seems however to have been a section of Byzantine opinion to which the notion of the Holy War was unacceptable (cf. Runciman., *Eastern Schism*, pp. 82, 83, citing *Alexiad*, X, c. 8).

[3] C. Diehl, *History of the Byzantine Empire* (Princeton, 1925), pp. 72–99; Runciman, *Crusades*, I, ff. 29–37; Grousset, *Croisades*, I, pp. iv–xx.

western Church was reluctant to abandon its general condemnation of war as evil, and apart from Spain, the militant expansion of Islam in the seventh century (itself an example of a Holy War, and an invitation to reprisals) inflicted less damage in the West than in the East. Not until after the re-establishment of the empire in the West under Charlemagne in 800 can there be detected the signs of a widespread change. The basis of Charlemagne's power was essentially secular, but there was no gainsaying that he acted in co-operation with the papacy as the avowed and militant agent of Christendom. He could declare that it was his special duty to defend the Church against its enemies, and Pope Stephen II could assure him that 'in as much as you wage war on behalf of Holy Church, your sins shall be remitted by the Prince of the Apostles'.[1] Such declarations might perhaps be regarded as the language of diplomacy, but the facts themselves gave them some substance. Charlemagne's defence of the papacy in Italy was not to be forgotten, and other consequences of his campaigns would be remembered with even greater effect. Did not his wars in Germany result in the forcible conversion of the Saxons to Christianity? And had he not undertaken an heroic, if unsuccessful, expedition against the Saracens in Spain which resulted in his defeat at Roncesvalles? Henceforth, the growing enthusiasm for the Holy War in western Europe would be inseparably connected with recollections of Charlemagne, and with the legends which grew up round his name.

The condition of Europe in the period following the death of Charlemagne was particularly suited for the further propagation of these ideas. Between 850 and 1000 western Christendom felt itself encompassed by enemies. The Saracens, having conquered Sicily, were threatening Italy, and were advancing inexorably northward in Spain. The Hungarians were pressing so vigorously from the east that the effects of their raids could be felt even in the neighbourhood of Paris. And from the north there took place fierce onslaughts from Scandinavia. In the midst of this crisis, which was both acute and very prolonged, it was not surprising that the political and religious motives for war should have become intermingled. Frankish, English and Italian writers at this time did not distinguish too precisely between those who were so strongly attacking Christendom. All alike tended to be designated as simply *pagani* or *infideles*, and the wars against them could be described not only as an effort of self-preservation, but also as the defence of the Faith. And

[1] Erdmann, *op. cit.*, pp. 19, 20.

so it might also appear in reality. The defeat of Guthrum at Chippen-
ham in 878 was followed by his conversion to Christianity, and in like
manner it was the conversion of Rolf the Viking after his defeat at
Chartres in 911 which marked the true beginning of medieval Normandy. Not without reason did Otto the Great declare some forty years
later that 'the protection of our Empire is inseparably bound up with
the rising fortunes of Christian worship', and it was appropriate that he
should carry with him sacred relics when he advanced in 955 to his
victory over the Hungarians at the Lechfeld.[1] By the opening of the
eleventh century the minds of men in western Europe had been
conditioned to the idea of a Holy War.

II

And now began a deep-seated movement which was to affect all Europe,
and in which the Normans were to play a dominant part. It was due in
the first instance to a variety of general causes, some political, some
psychological and some more strictly ecclesiastical, but these were all
linked together and in all of them the Normans found themselves particularly concerned. Chief among them was the fact that, as the eleventh
century advanced, western Christendom no longer found itself in a
state of defence since the great wars of the preceding period had removed the insistent pressure on its frontiers. During the first quarter of
the eleventh century for example, the Scandinavian impact upon the
West began to lose its force and to change its character, and after the year
1000 Hungary could be regarded as a Christian kingdom. The conversion of the north and the conversion of the Hungarians were in fact
events of wide political significance, and it was symbolic of the change
that eleventh century Norway could produce a sainted King in Olaf
(who had been received into the Church by an Archbishop of Rouen)
and that Hungary should at about the same time be ruled by St
Stephen.[2] A new pattern of politics was given expression when in 1027
Cnut the Great made his famous visit to the shrines of Rome, while in
the south, Islam, though still possessing Sicily and much of Spain, was
being successfully resisted by the Macedonian emperors. In short
western Europe had been freed from the constant threat of attack, and
any religious war that it might undertake in the future would be
offensive, rather than defensive, in character. It would be waged in

[1] M. Bloch, *Feudal Society*, p. 83.   [2] *Ibid.*, pp. 13–14; 31–5.

the hope of expanding the frontiers of Christendom rather than of ensuring its continued existence.

This development was accelerated by a growing awareness in western Christendom of its unity and militant purpose. By the opening of the eleventh century, the ecclesiastical reforms propagated by the Burgundian monastery of Cluny and its offshoots were already beginning to impart new vigour to the western Church, and at the same time there were arising those feudal aristocracies whose privileged place in society was to depend upon the specialized performance of military service. These two movements were distinct, and they were sometimes brought into collision. But their influence upon each other has already been noted in the early development of Normandy,[1] and it was not only in the Norman duchy that this was felt. Elsewhere also were the new magnates to be lavish benefactors of the Cluniac houses, whilst Cluny was soon to call on their armed support. A similar temper might also be detected in the developing zeal for pilgrimages which marked the age,[2] and it is perhaps significant that Cluny not only advocated the pilgrimages on religious grounds but supervised many of the pilgrim routes. At all events an ever-increasing stream of pilgrims began to move across Europe, and particularly towards the three great focal points: the basilicas of Rome; the shrine of St James at Compostella; and the Holy Places of Palestine.

A pilgrimage is an act of faith; it was sometimes regarded as an ultimate journey; and the numberless pilgrimages of the eleventh century were inspired by a belief that by such means the pilgrim might obtain spiritual benefit, and even perhaps expiate his sins. But the pilgrimages were also in some sense a collective work for the common salvation of Christians, and they contributed to a feeling of unity in Latin Christendom which otherwise it might have lacked. All classes were affected. Among the notorious sinners of the age, Fulk Nerra, the terrible count of Anjou, made three journeys to the Holy Land, and Geoffrey, count of Brittany, undertook the same expedition in 1008. Harold Hardraada, the Viking leader who was later king of Norway and met his death at Stamford Bridge, could in 1034 be found on the banks of the Jordan, and Sweyn Godwineson the elder brother of King Harold, fresh from murders in England and the rape of an abbess, started barefoot for Jerusalem

[1] Above, pp. 27, 28.
[2] The literature on these is very large. There may here be cited Alphandéry, *op. cit.*, pp. 10–31; Runciman, *Crusades*, I, pp. 38–51; P. Riant, *Scandinaves en Terre Sainte* (1895), *passim*.

in 1052, and died on the journey.[1] Such were among the prominent men who responded to this impulse, but the call was by no means confined to important personages. Rodulf Glaber, the chronicler, speaks of the 'innumerable crowds' of pilgrims,[2] and the evidence suggests that he was scarcely exaggerating. Rome the repository of so many relics was never more revered than at this time, and during the same years the pilgrimage to Compostella attracted a vast concourse from all quarters. Again, in 1064–5, a company estimated at no less than seven thousand persons left Germany for Palestine under the lead of their bishops.[3]

And in all this activity the Normans took a prominent part. In most of the great pilgrimages of the age they were fully represented, and the zeal for pilgrimage was zealously fostered in the duchy.[4] The Normans also possessed their own special pilgrimage shrine of St Michael 'in peril of the sea', and, as has been seen, they extended their special interest to that other famous shrine of Monte Gargano in the Abruzzi.[5] Again, in 1026 the great pilgrimage to Palestine which was led by Richard, abbot of St Vannes of Verdun, was sponsored by a Norman duke, and nine years later Duke Robert I, father of William the Conqueror, abandoned his duchy in order to make his famous pilgrimage to Jerusalem from which he never returned.[6] The ecclesiastical revival in the province of Rouen was now moreover fully prepared, and Normandy was brought to promote all the religious enthusiasms which were beginning to fire western Europe just at the time when the new aristocracies were being organized for military service. By 1050 all these distinct and related developments had thus combined to produce in western Christendom, and not least in Normandy, a climate of opinion more favourable than ever before to the prosecution of religious war.

The change was reflected even in the modes of popular devotion. Sword blessings, for example, multiplied, and there was an increase in the number of liturgical prayers for victory.[7] At the same time there was a developing cult of warrior saints.[8] The traditional cult of martyrs such as St Lawrence and St Sebastian, who were commemorated in the great basilicas of Rome, was of course continued, as was also the veneration of those others who had suffered death rather than serve in the Roman armies or resort to violence. But the temper of the mid-eleventh

---

[1] A.S. Chron., 'C', s.a. 1046, 1047, 1052; 'D', s.a. 1050 (equals 1049). Florence of Worcester, s.a. 1052.   [2] Bk. VI, ch. 6.   [3] Cf. Runciman, *Crusades*, I, pp. 43–8.
[4] Cf. L. Musset, in *Annales de Normandie* (1962), pp. 127–51.
[5] See above, pp. 38, 39.   [6] Douglas, *William the Conqueror*, 36, 37, 408, 409.
[7] F. Heer, *Medieval World*, p. 97.   [8] Erdmann, *op. cit.*, pp. 38–41, 46, and *passim*.

century was better represented in the waxing enthusiasm for St Michael the warrior archangel, so beloved of the Normans, and for St Gabriel 'chief of the angelic guards'. It would even appear that there may have been an early cult of St James in Spain as a man of peace, but in the eleventh century he was fully established as *Santiago Matamoros*, the slayer of the Moors. Had he not in the ninth century led the Christians to their victory at Clavijo, and might he not once more fight on behalf of Christendom?[1] It would of course be easy to exaggerate. The enthusiasms of the age were too manifold to be described under a single formula. But the general tendency is evident, and the inspiration thus generated was pervasive.

The most vivid literary expression of the idea of the Holy War thus propagated, was given in the *Chansons de Geste*, some of which clearly recall episodes in the Norman conquests.[2] Here, however, it will suffice to cite two poems the one dating from the beginning, and the other from the end of the eleventh century. The former written in Latin is concerned with the fabled exploits of a Norman duke; the latter is the famous *Chanson de Roland* itself; and both have direct relevance to the character of the Norman achievements between 1050 and 1100. Thus about the first decade of the eleventh century there was composed a Latin *Lament*[3] for the death of William Longsword, second duke of Normandy, who was assassinated by the enemies of Louis d'Outre Mer king of France on an island in the Seine in 942. The poem which certainly ascribed to the Norman duke, Christian and feudal virtues which he never possessed, is, by reason of its subject matter and its date, of peculiar significance as an early expression of the ideals of the Holy War. For this son of Rolf the Viking now appears as a Christian warrior laying down his life for his Faith, and in the cause of a Christian emperor. Here for instance is the Christian hero:

> When his father perished, then the unbelievers
> Rose against him, rose in armed rebellion
> These he vanquished, trusting in God's succour
> These he conquered with his own right arm.[4]

---

[1] A. Castro, *The Structure of Spanish History* (Princeton, 1954), p. 151; T. D. Kendrick, *Saint James in Spain*, 19–23.   [2] Cf. N. Mathieu, *op. cit.*, pp. 46–56.
[3] Ed. J. Lair, *Guillaume Longue-Epée*, 1893, pp. 66–68.

[4]
> Moriente infideles suo patre
> Surrexerunt contra eum bellicose
> Quos, confisus Deo valde, sibi ipse
> Subjugavit dextra forte

Thereafter was he treacherously killed to the sorrow of all good men, but he went at once to take his reward among the Blessed in Heaven.

> Now let all men weep for William
> Innocent yet done to death.[1]

Thus early had the notion of the Holy War taken root in the Viking province of Gaul.

Equally significant is the more famous *Song of Roland.* As will be recalled its thesis is the defeat of the rearguard of the army of Charlemagne in 778 by the Saracens at Roncesvalles in the Pyrenees, and the earliest complete form of the poem which we now possess is contained in a twelfth century manuscript preserved in the Bodleian Library at Oxford.[2] It is moreover generally believed that the poem in the form given to it in this Ms, or in a form very similar thereto, was compiled in the second half of the eleventh century, and perhaps between 1080 and 1100.[3] Concerning the ultimate origins of the *Roland*, however, a very long controversy has raged. It has been argued that the *Roland* should be regarded as a collective work deriving perhaps from a poet in the eighth century, whose work received constant additions and alteration for some two hundred and fifty years.[4] It has also been argued, and perhaps more convincingly, that the poem, as we now know it, was the work of a single poet of the eleventh century, who used for his purpose existing material some of which may already have been in verse form.[5] Between these two points of view a very large number of intermediate

---

[1] Cuncti flete pro Willelmo
  Innocente interfecto

[2] MS. Digby 23. Bédier (*Chanson de Roland – Commentaires*, pp. 63–7) claims 'precellence' for this text. It has subsequently been contended that better readings of some passages can be obtained elsewhere.

[3] Bédier, *op. cit.*, suggests 1098–1100. Pauphilet (*Romania*, LIX (1933), pp. 183–98) suggests 1064.

[4] E.g. R. Menendez Pidal, *La Chanson de Roland* (Paris, 1960), pp. 269–470, 500–1. Isolated references do not however do justice to this notable work which incidentally reviews many of the controversies of the present century.

[5] Bédier, *Les Légendes épiques*, 4 vols., esp. vol. III, pp. 183–455. Many points in Bédier's magnificent exposition have been successfully challenged, but his central contention that the *Roland* was the work of a single poet writing in the latter half of the eleventh century still commands wide though not universal, acceptance. This poet must, however, have had material ready for his use. The conjunction of the names Roland and Oliver as names for brothers which can be discovered as early as 1000 is evidence of earlier traditions, and a short note added between 1065 and 1075 to a tenth-century MS. of San Millan of Rioja has been held to indicate that some of this material had been early expressed in verse form and perhaps in a vernacular. A layman must express himself of these controverted topics only with extreme diffidence.

H

theories have been propounded. Nor is there need to debate further in this place whether the alleged author of the *Roland*[1] was a native of Normandy, or even the much more plausible hypothesis that the poem in its first form has some special connexion with the Normans.[2] It would appear, however, that the exploits both of William the Conqueror in England and of Robert Guiscard in the Balkans are attributed in the poem to the legendary Charlemagne,[3] and certainly the characters of the *Roland* as represented in the Bodleian Ms come from the whole period from 800 to 1085. Little or nothing in the poem as there set out is alien to the temper of the latter half of the eleventh century.

It is thus of particular interest that the whole poem is infused so notably with the notion of the Holy War which was developing to its climax in the West during the fifty years when the Normans were making their conquests. Charles the hero is conducting his unending war against the pagans, and 'the christians are right: the pagans are wrong'.[4] Charles is a man of supernatural age and superhuman sanctity. St Gabriel watches over his sleep and when he fights, the angel of God goes with him. He is moreover almost as much priest as King. He gives the priestly blessing; like a priest he signs with the Cross; and as only a priest can, he pronounces absolution. The same spirit animates his followers who form the subject of subsidiary themes, but who all help to fulfil the same central purpose. Turpin the Archbishop not only himself fights and slays and dies, but he also promises salvation to those of his companions who may fall in battle. And Roland is himself the final embodiment of these aspirations. He fights, it is true, for 'France'; he fights also as a great and faithful vassal of his lord. But he fights above all as a christian warrior. His famous sword, Durendal, is studded with Christian relics, and when he too comes to die:

> His right hand glove to God he offers it
> Saint Gabriel from his hand has taken it.
> Over his arm his head bows down and slips
> He joins his hands; so is life finished

[1] Cf. W. T. Holmes in *Speculum*, XXX (1955), pp. 77–81.

[2] Bédier, *op. cit.*, III; E. Faral, *Chanson de Roland*, p. 57 and most emphatically F. Lot (*Romania*, LIV (1949), pp. 463–73) have all denied the likelihood of any such connexion. There have, however, been some voices raised in an opposite sense. The whole matter is discussed by me (I fear inconclusively) in *French Studies*, XIV (1960), pp. 99–116.

[3] Cf. Douglas, *op. cit.*, pp. 101, 104, 105; H. Gregoire, *Bull. Acad. R. de Belgique – Classes des Lettres*, XXV (1938); and *Byzantion*, XIV (1939), E. Li Gotti, *La Chanson de Roland e i Normanni* (1949).

[4] Vv. 1015, 1016.

God sent down his angel Cherubin
And Saint Michael we worship in peril
And by their side Saint Gabriel alit
So the Count's soul they bore to Paradise.[1]

The notion of the Holy War fostered over so many years and by such diverse means has been given a full, and perhaps a final, expression.

III

The chief beneficiaries of the enthusiasms which had thus been generated were to be the papacy and the Normans. Indeed, the conception of the Holy War could hardly have been translated into terms of practical action apart from the co-operation between them. It is quite true that as early as the ninth century the papacy had begun to take the lead in this matter which was clearly at that time of direct relevance to the survival and to the unity of Latin Christendom. Thus in 848 Pope Leo IV promised heavenly rewards to those who fell fighting for the truth of the Faith, the safety of their homes, and the defence of Christendom; whilst some thirty years later Pope John VII declared that warriors killed in battle against the pagans might be assured of their salvation.[2] The papacy was, however, very soon, to enter on a period of prolonged political decline, and the concept of the Holy War was for long to be used to enhance the power, or to enlarge the posthumous prestige, of secular rulers.[3] Not until the pontificate of Leo IX who ascended the papal throne in 1049, was the papacy ready to assert itself as the natural leader in any Holy War in which Latin Christendom might be engaged. And it was only with Norman support that during the next fifty years the claim was to be widely acknowledged.

The acts of Leo IX in 1053 thus challenge immediate attention. In that year the pope not only proclaimed the Holy War with a precision which none of his predecessors had attempted. He also declared the war not against pagans but against Christians, and indeed against those very Normans who were soon to derive such benefits through posing as the soldiers of Christ. Indeed, when Leo IX decided to oppose the Normans

---

[1] Vv. 2389–96. Trans. C. K. Scott Moncrieff.
[2] Alphandéry, *op. cit.*, 16.
[3] A. Gieyztor in *Medievalia et Humanistica* (V and VI) has shown that the so-called 'crusading bull' of Sergius IV (1009–1012) was in fact a later concoction.

in Italy, he did so as the declared leader in a war to be waged specifically for 'the deliverance of Christendom.'[1] The religious character of the
enterprise was in fact continuously asserted by the pope and repeatedly
stressed by the chroniclers who recorded it. The German and Italian
troops who Leo had collected were blessed by the pope from the walls
at Benevento; they were absolved from their sins, and such penances as
they had incurred were remitted.[2] They were further assured that,
should they fall in battle, they would be received as martyrs into
Heaven. Before the engagement the pope is reported to have cried 'If
any of you should die to day he will be received into Abraham's bosom',
and on his death bed we are told that Leo exclaimed 'Truly I rejoiced
in our brothers who were killed when fighting for God in Apulia. For
I saw them numbered among the martyrs and clad in shining golden
robes'.[3] Here, in truth, was the Holy War proclaimed and led by a
pope. But it was directed against those who were soon to be its foremost
champions.

The defeat of the papal army on 18 June 1053 was thus of particular
relevance to the concept of the Holy War and to the part played by the
Normans in its development. It might indeed have proved fatal to the
claim that the papacy could call on the military support of Christendom,
and might employ spiritual sanctions in order to promote papal policy
by force of arms. As Leo of Ostia, the chronicler, was soon to observe,
trial by battle had taken place at Civitate, and God had given victory
not to the pope but to the Normans.[4] How was this to be explained?
It seemed specious to suggest that the Swabians had been judged un-
worthy to be the soldiers of Christ, and it is significant that Peter
Damien, who was so staunch a supporter of the reforming papacy,
should have reluctantly concluded that the military policy of Leo did
nothing to enhance his reputation.[5] Certainly, the position both of the
papacy and of the Normans in relation to the concept of the Holy War
had been radically disturbed by the events of 1053, and it was not to be
stabilized until the reconciliation between them six years later. The

[1] Leo IX to the Emperor Constantine IX (*Pat. Lat.*, CXLIV, col. 774. Leo's policy in this
respect is discussed exhaustively by Erdmann *op. cit.*, pp. 107–17, and by Rousset, *Premiere
Croisade*, pp. 45–9.

[2] Ann. Benevent., s.a. 1053; Amatus, III, c. 40.

[3] Ann. Benevent., s.a. 1053; *De Obitu sancti Leonis* (*Pat. Lat.* CXLIII, col. 527; Wido. *Vita
Leonis, ibid.*, col. 499).

[4] Normanni *Dei Judicio* extitere victores (*Pat. Lat.*, CLXXIII, col. 690). Compare the
account of the Battle of Hastings by Eadmer, *Hist. Nov.*, ed. Rule, p. 9.

[5] *Pat. Lat.*, CXLIV, col. 316.

importance of the synod of Melfi in 1059 to the establishment of Norman power in Italy has already been noted.[1] But the consequences of the alliance which was then effected between the papacy and the Normans were to stretch far beyond the peninsular, and it is significant that Archdeacon Hildebrand had been an active agent in bringing it about. For what occurred in 1059 assisted him as pope in overcoming the setback which Leo IX had received in 1053. As Gregory VII he was effectively to proclaim against secular rulers that, if need arose, it was the right and duty of the papacy to call on the armed strength of Christendom for the assertion of Christian rights under papal direction.[2]

Between 1059 and 1085 the papacy, progressively freed – and largely by Norman support – from dependence upon the western empire, was to show itself ever more ready to urge the new military aristocracies towards war on behalf of the needs of Christendom as interpreted by Rome. It was providing them with consecrated banners under which to fight. It was promising beatitude to warriors who were killed in battle.[3] The development was of course gradual. Before the time of Urban II, for instance, the bestowal of a papal banner might be regarded merely as a form of feudal investiture, and the soldiers of St Peter – *milites sancti Petri* – might denote the vassals of the papacy as well as those who took up arms on behalf of the Faith. There is, however, no mistaking the manner in which during these years the Hildebrandine papacy made enthusiasm for the Holy War a unifying sentiment in the West. The *militia Christi* were no longer visualized as hermits or as the ascetic 'Athletes of Christ' or that army of praying monks whose duties had been set out in the military metaphors of St Benedict.[4] Now it had come to denote the armed might of the West mobilized for war under papal leadership. As will be seen there would be plenty of opportunity for these inspirations to be distorted and degraded. It remains true, however, that during the decades which separated the synod of Melfi (1059) from the death of Gregory VII in 1085, there had begun to be propagated from Rome something that might not inaptly be described as a theology of armed action.

The attempt made by the Hildebrandine papacy to identify the objects of a Holy War with the implementation of papal policy lends a

[1] See above, pp. 55, 56.
[2] Erdmann, *op. cit.*, ch. v.
[3] *Ibid.*, chs V–VII.
[4] T. S. R. Boase in *History*, XXII (1937), pp. 112–14. Bohemund was actually hailed as an Athlete of Christ on his tomb at Canosa (Berteaux, *L'Art dans l'Italie meridionale*, pp. 312–16).

special interest to the support given by the popes to the military adventures of the Normans. In 1061–2 for instance (some three years after the synod of Melfi) Alexander II gave his blessing and a banner to Normans fighting in Sicily,[1] and in 1064 the Normans (perhaps with papal approval) were prominent in the expedition which captured Barbastro from the Saracens and placed the city for a time under Norman governorship.[2] Two years later the pope gave Duke William a banner for his invasion of England, and in 1070 the Duke was solemnly acclaimed by papal legates at Winchester as king.[3] Even the disputes between Gregory VII and Robert Guiscard were not permanently to affect this association. For in 1080 that pope, in a notable letter, commended to the bishops of Apulia and Calabria the project against the eastern empire of 'our most glorious son Duke Robert',[4] and ordered that all those who followed him to war should bear themselves fittingly as the soldiers of Christ. The duke of Apulia, it will be recalled, had recently been three times excommunicated. But the alliance between the papacy and the Normans was once more fully revived, and Guiscard in his turn was to fight under a papal banner outside Durazzo.[5]

The full implications of this strange alliance can only be appreciated in connexion with the slow development of the notion of the Holy War. Of course some of its immediate consequences could be variously interpreted. It might, for instance, be contended at Rome that the Normans were receiving no more than the support due to faithful liegemen from their overlord. Robert Guiscard had, after all, never ceased to profess vassalage in respect of the duchy of Apulia, and one of the most advertised consequences of William's invasion of England was the alleged restoration of the payment of 'Peter's Pence' to Rome. Nevertheless, the basic fact remained that the papacy had, with Norman assistance, made the concept of the Holy War a matter of practical politics for western Christendom just at the time when the great Norman conquests were being made. And the two movements had become inseparably connected.

No consideration of the Norman successes during the latter half of the eleventh century can thus avoid asking how far these were conditioned

[1] Setton and Baldwin, *Crusades*, I, p. 62

[2] Erdmann, *op. cit.*, 88, 89, 124; M. Villey (*La Croisade*, p. 69) thinks that the pope's share has been exaggerated. There is no doubt however that the Normans played a large part in the expedition (Douglas, *French Studies*, XIV (1960), p. 111).

[3] Ord. Vit., II, p. 199. The papal banner may be seen in the Bayeux Tapestry.

[4] Reg., VIII; Jaffé, *Monumenta Gregoriana*, pp. 435, 436.

[5] Will. Apul., IV, vv. 408, 409.

by a genuine enthusiasm on the part of the Normans for the ideals of the Holy War, or, alternatively, how far they were facilitated by an unscrupulous exploitation of these ideals by the Normans for their own ends. Yet to answer such questions involves examining the emotions and intimate thoughts of men who can only be judged by their public acts at a time when propaganda was becoming a much used weapon of policy.

Fortunately, however, contemporary narratives survive which admirably illustrate Norman sentiments during the great age of Norman expansion. William of Poitiers and Amatus of Monte Cassino, William of Apulia and Geoffrey Malaterra were all perfervid admirers of the Normans, and like the anonymous author of the *Gesta Francorum*, all wrote for Norman patrons and sought to address a Norman audience. While therefore they may justly be accused of partiality, they can be cited with confidence as expressing the sentiments of those to whom their works were addressed, or at least of indicating the manner in which the Normans of this age would have liked their exploits to be regarded. The unanimity of these four distinct writers is here in every way remarkable. They all of them make use of epic and legendary material which was evidently common to the whole Norman world,[1] and they all attempt to justify the Norman exploits of the age by reference to religion, and in relation to the Holy War.

There was, of course, an obvious occasion for enlarging on this theme in connexion with the Norman invasion of Sicily which, though undertaken for the purpose of secular conquest, none the less had the effect of ending Saracen domination over the island. Even so, some of the descriptions supplied by Amatus and Malaterra are surprising. Before embarking from Italy to Sicily in 1061, Robert Guiscard, according to Malaterra, preached something like a sermon to his troops, bidding them obtain remission from their sins before embarking upon so sacred a venture.[2] Even more noteworthy is the account given of the battle of Cerami in 1063. Faced, it is said, by an overwhelming Moslem force recruited from Sicily and North Africa, Count Roger, in his turn exhorted his followers in terms only applicable to a Holy War. Numbers could never prevail against them, he said, since they were the stalwart soldiers of the army of Christ. Nor was this all. In the ensuing battle, St George is made to appear fully armed, riding on a white horse and

[1] Cf. M. Mathieu, ed., *Guillaume de Pouille*, pp. 46–53.
[2] Malaterra, II, c. 9.

bearing a shining banner. Thus accoutred, he led the Normans to their victory.[1]

The temper of this account is certainly daunting, but it might be paralleled by the description supplied by both Malaterra and Amatus of the capture of Palermo. Before the assault Robert Guiscard declares to the Normans that Christ is their leader, and the first Norman on the wall makes a great sign of the cross over the city. The triumphant entry of the Normans into Palermo was yet more remarkable. The Norman column – led it is said by Robert Guiscard, Count Roger and other notables – proceeded at once to the great church of St Mary. This they found had been turned into a mosque. It was immediately cleansed, and a Greek archbishop, named Nicodemus, was found living in poverty in the suburbs. He was escorted in state to St Mary's, and then Mass was solemnly sung before the armed and reverent company. It might be thought that the religious mission of the Normans had been sufficiently stressed in this narrative. But Amatus had still something else to record. Before the Mass was ended, he says, angels descended from on high, and the whole church was filled with music and light.[2]

The supernatural element in these stories is indeed remarkable even in accounts of a war in Sicily which might be alleged to have had religious connotations. More surprising however are such sentiments when they are attributed to the leaders of the early Norman wars in Italy which were waged against Christians, and with savage violence. Yet Richard of Capua and Robert Guiscard could be described by Amatus as the 'Lord's Anointed' and all the Norman conquests, not only in Sicily but also elsewhere, were directly attributed by Malaterra to the guidance of God.[3] Robert Guiscard, 'the most Christian Duke', was apparently favoured specially in this respect, and Amatus can actually add that it was Jesus Christ Himself who assured him of his victories. The hand of God, we are assured, was with him in everything he did. A long string of visions and miracles was cited in support of this assertion, and it could even be claimed that this crude and brutal warrior was under the special protection of Our Lady.[4] It is hardly surprising therefore to learn that when Guiscard decided to carry his conquests from Italy to Sicily, he too should have proclaimed his sacred

[1] Malaterra, II, c. 33. After the battle Roger sent four captured camels as a present to Pope Alexander II.
[2] Amatus VI, cc. 19, 20; Malaterra, II, c. 45. A seal of Roger II bears the inscription *Jhesus Christus vincit*, recalling the old imperial formula (Kantorowicz, *Laudes Regiae*, p. 8).
[3] Malaterra, IV, cc. 6, 9 etc.   [4] Esp. V, cc. 1–3.

mission: 'My desire' he is made to exclaim 'is to deliver Catholics and Christians from the Saracens and to be the instrument of God's vengeance'. And during the ensuing campaigns he is constantly represented as urging his followers to religious exercises. Let them go into battle fortified by the Sacrament. Let them trust in God rather than in numbers, and rely on the Holy Spirit who will give their righteous cause the victory.[1]

It is easy to dismiss such assertions with impatience or disgust. Yet here is the authentic voice of the eleventh century speaking about some of its most representative characters, and these descriptions, designed to justify the Norman exploits in Mediterranean lands may at all events be legitimately compared with the account given by William of Poitiers of the Norman invasion of England. The battle of Hastings was fought three years after that of Cerami, and six years before the capture of Palermo. It can thus be regarded as chronologically part of the Norman enterprise which reached a climax during this decade; and the detailed commentary given by William of Poitiers of the Norman Conquest in the north is informed with precisely the same temper as pervades the descriptions given of the Norman ventures in the south by Amatus and Malaterra. In the opinion of his latest editor, William of Poitiers, when describing the Norman Conquest of England, found himself committed to a passionate belief in the essentially Christian mission of the Normans.[2]

This belief might indeed be said to colour all his interpretation of William's expedition against England in 1066. The murder of Alfred the Atheling in 1036, it was claimed, called for divine retribution on the son of his murderer. Stigand, a schismatic archbishop occupied the throne of St Augustine. The solemn promise of a venerated king had been set aside, and the violation of an oath sworn by Harold upon sacred relics demanded the punishment of a perjured usurper. Like Robert Guiscard before his invasion of Sicily, William of Normandy is thus depicted as the agent of Divine vengeance, and in the event the duke was to fight at Hastings with consecrated relics round his neck.[3] Even a miraculous element in the enterprise was soon to be discovered. Very early in the twelfth century, the English, or half-English, Eadmer, who was born about 1060, was to compose his *History*, and in it he described the battle of Hastings. So heavy were the losses inflicted on

[1] Amatus, V, c. 23 and *passim*. Cf. Rousset, *op. cit.*, 37, 38.
[2] R. Foreville, *Guillaume de Poiters*, pp. xliv–xlvi.
[3] Will. Poit., pp. 147, 173–9 and *passim*.

the Normans he says that in the opinion of survivors whom he had questioned, the Normans must have been defeated had not God Himself intervened. Therefore, concludes Eadmer, the Norman victory at Hastings must be considered as 'without doubt entirely due to a miracle of God'.[1]

It is not of course the truth or falsity of these various assertions that is here in question, but the fact that they were made and were widely believed. As in Italy, as in Sicily, and as later in the Balkans, so also in England the Norman invasion was made to appear in the nature of a Holy War, and thus in Europe it was to be widely regarded. In fact, a religious excuse, when added to the lure of plunder, undoubtedly assisted Duke William in 1066 in attracting to his expedition many volunteers from widely scattered lands in Europe. The unanimity of sentiment among all these writers about the various Norman exploits in this period is in fact highly remarkable, and the same emotions were to be invoked to explain and justify the Norman ventures right down to the end of the eleventh century.

Thus the expedition of Robert Guiscard in 1081 against the eastern empire was most emphatically given the character of a Holy War both by the duke of Apulia himself and by Pope Gregory VII,[2] whilst Roger vigorously voiced the same claim throughout the final stages of his conquest of Sicily. In his charters he could style himself (in Greek) the 'champion of the Christians', and (in Latin) as 'strong in the protection of God, girt with the heavenly sword, and adorned with the helmet and spear of heavenly hope'.[3] It was surely sufficient; but it is perhaps more significant that in his bull announcing the foundation of the bishopric of Catania, Urban II could in his turn salute Count Roger as the 'propagator of the Christian Faith'.[4] In the light of all this there was perhaps some excuse for Malaterra's description of Roger's seizure of Malta in 1090 as a war for the rescue of Christians, and its success as directly attributable to the intervention of God. Had not the captive Christians in the island moved to meet the Norman conqueror with wooden crosses in their hands and chanting *Kýrie eléison*.[5] Three years earlier, the long siege of Castrogiovanni had come to an end when the Emir

[1] Eadmer, *Historis Novorum*, ed. Rule, p. 9; *absque dubio soli miraculo Dei ascribenda est.*
[2] See Gregory VII's letter (Reg., VIII, 6; VIII, 8 – Jaffé, *Monumenta*, pp. 435–6, 437–8.
[3] Diploma of 6 May 1098 cited by Caspar, *Roger II*, p. 632; diploma for Mazzara in 1093 printed by Starrabba in *Contributo*, p. 48. Cf. Jordan in *Moyen Age*, XXXIII, p. 240.
[4] Jaffé–Loewenfeld, no. 5460.
[5] Malaterra, IV, c. 16 – an astonishing passage.

Ibn Hamoud, a descendant of the holy family of Ali, and related to the Khalifs of Cordova, had surrendered to Count Roger and become a Christian.[1]

To assess the quality of sentiments that were so loudly and equivocably expressed is extremely difficult, and it would be credulous indeed to accept these statements at their face value.[2] It seems monstrous to associate religious motives with the depredations of the Normans in Italy before 1059, and a close association between St Januarius and Richard of Capua might well appear incongruous. Even more repulsive is the attribution of the successes of such a man as Robert Guiscard to the special favour of Our Lord and Our Lady. Again, the boastful self-righteousness of William of Poitiers is displeasing, even if William the Conqueror did show favour to the Church. Perhaps, however, it is in connexion with the career of Roger, the Great Count, that the claims of the Normans to have been the champions of Christendom meet their most interesting test. Certainly, Roger was to wrest Sicily from the Saracens. But it must be remembered that this man, for whose sake the miracle of Cerami was granted, had shortly before entered Sicily as the ally of the Moslem emir of Syracuse. And three years after the religious ceremonies which celebrated the capture of Palermo he made a solemn treaty to their mutual advantage with Tamin, the Sultan of Mehdia who had been striving to regain Sicily for Islam.[3]

Roger was, moreover, never reluctant to employ Saracen mercenaries against his fellow Christians. Robert Guiscard had taken Saracen troops with him when, as the ally of the pope, he sacked Rome in 1084, and Roger's later employment of such troops was to be constant. Thus he used them in South Italy in 1091, in 1094 and in 1096.[4] Finally he brought a very large contingent of Saracens to the siege of Capua in 1098, and this last incident was to be particularly revealing. For St Anselm, in exile from England, was himself outside Capua at that time, and not unnaturally wished to seize the opportunity of trying to convert these Saracens to the faith of Christ. This, however, Roger resolutely refused to allow. Doubtless, he felt that such an attempt might impair the efficiency of his Moslem troops.[5]

[1] *Ibid.*, IV, c. 6.
[2] It should be remembered that similar assertions were made (though not so extensively) on behalf of others in this period: notably in connexion with the Pisan expedition against the Saracens of Mehdia in 1087.
[3] Mas Latrie, *Traités de Paix et de Commerce*, 28.
[4] See above, p. 84.
[5] Eadmer, *Vita Anselmi*, ed. Southern, pp. 110–12.

The Norman leaders appear often to have used the religious impulse as the thinnest cloak for wanton aggression. None the less, in view of the emotional climate of the eleventh century, it would be rash to dogmatize too freely about their motives. Robert Guiscard's devotion to St Matthew was notorious, and it may even have been sincere; whilst his benefactions to the Church, were lavish.[1] Again, Roger I will be found to have been the veritable founder of the second Sicilian Church whatever may have been the inspiration of his ecclesiastical policy. Even more hazardous would it be to pass a hasty judgement upon the quality of the sentiments attributed to the Norman warriors by the reputable chroniclers who recorded their acts. Malaterra insists for instance that it was the Norman practice to confess and communicate before battle; so does Amatus; and so does William of Apulia, whilst William of Malmesbury, writing at a slightly later date, makes a similar statement in connexion with the battle of Hastings.[2]

These are, to some extent, suspect witnesses, but assertions of the same type were made about the Normans by writers such as Leo of Ostia and Rodulf Glaber who were outside the immediate Norman circle, and in 1081 some of the followers of Robert Guiscard seem to have given good heed to the instructions of Pope Gregory VII to regard themselves as the instruments of the Divine Justice. Before the assault on Durazzo in that year, we are told, there were scenes of exceptional religious enthusiasm among the Normans who later went into battle singing hymns.[3] Such statements when made by friends of the Normans must be treated with proper caution, but it is otherwise with testimony on such matters supplied by their enemies. Anna Comnena, the Byzantine princess, had good reason to hate the Normans in general, and Robert Guiscard in particular, and she described in some detail the first engagement fought between Guiscard and her beloved father, the Emperor Alexis I. The night before the battle she says,

> Robert Guiscard left his tents standing empty and moved with all his force towards the church built long ago by the Martyr Theodore. And there throughout the night they sought to propitiate God, and they also partook of the Immaculate Sacred Mysteries.[4]

[1] See below, p. 147. He took an arm of St Matthew with him on his expedition against Durazzo.
[2] Malaterra, II, cc. 9, 33; III, c. 27; Will. Apul., III, vv. 109, 110; Will Malms., *Gesta Regum*, p. 32.
[3] Malaterra, III, c. 27.
[4] Anna Comnena, *Alexiad*, IV, c. 6: trans. Dawson, p. 108.

In the light of all the evidence it would be hazardous to deny that on occasion the Norman warriors were persuaded that they were the chosen agents of God, or that some such conviction may have contributed to their success in arms.

Be that as it may, there can be little question of the efficiency of what Amatus called the spiritual strategy of the Normans in this age. Nor can there be any doubt that sentiments derived from the conception of the Holy War, and propaganda inspired by them, served to promote and to link together all the Norman achievements in the latter half of the eleventh century. These could of course be voiced with special and peculiar emphasis during Bohemund's Syrian campaign which in 1099 led to the foundation of the Norman principality of Antioch. But the same religious emotions, real or assumed had, long before the First Crusade, been made to colour all the armed enterprises of the Normans in Europe. And the strength of these enthusiasms may be gauged by the traditions they established. For they were to endure. Did not Dante in the fourteenth century, when contemplating the Blessed in Paradise, place Robert Guiscard alongside Charlemagne among the champions of Christendom in the Heaven of Mars?[1]

[1] Paradiso, canto XVII, esp. vv. 43–9.

Chapter 6

THE NORMAN WORLD

I

Despite their individual features, all the enterprises undertaken by the Normans between 1050 and 1100 can be regarded as forming part of a single movement that was everywhere marked by common modes of action and co-ordinating principles of policy. As a result, there was formed something which may not inaptly be described as the Norman world of the eleventh century.[1] Contemporary writers seem in fact to have been very conscious of this. Thus the surviving version of the chronicle of Amatus of Montecassino (whose theme was the exploits of Richard of Capua and Robert Guiscard) opens with a chapter which brings together as a single endeavour the Norman conquest of England, complete with the comet, the Norman share in the capture of Barbastro from the Saracens in Spain, and the Norman campaigns in Italy.[2] Similarly, Geoffrey Malaterra (who, to be sure, had been a monk in Normandy before he migrated to Calabria) began his history of the Norman conquest of Sicily under the leadership of Roger the 'Great Count' with a description of the establishment of Rolf the Viking ('Rodlo') in tenth-century Neustria.[3] Meanwhile similar sentiments had been expressed at the other end of Europe by William of Poitiers who could not only brag of the wisdom and valour of the Normans at home, but could bid their English enemies remember that the Normans had taken possession of Apulia, were subduing Sicily, and had brought fear to the Saracens.[4]

These chroniclers were, it would seem, substantially independent of each other but they are united in voicing sentiments which might serve to link together all the Norman world in their time. And the composite

---

[1] The close connexions between England and the Norman kingdom of Sicily in the twelfth century were illustrated in two notable articles which after a generation have not lost their value (C. H. Haskins in *Eng. Hist. Rev.*, XXVI (1911), pp. 433–47, 641–65; and E. Jamison in *Proc. Brit. Acad.*, XXIV (1938), pp. 237 et seq). It is not however always realized how fully these connexions were foreshadowed in the relations which developed throughout all parts of the Norman world between 1050 and 1100.

[2] Amatus, I, c. 1–14.   [3] Malaterra, I, c. 1.   [4] Will. Poit., 228.

tradition which they severally helped to establish was to be notably developed by writers of the next generation. Ordericus Vitalis was himself mainly concerned with the history of the Anglo-Norman kingdom, but he never lost interest in Norman exploits in the Mediterranean lands, and he evidently took steps to inform himself about them. He expressed his admiration for the work of Geoffrey Malaterra, and it is not impossible that he used the lost Latin original of the chronicle of Amatus.[1] With similar sentiments, William of Malmesbury when writing about 1125 his 'History of the Kings of the English', has much to say not only about the Normans in France, but about the Normans in Italy, in Sicily and in Syria. And he too was in this respect reasonably well informed. He could give a striking description of the tomb of Robert Guiscard at Venosaul[2] (which has now disappeared), and he summed up his interpretation of the career of Bohemund of Taranto in a telling epigram. The future prince of Antioch had been brought up in Apulia, but he was none the less a Norman.[3]

Thus was the unity of the Norman world envisaged by the Norman chroniclers. And there are good reasons for supposing that a similar conviction was held by many of the chief architects of the Norman achievement. According to the *Carmen*, Duke William encouraged his troops at the battle of Hastings by bidding them remember the great deeds that had already been done by their compatriots in Apulia, Calabria and Sicily, and the Conqueror, we are told, was wont to refresh his courage by reflecting on the valour of Robert Guiscard.[4] Similarly Tancred lost no time in informing his uncle, Duke Roger 'Borsa' of Apulia, of the Norman triumph in the great battle of Antioch, and Bohemund was in due course to send the captured tent of Kerbogha as a trophy to adorn the church of St Nicholas at Bari.[5] Norman prelates such as Geoffrey, bishop of Coutances, and Odo, bishop of Bayeux (who was also earl of Kent) in their turn thought it quite appropriate to demand from their kinsfolk in Italy money to help them rebuild their cathedrals at home; whilst at a slightly later date, it was noted as a source of pride that the chant of St Évroul rose to God from Calabrian abbeys.[6] Correspondingly, the attainment of royalty, with all that it implied, by a Norman duke was of immediate interest to the Normans in many lands. William's coronation, at Westminster in 1066 was

---

[1] Jamison, *op. cit.*, p. 245. [2] *Gesta Regum*, II, p. 322.
[3] *Ibid.*, II, p. 400: Loco Appulus, gente Normannus.
[4] *Ibid.*, II, p, 320. [5] Röhricht, *Regesta*, no. 9. [6] Ord. Vit., II, p. 91.

noted with pride in Italy, and a later writer reported that in 1087 news of the Conqueror's death outside the walls of Rouen passed with incredible speed to Italy and there caused consternation among the Normans.[1]

Among the Norman rulers in the south, also, the same feeling of Norman unity is to be discerned. Robert Guiscard seems never to have forgotten his upbringing in the Cotentin, and Roger the 'Great Count' always retained recollections of his early association with St Évroul. After Robert Guiscard's death, moreover, the same sentiments persisted despite the rivalries which broke out among those who contended for his inheritance. Count Roger of Sicily was in every way a more powerful man than his nephew Roger 'Borsa', who inherited the duchy of Apulia from Robert Guiscard, but the 'Great Count' none the less seems to have recognized the duke of Apulia as his feudal superior.[2] And a yet more striking demonstration of Norman solidarity came in 1096. In that year all the Norman forces – those of the rivals Roger of Apulia, Roger of Sicily and Bohemund of Taranto – could unite in a campaign against Amalfi. Nor was this all: for in the same year they were to be met by the Crusaders coming from the north. In these circumstances we are told, Roger, the duke of Apulia, not only welcomed Robert, duke of Normandy, the Conqueror's son, but treated him, throughout a whole winter, as his natural lord.[3] Evidently, the duke of Normandy in the last decade of the eleventh century was still regarded in some sense the suzerain of all the Normans everywhere.

These sentiments of Norman solidarity are in themselves of high interest. But what gave them actuality were the personal relationships which were established among the Normans at this time. No aspect of the Norman conquest of England for example is more remarkable than the close cohesion between the small group of Norman families which, between 1070 and 1087, acquired almost half the territorial wealth of England while retaining (and increasing) their recently won possessions in Normandy. If a list were to be made of the principle figures in England under William the Conqueror it would be largely composed of precisely those names which had become prominent in the duchy during his reign as duke. There were, in the first place, the king's half brothers Odo, bishop of Bayeux, now earl of Kent, and Robert, count of Mortain, now established in Cornwall, together with such as Geoffrey

[1] Ord. Vit. III, p. 249.   [2] Eadmer, *Vita Anselmi* (ed. Southern, p. 111).
[3] Fulcher of Chartres, I, c. 7; Ord. Vit., II, p. 91

of Montbrai, bishop of Coutances, with land all over England, Roger Bigot from Calvados, Robert Malet from near Le Havre, and Richard fitz Gilbert of Tonbridge and Clare from Brionne. It was, in fact, with the new feudal families of Normandy that England was now to be concerned – families such as those of Beaumont and Montgomery, of Giffard from Longueville-sur-Scie, of Montfort from the Risle, and of Warenne from Bellencombre, not to mention the comital dynasties of Evreux and Eu. Such was the Norman aristocracy which after 1070 dominated the political scene alike in Normandy and in England.[1]

Between 1066 and 1087 the interests of most of the greater Anglo-Norman families stretched indiscriminately across the Channel, and inter-marriages strengthened the ties between them. At the same time these magnates were able to reproduce in England much of the control over their dependents which they had previously established in Normandy. The chief sub-tenants of a Norman magnate in England in the time of William the Conqueror might well hold lands widely scattered through the English shires, but they often themselves bore territorial names which show that their families had been near neighbours of their lords in Normandy. This is, for instance, particularly noticeable in the case of the baronies of Robert Malet, Richard fitz Gilbert and the count of Eu, but many other illustrations could be supplied, and it might be noted how the dependence of the family of Clère upon Tosny which was recorded in preconquest Norman charters was to be continued in eleventh and twelfth century Yorkshire. Soon, too, the same associations would be yet further extended. By 1086 Norman families with their dependents were beginning to be established in Wales; and in Scotland the development was in time to be even more remarkable. It is true that the establishment of Norman families, and the successful propagation of Norman ideas in Scotland only reached its climax in the twelfth century. But the process may surely be said to have begun in 1072 when William the Conqueror brought his Norman followers to Scotland, and claimed authority over Malcolm, the Scottish king.[2]

These men were certainly rapacious and violent. There was thus always a danger of dissensions among them, and of rebellion against the king. But generally, the great Anglo-Norman families of this age were conscious of their common interests, and conscious also that they shared

[1] Douglas, *William the Conqueror*, ch. II; Loyd, *Anglo-Norman Families*, *passim*.
[2] Cf. G. W. S. Barrow, 'Les familles normandes d'ecosse', *Annales de Normandie* (Dec. 1965), pp. 495–516.

these with their king. Thus they sought to prevent disunion among themselves, and also co-operated with the king in the government of the con-
joint realm he had created. Men such as Robert and Henry of Beaumont,
Roger II of Montgomery, Robert count of Mortain, Odo bishop of
Bayeux and earl of Kent, appear as often in the Norman as in the
English courts of King William between 1066 and 1087.[1] Such conditions might of course be modified by modes of inheritance, and a
practice grew up whereby the eldest son inherited the Norman lands,
and the second received the English estates of the house.[2] It is true, also,
that for nineteen years, between 1087 and 1106 Normandy and England
were politically divided. Nevertheless despite these developments, the
greater Anglo-Norman families generally maintained their integrity
during this age. And this in its turn undoubtedly contributed both to the
political unity of the Anglo-Norman realm, and also to the special place
it occupied in the eleventh-century Norman world.

The close personal associations among the Normans were extended
not only over Normandy and England but also over all the countries
which the Normans conquered. The account given by Ordericus
Vitalis of the early benefactors of St Évroul is for instance here of considerable interest since it may now be supplemented by earlier evidence
taken from Italy. Thus among those who in 1095 witnessed a gift for the
bishopric of Chieti by Count Robert of Loritello (a nephew of Robert
Guiscard) was a certain William 'de Scalfo'.[3] This was none other than
William of Échauffour, and his father was the famous Arnold of Échauffour, whose long career of acquisitive violence had brought him at last
into conflict with Duke William about 1059. Arnold, we are told, was
in revolt against the duke for nearly three years, and at length he departed for Italy, where

> He visited his friends and relatives who had great possessions in Apulia,
> and eventually he returned to Normandy with a very large sum of money.[4]

He seems to have purchased a reconciliation with the duke, and to have
died about 1063. But by this time another of Arnold's sons, named Ber-
enger had so advanced in the Church as to become Abbot of Robert
Guiscard's monastic foundation of Holy Trinity at Venosa. It is hardly
surprising therefore that with such patronage William, after his coming

---

[1] *Regesta Regum*, II, *passim*.   [2] Douglas, *op. cit.*, p. 361.
[3] Jamison in *Studies presented . . . to M. K. Pope*, p. 204, citing *Regesto delle Pergamene – di Chieti*, ed. A. Balducci, I (1926), App. iii, pp. 92–4.
[4] Ord. Vit., II, pp. 84, 93.

to Italy, rapidly prospered in the service of the great duke of Apulia.[1] It is probable that he participated in Guiscard's wars both in Sicily and the Balkans, and before the end of the eleventh century he had become possessed of no less than thirty fortified strongholds in southern Italy.[2]

But of all the Échauffour connexions the most important in Italy was Arnold's half-brother, William of Montreuil, styled in the south (somewhat euphemistically) 'The Good Norman'. William of Montreuil[3] married a daughter of Richard, prince of Capua, and made his fortune in Italy as the ally, and later as the enemy, of his father-in-law. In due course he moved to Rome where he entered the service of Pope Alexander II, and this in turn was to prove advantageous to him for he

> received the standard of the Pope, and reduced the Campania by force of arms, thus bringing the natives who had been cut off by various schisms from Catholic unity back to submission to St Peter the Apostle.[4]

A better example of Norman methods and propaganda could scarcely be found, and the result was so successful that before his death William Montreuil already possessed large lands within the principality of Capua and had acquired the duchy of Gaeta. A reference to William of Échauffour, his father, and to his uncle, the 'Good Norman', is thus sufficient to indicate the manner in which between 1050 and 1100 the influence of this family was spread by its various members. Nor need there be any doubt of the peculiar Norman fervour with which they regarded their activities. Their achievements, they claimed, 'had brought terror to the "barbarians" in England and Apulia, in Thrace and Sicily'.[5]

A similar pattern could probably be traced in the history of many other Norman personalities at this time. Richard of Aversa, the first Norman prince of Capua, married a daughter of Tancred of Hauteville, so that Jordan I, prince of Capua from 1078 to 1090, was the nephew of Robert Guiscard, the Norman duke of Apulia and Calabria.[6] Again, Robert 'Curthose' the eldest son of William the Conqueror married Sybyl who was the daughter of a Norman count of Conversano near Bari, and herself a grand-daughter of Robert Guiscard.[7] The intimate relationship of the house of Hauteville with the counts of the

---

[1] Ord. Vit. II, pp. 48, 65, 90. [2] Ménager, *Quellen und Forschungen*, p. 45.
[3] Chalandon, *Domination normande*, I, pp. 215–26. [4] Ord. Vit., II, p. 87.
[5] Ord. Vit., interp. Will. Jum., ed. Marx, p. 163; 'ex his filiorum et nepotum militaris turma propagata est quae barbaris in Anglia vel Apulia seu Trachia vel Siria nimio terrori visa est'.
[6] Amatus, VII, c. 2; Malaterra, I, c. 4.
[7] Chalandon, *op. cit.*, I, pp. 180, 181. She was renowned for her beauty (Ord. Vit., IV, p. 78).

Principate, of Loritello and Catanzarro, will hereafter be disclosed, and many important members of the contingent which followed Bohemund of Taranto to Antioch in 1096 will be found to have been of his kindred in southern Italy.[1] Similarly, among the barons of Bohemund's uncle, Count Roger of Sicily, there were several whose names perhaps suggest that they had recently arrived from the north. There was for instance Robert of Sourdeval in the Cotentin, who in 1093 took part in the recovery of Catania, and who in 1095 witnessed a Norman charter of privileges in favour of the monastery at Lipari.[2] There was also Roger of Barneville, likewise in the Cotentin, who, at Palermo in 1086, attested Roger Borsa's grant for La Cava, and in the next year witnessed a privilege for the cathedral of Palermo. He evidently prospered, and he met his death in 1098 or 1099 during the siege of Antioch.[3]

The connexions of these men with the kinsfolk they had left behind in Normandy might be hard to illustrate in detail, but sometimes more precision can be obtained. Thus a Norman charter of 1027–35 for the abbey of Jumèges shows the family of Pantulf as dependents of the house of Montgomery in the neighbourhood of Sées, and some fifty years later precisely the same relationship was reproduced in Shropshire where in 1086 William Pantulf was one of the chief barons of Roger II of Montgomery who was then earl of Shrewsbury.[4] Thus had the interests of Pantulf been extended from Normandy to England. But they had already stretched into Italy. For as early as 1075 this same William Pantulf had visited Apulia, and after his return to the north he was suspected of complicity in the murder of the Countess Mabel of Bellême. He cleared himself of the charge and later revisited Apulia where he found favour with Robert Guiscard. Returning to England once more, he added to his possessions on both sides of the Channel, and though his later career was chequered, he survived until after 1102 when Henry I placed him in charge of the castle of Stafford. Certainly, the house of Pantulf had extended its influence between 1050 and 1100. But it never lost its Norman allegiance. It is reported for instance that Robert Guiscard promised William Pantulf large estates in Apulia including three fortified townships if he would stay in Italy. But this subtenant of Montgomery refused. He had been rewarded by his lord with lands in Shropshire, and his family home was in Normandy. Therefore he

[1] See below, pp. 163, 175, 176.
[2] E. Jamison, *op. cit.*, p. 207.
[3] *Ibid.*; cf. *Guillaume, op. cit.*, App. 'E', ii.
[4] *Chartes de Jumièges*, ed. Vernier, I, no. xiii; *Domesday Book* I, fols 257, 257b.

returned to the north bringing back with him from Bari a tooth of St Nicholas for the monastery which he had founded at Noron.[1]

So widely stretched were Norman relationships at this time that families from outside Normandy were sometimes able to take surprising advantage of them. Not the least interesting among the minor characters of Norman history between 1050 and 1100 are, for instance, three men who all took their name from the little township of Cioches near Béthune.[2] Two of them, Sigar and Gunfrid 'de Cioches', who had evidently assisted the Conqueror had, before 1086, acquired extensive lands in four English shires. The third, Arnulf 'de Cioches' who was a cleric was made tutor to Cicely, Duke William's daughter, who was later abbess in Caen, and he subsequently became chaplain to Duke Robert in Normandy. In that capacity he accompanied the duke in 1096 to Apulia and Syria, and finally, by Robert's suggestion, he was in 1099 appointed patriarch of Jerusalem.[3] These three men therefore from the same Flemish village all rose to prominence through their association with William the Conqueror: the laymen to be rewarded with lands in England as tenants-in-chief of the Norman king; the cleric to serve the Conqueror's daughter and his son, and at last by Norman influence to be appointed Latin patriarch of Jerusalem at the culminating moment of the First Crusade.

II

The unity of the Norman world at this time was fostered not only by secular Norman magnates, but also by Norman prelates who during these decades carried the influence of the province of Rouen over much of western Christendom. Partly this was due to the prestige which was beginning to attach to the Church in Normandy, but more particularly could it be attributed to the conquests which naturally tended to introduce Norman ecclesiastical ideas and personalities into the regions that had been subdued. Certainly, the results were soon apparent. From this time must have begun the long-standing connexion between the rites of Rouen, Salisbury and Hereford, and it has been observed how strong was the Norman influence on the liturgical development of the Church in southern Italy and Sicily.[4]

[1] Ord. Vit., II, pp. 428–33; III, pp. 220, 221; IV, p. 173.
[2] Douglas in *Trans. Bristol and Glos: Archaeological Soc.*, vol. LXXXIX (1966), pp. 28–31; W. Farrer, *Honours and Knights Fees*, I, pp. 20–9; C. W. David, *Robert Curthose*, App. 'C'.
[3] His later career was stormy.
[4] E. Bishop, *Liturgica Historica*, pp. 276–301; E. Kantorowicz, *Laudes Regiae*, pp. 157 et seq.

Such results were, it is true, only to be fulfilled in the future, but already in the latter half of the eleventh century the ecclesiastical connotations of the spread of Norman power were being to some extent reflected in the liturgy of the Church. Before 1066 a litany sung on important Church festivals in the cathedral of Rouen contained a special acclamation in favour of Duke William, and no such particular salutation is known to have been used in any similar litany at that time in favour of any other lay magnate who was not of royal or imperial rank.[1] No strict parallel could be found to this in Norman Italy, but in this respect it is noteworthy that Robert Guiscard (who was assuredly not an anointed *rex*) was specifically named in the *Exultet* that was sung at Mass on Holy Saturday in the cathedral of Bari.[2] It is not without interest that the use of Rouen was to persist in Sicily until the sixteenth century, and a similar correspondence could be detected in the eleventh-century interests of the Faithful. At that time the pilgrimage to St Michael ('whom we worship in peril') in Normandy could be matched by the special Norman devotion to the Apulian shrine of St Michael at Monte Gargano, and St Lô whose patronage pervaded the Cotentin, was apparently venerated at Palermo during the last quarter of the eleventh century. Similarly, while Norman devotions were systematically introduced into England during the reign of William the Conqueror (often to the high displeasure of English churchmen) the cult of St Nicholas of Myra became at the same time almost as popular in Normandy as it was at Bari.[3]

The ecclesiastical connexions which developed through the lands dominated by the Normans were, of course, promoted chiefly by the appointment of Normans, or of Norman nominees, to high offices in the Church. Just as the revival in the province of Rouen had been predominantly, though not exclusively monastic, so also was the extension of Norman power everywhere marked by the appointment of abbots who had been trained in Normandy. In England, in particular, between 1066 and 1100 a large number of Normans replaced English abbots who had died, or been removed, from office. Thus Turold came from Fécamp to Malmesbury, and Thurstan from Caen to Glastonbury, and if both these appointments were unhappily oppressive, others were more successful. Paul, formerly a monk at Le Bec presided with dignity over

---

[1] Kantorowicz, *loc. cit.*; Douglas, *William the Conqueror*, pp. 154, 249, 250.
[2] L. Duchesne, *Christian Worship*, trans. McClure (S.P.C.K., 1917), Appendix, p. 545.
[3] Ord. Vit., II, pp. 107, 178; III, pp. 205–21.

St Albans, and Serlo from Le Mont St Michel with success over Gloucester. At the same period, Ely passed eventually under the rule of
Simeon from St. Ouen, and the Confessor's abbey of Westminster received in succession two notable abbots from across the Channel,
namely Vitalis from Bernay, and Gilbert Crispin from Le Bec. All these
appointments were in fact made during the reign of William the Conqueror himself, and the process was extremely rapid. Nine years after
the battle of Hastings, of the twenty-one abbots who attended a council
in London only thirteen were English, and of these only three remained
in office in 1087. By the end of the eleventh century monastic life in
England had passed substantially under the control of Norman abbots.[1]

Equally remarkable was the monastic advance from Normandy into
the Mediterranean lands, and here in one instance exceptionally full
testimony is available since the abbey of St Évroul was so fortunate as to
house the historian Ordericus Vitalis. St Évroul was to give abbots both
to Crowland and to Thorney, but it was in the south that its influence
was most signally extended. Partly this was due to the fact that about
1059 the abbot of St Évroul was Robert II of Grandmesnil who belonged to a great Norman family[2] which was then in conflict with Duke
William. He escaped to Italy where he elicited some support from Pope
Nicholas II, but after returning to Normandy he failed to get himself
reinstated. He, therefore, fled once more to Italy and this time he took
with him many monks from St Évroul.[3] These were installed in 1062
under their former abbot in the monastery of St Eufemia in Calabria
which was then founded by Robert Guiscard. Shortly afterwards when
the abbey of Holy Trinity at Venosa was set up by Robert Guiscard this
was subjected to St Eufemia, as was also the abbey of St Michael at
Mileto which was founded by Count Roger before 1080. To both these
houses monks from St Évroul were given as abbots, and after the death
of Robert of Grandmesnil the movement spread over into Sicily. In
1091 Count Roger established the Benedictine house of St Agatha at
Catania appointing as abbot a Breton monk named Anscher from
St Euphemia, and Pope Urban II forthwith promoted this same
Anscher to be the newly restored Latin bishopric of Catania. Finally
from St Agatha and from Catania there were to derive three more
monasteries – St Leo in Pannachio, St Mary at Robere Grosso, and
St Mary in Licodia – which might be described as the Sicilian

[1] Knowles, *Monastic Order*, pp. 100–8.
[2] See Genealogy 7. [3] Ord. Vit., II, pp. 89, 90, 99.

great-grand-daughters of the distant Norman monastery in the forest of Ouche.[1]

St Évroul was not in the first rank of Norman abbeys, and though the great extension of its influence overseas was facilitated by exceptional circumstances, and recorded in exceptional detail, it should not be regarded as unique. Perhaps the most notable of all Count Roger's monastic foundations was the great Benedictine abbey of St Bartholomew in Lipari islands, and though nothing is known of the origins of Ambrose, its first abbot, he may conceivably have been a Norman and he was certainly a Norman protégé. Again, about 1085 Count Roger persuaded Norman monks returning from a pilgrimage to Jerusalem, to remain in Calabria where in due course he established them in the priory of St Mary at Bagnara, from which was subsequently to spring both the cathedral community of Cefalù in the north of Sicily, and the monastery of St Mary at Noto in the extreme south.[2] Such were, however, isolated instances of the progress of Norman monasticism in the south, which forms a fitting counterpart to the process whereby, during the same years, the monasteries of England passed under Norman control.

More important, however, as a factor in promoting the unity of the Norman world was the widespread appointment of secular prelates of Norman allegiance. The catastrophic effects of the Norman conquest upon the episcopate in England are for instance well-known. By 1080 only two of the occupants of English sees were not of Norman birth or training. Among the bishops who had thus been appointed were the unsatisfactory Herfast of Norwich, and the mundane Remigius of Lincoln, together with the saintly Osmund of Salisbury, the learned Robert of Hereford, Walcher of Durham and Gundulf of Rochester who built the Tower of London. It was a notable group that was derived mainly from the secular church in Normandy. The contribution of Norman monasteries to the English episcopate during these years was subordinate, but it was none the less remarkable. Le Bec, for example, gave to Canterbury, in Lanfranc and Anselm, two of her greatest archbishops and the former based his policy as a metropolitan in England on his previous experience in the province of Rouen.[3]

There were of course special opportunities offered in this respect to King William and Archbishop Lanfranc, but in the south too a similar

[1] L. R. Ménager, in *Quellen und Forschungen*, XXXIX (1959), pp. 1–19; 22–49; 58, 59; L. T. White, *Latin Monasticism in Sicily*, pp. 47–51.

[2] White, *op. cit.*, pp. 55, 77–100.

[3] Douglas, *William the Conqueror*, pp. 324–50.

development took place. Robert Guiscard, like William the Conqueror, consistently introduced prelates of the Norman allegiance into his newly won dominions. In Apulia the archbishops, Gerard of Siponto, Bizantius of Trani and Dreux of Taranto, who made their appearance at this time, all owed their appointments to Robert Guiscard, and while Bizantius belonged to the local clergy, Dreux was a Norman by birth, and Gerard was a German monk of notorious Norman sympathies from Monte Cassino.[1] In Calabria the situation was less clear, but William who became archbishop of Reggio in 1082 had for long been associated with Robert Guiscard, and was perhaps himself a Norman, whilst John who became bishop of Squillace in 1096 owed his appointment to his support of Count Roger.[2]

It was in Sicily, however, that was most clearly demonstrated how closely Norman influence in the Church followed the Norman military successes. The reconstitution of the Sicilian Church in the time of Count Roger will appear as one of the greatest of the Norman achievements in this age,[3] and the men who were then appointed to the newly established Sicilian bishoprics were naturally men with Norman sympathies.[4] Nearly all of them came from north of the Alps and some of them were certainly of Norman blood. Thus Robert who, in, or shortly after, 1081 became bishop of Troina was probably a Norman, and Stephen who is recorded about 1088 as bishop of Mazzara, south of Trapani, came from Rouen. Gerland who appears as bishop of Agrigento in 1093 derived from France, whilst the Breton Anscher who in 1092 was bishop of Catania had been a monk of St Évroul.[5] A Norman partisan was made archbishop of Palermo as early as 1073, and Normans were soon to obtain canonries in that cathedral church.[6] The inexorable extension of Norman influence at this time in the Sicilian Church was thus in every way notable, and it was soon to be matched in Syria when, as the direct protégé of Roger's nephew, Bohemund, Bernard of Valence was installed as the first Latin patriarch of Antioch.[7]

The effect of these appointments upon the politics of Christendom will appear later. Here they are noted as demonstrating how the Norman advance during this half century was extended in the Church. Lanfranc and Anselm for example were neither of them Normans, but

[1] J. Gay, *L'Italie méridionale et l'empire byzantine*, pp. 350, 551.
[2] Leib, *Rome, Kiev et Byzance*, pp. 54, 130, 131.   [3] See below, pp. 136–8.
[4] Ménager in, *Rev. Histoire ecclesiastique*, LIV, pp. 15–18.
[5] Malaterra, III, c. 18; IV, c. 7; Starrabba, *Contributo*, p. 48; *Pat. Lat.*, CLI, col. 339, no. 59 col. 510, no. 242.   [6] Ménager, *loc. cit.*   [7] Below, pp. 166, 167.

both owed their appointments as archbishops of Canterbury to Normans, and both were influential far outside the country where most of
their work was done. As early as 1059 Lanfranc, already well known as a
scholar, was present at the famous Easter council at Rome where he
heard pronounced the famous papal decrees against lay investiture
before pleading the cause of William in respect of the duke's marriage.
And many years later in 1098 Anselm was to be found at the council of
Bari where at the request of the pope he argued as a doctor of the
Church the Latin case against the Greeks in the matter of the *Filio-que*
clause in the Nicene creed.[1] During the same years Norman monasticism
was making its own conquests which were symbolized in the appointment of the Norman abbots who came to preside over so many of the
monasteries of England, of Calabria and of Sicily. And in the secular
Church the consequences were equally striking. These men of Norman
birth or of Norman allegiance, who in so short a time secured most of
the bishoprics of England, and so many of the sees of Apulia and Sicily,
who became archbishops of Canterbury, York, Reggio and Palermo,
and Patriarchs of Antioch and Jerusalem, had undoubtedly their own
contribution to make to the consolidation of the Norman world.

III

The extension of Norman influence in the Church during these decades
was the essential counterpart of the Norman success in arms, and the
Norman world of the eleventh century was formed by the advancement
of prelates as well as by the creation of secular lordships. The two developments were inseperably blended since they were both promoted by the
same set of people. During these years small groups of inter-related
great families were established as dominant not only in England and
Apulia but also in Sicily and Antioch, and these groups were, moreover,
closely connected. The small and compact aristocracy which came to
dominate England between 1070 and 1100 has frequently been illustrated.[2] The widespread connexions of the Hauteville family are likewise famous, and only less notable were those of the princely house of
Capua.[3] Again among the dominant families in feudal Antioch were
those of Sourdeval, La Ferté-Fresnel, Vieux-Pont and Barneville, all of

[1] Hefele-Leclerc, *Hist. des Conciles*, V, pt. i, pp. 457-60.
[2] Cf. Corbett in *Cambridge Medieval History*, V, ch. XV; Douglas, *op. cit.*, chs. 4 and 11.
[3] Chalandon, *op. cit.*, I, p. 121 and Genealogy 2.

whom were also active in the north during this time.[1] It is in fact wholly remarkable how many of the widespread Norman achievements of these years, both secular and ecclesiastical, were made by men who were the brothers and cousins of each other fully conscious of their kinship and conscious also, whether as prelates or lay lords, of their common and militant purpose.

Nowhere, in short, could the interrelated character of Norman enterprise in this age be better illustrated than from the history of particular families. Among these the family of Tosny[2] might be taken as a first example since as early as 1015–16 Ralph II of Tosny, then a landowner in middle Normandy, was apparently fighting in defence of Salerno against the Saracens. Even more significant, however, were the ventures of his son and successor Roger I of Tosny. This man inherited his father's lands in Normandy, but early in life he departed for Spain where he distinguished himself in war against the Saracens, and on his return, by way of Conques in Rouergue, he founded at Chatillon-Conches, in Normandy, a monastery in honour of Ste Foye. His adventures earned him the nickname of 'the Spaniard', and his fame was such that it was recorded by writers outside Normandy. Indeed, legend was later to attach to some of his deeds, but he is known to have taken a full part in the disturbances which followed the accession of Duke William in 1035 and he died a few years later. His son and successor Ralph III of Tosny, was likewise instrumental in extending the influence of Normandy, but he carried the interests of the family to England. He fought both at Mortemer in 1054 and Hastings in 1066, and in due course he was rewarded with lands in no less than seven English shires. Thus three successive generations of the family of Tosny, which remained strongly established in Normandy, contributed to the Norman impact on Italy, Spain and England.

Also from central Normandy came the family of Crispin,[3] which was established during the second quarter of the eleventh century by Gilbert Crispin I, who was a close supporter of Duke Robert I, and who became castellan of Tillières. He had several sons, of whom three may here be mentioned. The eldest, Gilbert, succeeded his father at Tilliéres. The

---

[1] Cahen, *Syrie du Nord*, p. 535; Ord. Vit., II, p. 356; III, p. 197; IV, pp. 342, 344; V, p. 106.
[2] G. H. White in *Complete Peerage*, XII (1), pp. 753 et seq.
[3] See Genealogy 8 which is based on A. Robinson, *Gilbert Crispin*, pp. 1–18. The main source for the early filiations of the Crispins is a 'Narrative' given in an appendix to Milo Crispin's *Life of Lanfranc* and probably written by him. It is printed in *Rec. Hist. Franc.*, XIV, pp. 268–270. A narrative of this type needs to be treated with proper caution, but it can be confirmed in most important particulars.

second, William, was castellan of Neaufles, and having formed a close friendship with Herluin, he became one of the earliest benefactors of the abbey of Le Bec, thus associating himself with one of the most influential Norman developments of the eleventh century.[1] But it was Roger Crispin,[2] the third of the sons of Gilbert I, whose career was so spectacular as early to form the subject of legend. In 1064 he was at Barbastro, and after that victory, the city was apparently placed in his charge. Later, however, it seems to have been recaptured by the Saracens, and Roger thereupon left Spain, and went to southern Italy where he remained for some years. Finally, he moved east once more, and sought service with the emperor at Constantinople. Not surprisingly, he proved unreliable, but he fought, apparently without much enthusiasm, at Manzikert in 1071, and he must have died shortly afterwards. Meanwhile, his nephew Gilbert Crispin[3] (William's son) had begun an influential career in the Church. Early in life, he entered le Bec as a monk. He was a close friend of St Anselm, and about 1085 he crossed the Channel to become a most distinguished abbot of Westminster. Between 1060 and 1090, therefore, three members of the family of Crispin, namely William Crispin, his brother and his son, entered into the history of Spain, England and the eastern empire.

It was not, moreover, only by the greatest among the Norman families such as those of Tosny and Crispin that Norman action was extended and correlated at this time. Before 1066 for example there was established at Tilleul-en-Auge near Lisieux a certain Humphrey[4] who, we are told, came over to England with his son Robert at an early date and was treated with honour by Edward the Confessor. Humphrey, and presumably also Robert, took part in the expedition of Duke William in 1066, and afterwards he was made the castellan of Hastings castle. He returned to Normandy in 1069 and henceforth his career was to be overshadowed by that of his eldest son. Robert became one of the chief tenants of Hugh of Avranches, earl of Chester, and established himself at Rhuddlan where he built a castle from which he took his title. He waged a continuous and very brutal war against the Welsh, and was in fact one of the chief agents of the first Norman penetration into Wales.[5]

[1] *Narrative*; R.A.D.N. nos. 55, 105, 110, 128, 156, 188, 189; Will. Jum., 117; Porée, *Hist. du Bec*, I, pp. 128, 177, 179.

[2] *Narrative*; Amatus, I, c. 5–8; Runciman, *Crusades*, I, p. 62.

[3] Robinson, *op. cit.*, pp. 19–84.

[4] See Genealogy 9. On him see Ord. Vit., II, iii, p. 186; III, pp. 280–3. Cf. J. F. A. Mason in *Eng. Hist. Rev.*, LXVI (1956), pp. 61–9.

[5] J. Lloyd, *History of Wales*, II, pp. 384–94; Beeler, *Warfare in England*, pp. 205–10.

He thus won for himself a prominent place in the new Anglo-Norman aristocracy, and is to be found attending the Conqueror's courts in England.[1] By 1086 he had secured large estates both in England and in the Welsh march.[2] But after the Conqueror's death he supported Robert Curthose against William Rufus, and he was himself killed by his Welsh enemies on 3 July 1088 in a bloody but picturesque engagement near Great Orm's Head.[3]

Meanwhile, Robert of Rhuddlan's two brothers William and Arnold had become monks at St Évroul, and William migrated in due course to St Euphemia in Calabria. There he became first prior, and then after the death of his uncle, Robert of Grandmesnil, in 1088, the second abbot of that famous house. He witnessed a diploma of Roger Borsa for Mileto in 1087, and also in 1091 Count Roger's foundation charter for St Agatha's at Catania.[4] He may thus be said to have played a significant part in the history of the Normans in the south. At all events the family record is impressive. Humphrey of Tilleul and his sons Robert and William belonged to what in 1060 might be called a Norman family of the middle rank. Yet within three decades they had entered into relations with Edward the Confessor, William the Conqueror, Robert Guiscard and Roger the 'Great Count', whilst their activities had stretched northwards as far as Gwynned, and southwards to eastern Sicily. All the more remarkable therefore was it that the family solidarity should remain intact. Yet so it proved. On the death of Robert of Rhuddlan in 1088 his youngest brother, Arnold, crossed the sea to England to bring back the body, pickled in salt, to St Évroul, and then himself journeyed to Italy to collect from his wealthy kinsfolk in the peninsular money which enabled a splendid monument to be erected to the warrior hero of the family in the Norman monastery which they favoured.[5]

Perhaps, however, the unified character of the Norman achievement in this age is best exemplified in the family of Grandmesnil.[6] Robert II of Grandmesnil has already been noted in connexion with the contribution made by the monastery of St Évroul to the Norman monastic colonization of south Italy and Sicily, and he certainly played his own personal part in that notable movement. As Abbot of St Évroul, in 1059,

---

[1] *Regesta*, I, nos. 140, 220, xxxii.
[2] W. Farrer, *Honors and Knights Fees*, II, 13, 51, 215–25; J. G. Edwards, *Proc. Brit. Acad.*, XLII (1956), pp. 159–63.   [3] Lloyd, *op. cit.*, II, pp. 390, 391.
[4] Ménager, *Quellen und Forschungen*, XXXIX, p. 20.
[5] Ord. Vit., III, pp. 286, 287.   [6] See Genealogy 7.

he twice had to fly from Normandy to Italy, and the influence of the monks who followed him from St Évroul to the peninsular was pervasive. Robert of Grandmesnil in close association with the Robert Guiscard, thus himself became a considerable figure in the western Church, and his prestige was strong enough in 1077 – some seventeen years after his exile – to allow him to revisit his relatives in Normandy. On that occasion, King Philip I of France wished him to be made bishop of Chartres, but his interests always remained in the south, and there his influence was continuously to spread until his death in 1082.[1]

The career of Robert of Grandmesnil is in truth notable, but the exploits of Hugh his brother were equally important. These, however, were concerned with secular rather than ecclesiastical affairs, and were directed northward rather than towards the south. Hugh I of Grandmesnil is, indeed, a familiar figure in Anglo-Norman history. Born about 1014 he, like his brother, incurred Duke William's displeasure in 1059, but he was reconciled to the duke before 1066. One of the most prominent members of the new feudal aristocracy in Normandy, he then joined William's expedition, fought at Hastings, became custodian of Winchester in 1067, and was at length established at Leicester. He later became one of the Conqueror's closest counsellors, and he was to obtain for his house an immense share of the spoils of conquest. He came eventually to be one of the richest of the new landowners in England possessing for example no less than sixty-seven manors in Leicestershire and twenty in Nottinghamshire. Powerful on both sides of the Channel, he was always active in the politics of the Anglo-Norman realm, and he survived, vigorous to the last, until 1094.[2]

Hugh I and Robert II of Grandmesnil thus carried the influence of Normandy both into the feudal structure of England and into the ecclesiastical structure of Calabria and Sicily. And their work was to be carried on by the next generation. After Hugh I's death his eldest son, Robert III, inherited the family lands, but his second son, William,[3] had already departed as a youth to Italy where he married Mabel, daughter of Robert Guiscard, and won for himself very large estates, the centre of his honour being the old Byzantine stronghold of Rossano in southern

[1] Ord. Vit., II, pp. 73–91; 431; III, p. 185; Jaffé, *Monumenta Gregoriana*, p. 301 (Reg., V, ii); Amatus, VIII, c. 2.

[2] *R.A.D.N.*, no. 137; *Regesta*, I, nos. 109, 110, 140, 169, 170; D.B., *passim*; Will. Poit., p. 197; Ord. Vit., II, pp. 133, 167, 186; III, p. 413. After his death his body pickled in brine, was clothed in a monastic habit and brought from England for burial at St Evroul.

[3] Malaterra, IV, c. 8; *Gesta Francorum*, p. 56; Ord. Vit., III, pp. 171, 308, 360, 455; Hagenmeyer, ed., *Gesta Francorum*, p. xxxii; Jamison, *op. cit.*, p. 200.

Calabria by the Ionian sea. In 1081 he accompanied Guiscard to the siege of Durazzo, and at some period of his life, he was at Constantinople with an official title at the imperial court. He took his full share in the disturbances which followed Guiscard's death, and in 1094 Count Roger of Sicily brought Saracen troops against him at Castrovillari near Cozenza. But William of Grandmesnil had become firmly established at Calabria and there he prospered. Meanwhile, his younger brother, Yves, had received their father's English lands, but he pawned these in order to join the First Crusade. The last scene in this family history that needs here to be recorded is that of Yves together with his elder brother William and his younger brother Aubrey engaged (albeit with little distinction) at the siege of Antioch in 1099.[1] The history of the family of Grandmesnil during the last four decades of the eleventh century may thus be cited to illustrate the character of Norman enterprise at that time. Hugh I rose to power with William the Conqueror, Robert I and William in association with Robert Guiscard, but here too the family interest was integral and it was always maintained.[2] Firmly based upon Normandy it operated over England, Italy and Sicily, and stretched at the last into Syria.

These family records demonstrate, perhaps more clearly than could any literary generalizations, the interconnexion between the various zones of Norman action at this time. Roger I of Tosny and Roger Crispin in Spain; William of Grandmesnil and his brothers in Italy, Sicily and Syria. Hugh of Grandmesnil in England; Robert of Rhuddlan in Wales; Robert II of Grandmesnil and Gilbert Crispin in two widely separated provinces of the western Church – these were all engaged on a common enterprise which was in due course to create a wide-stretched dominion comparable even to that which Durendal the sword of Roland won for Charles, the fabled emperor:

> So many lands he's led his armies o'er,
> So many blows from spears and lances borne
> And such rich kings brought down.[3]

Indeed, the spirit which was made to animate Norman endeavour before the eleventh century had closed was not unlike that of the eleventh century *Roland*, and some of the similarities between them were

---

[1] *Gesta Francorum*, p. 56.

[2] As late as 1130 a member of the family gave up his Italian estates to return to his kinsfolk in Normandy (Ord. Vit., III, p. 435).

[3] *Chanson de Roland*, vv. 538–42, trans. Scott Moncrieff.

soon to be further illustrated. There is, for instance, no better example of the peculiar nature of Norman patriotism than that expressed in the harangue which Ailred of Rievaulx, the biographer of Edward the Confessor, attributed to the aged Walter Espec, leader of the English army against the Scots at the battle of the Standard in 1138. Here the successes of the Normans in England, Apulia, Calabria and Sicily are not only extrolled; they are treated as parts of a single venture.[1] Similarly, Henry of Huntingdon,[2] speaking in the same vein through one of his own characters, recalls to 'the magnates of England and the illustrious sons of Normandy', that through the valour of their fathers, 'fierce England fell captive, sumptuous Apulia was made to flourish anew, whilst far-famed Jerusalem and noble Antioch were brought to surrender'. The praise is extravagant, and the boasting distasteful. But the rhetoric was certainly expected to exercise a wide appeal.

Writers in Normandy and England by this time were taking pains to study the available chronicles about the Normans in the Mediterranean in order to supply their own compatriots with information about adventures in which they claimed a share. And their own comments on these happenings are often illuminating. Thus, some forty years after the event, Ordericus Vitalis made the dying Robert Guiscard address his followers in these terms:

> We were sprung from poor and obscure parents, and leaving the barren fields of the Cotentin, and homes ill-supplied with the means of subsistence, we set out for Rome. Only with much difficulty did we pass beyond that place, but afterwards, with God's aid, we got possession of many cities. But we ought not to attribute our success to our own valour but to divine providence – Recollect what great deeds the Normans have wrought, and how often our fathers have resisted the French, the Bretons, and the people of Maine. Recall the great exploits which you yourselves performed with me in Italy and Sicily when you captured Salerno and Bari, Brindisi and Taranto, Bisignano and Reggio, Syracuse and Palermo.[3]

Had not the 'rich region of Bulgaria' also fallen to their arms? And yet all this was due to the fulfilment of the Divine purpose. It is of course highly rhetorical but to some extent the boasting was warranted by the facts. The whole tenor of the speech may recall the Charles of the *Roland* who 'conquered Pouille and the whole of Calabrie' and who (unlike his historical prototype) also 'crossed over the bitter sea to England'.[4]

[1] *Chronicles of – Stephen, Henry II and Richard I*, ed. Howlett, II, pp. 318, 319.
[2] *Historia Anglorum*, ed. Arnold, pp. 261, 262.
[3] Ord. Vit., III, p. 184.   [4] *Chanson de Roland*, vv. 371, 372.

The enthusiasm voiced by such as Ordericus Vitalis and William of Malmesbury for the Norman achievement may be regarded as the retrospective expression of the spirit which had pervaded the Norman world when the Norman conquests were being made. Not for nothing was Rouen soon to be hailed as an imperial city and saluted as a second Rome.[1] The Norman people (it was said) had gone forth thence to subdue many lands. Thus had Brittany and England, Scotland and Wales been subjected, and thus had another son of Rouen become master of 'Italy, Sicily, Africa, Greece and Syria'. The final reference to the conquests made by Roger II in Africa is perhaps itself of interest for in view of the religious character so persistently ascribed to the Norman wars of the eleventh century there was something appropriate in the fact that the dominion of a grandson of Tancred of Hauteville should regain for Christendom the diocese of Hippo and the home of St Augustine.

Assuredly by the end of the eleventh century the Norman world was a reality, proud of its self-asserted Christian mission and proud also of its armed might which had by 1100 been stretched from Abernethy to Syracuse, from Brittany to Antioch. Over all the wide lands which the Normans had come to rule there had been made to prevail a certain community of sentiment based partly on self-interest, but partly also on genuine political and religious emotions. These interconnexions were moreover further strengthened by the submission of so many scattered countries to a limited number of Norman families whose members kept in constant touch with each other, and whose common interests were further promoted by frequent intermarriage. Thus was produced that particular type of Norman pride and Norman purpose which contributed substantially to the Norman success, and also to the special impact which was to be made by the Normans between 1050 and 1100 on the politics of Christendom.

[1] This anonymous poem of mid-twelfth century date is printed in Ch. Richard, *Notice sur l'ancienne bibliotheque de la ville de Rouen* (1845), pp. 37 et seq.; and in part by C. H. Haskins, in *Norman Institutions* (1918), p. 37.

Chapter 7

THE POLITICS OF CHRISTENDOM

I

Between 1050 and 1100 the Normans exercised upon the politics of Christendom an influence out of all proportion to their numbers. The major Norman undertakings of this age all entailed ecclesiastical as well as secular consequences, and their success was achieved at a time of critical change in the Church at large, when papal policy was itself being profoundly modified. As is well known, the eleventh century was a great age of ecclesiastical reforms directed against such abuses as clerical immorality, the traffic for money in ecclesiastical offices, and the undue influence of self-interested magnates in the affairs of the Church. But with these reforms in their earlier stages, the papacy had little to do. They were the work of monasteries such as Cluny, or of prelates in particular provinces such as Lorraine, or of enlightened secular rulers such as the Emperors Henry II and Henry III.[1] Not until the papacy had emancipated itself from the political decadence in which it had fallen during the tenth century[2] could Rome begin to play her proper part in the reforming movement.

The beginnings of this transition can however hardly be placed before the middle of the eleventh century. Despite the fact that the reforms were already being preached in Burgundy, and Lorraine, the reigns of the popes between 999 and 1012, particularly those of John XVII and John XVIII were a disgrace to the papal office, and though the vigorous pontificate of Benedict VIII from 1012 to 1024 foreshadowed a return to better conditions, the lapse after his death was lamentable. The scandals relating to the period 1024 to 1048 were later exaggerated

[1] A. Fliche, *Réforme grégorienne*, I, pp. 39–139.
[2] Liutprand of Cremona (*Pat. Lat.*, CXXXVI, cols. 690 et seq.) and Benedict of St Andrew (*Pat. Lat.*, CXXXIX, cols. 10–56) give lurid details. Possibly they exaggerate, particularly in respect of the influence of Marozia ('*Scortum impudens satis*'). But the truth was sufficiently deplorable. The most judicious study is P. Fedele, 'La Storia di Roma e del Papato nel secolo X' (*Arch. R. Soc. Romana di Storia Patria*, XXXIII, XXXIV) (1910, 1911). See also, L. Duchesne, *L'État pontificale*, pp. 285–305.

in the propaganda both of imperialist and papal writers, but the confused history of the papacy in the time of the notorious Benedict IX and his immediate successors reflected deplorable conditions which were made worse by the savage civil war that raged through the city of Rome.[1] A turn for the better was not taken until 1046 when the emperor Henry III crossed over the Alps to assert his imperial rights in Italy. At Rome he restored some sort of order, and after a council held at Sutri, he set up an imperial nominee as pope with the title of Clement II.[2] A period of confusion followed. But a new and happier era in papal history began in 1049 when Leo IX, formerly bishop of Toul, began his notable pontificate. Leo IX was at once the nominee of Henry III, and the first of the eleventh century popes who sponsored the reforms both north and south of the Alps. His accession therefore marked not only a climax in the German influence at Rome, but also the assumption by the papacy of a leading position in the reforming movement with which the emperor himself was already so deeply committed.[3]

Moreover, these dramatic events took place just at the time when the Normans were establishing themselves in Italy at the expense of all their rivals, and not least to the loss of the western empire. Leo, as the protégé of Henry III was thus brought, almost inevitably into conflict with the Normans. His condemnation of the marriage of Duke William of Normandy with Matilda of Flanders at the Council of Rheims in 1049 was not unconnected with the politics of the empire, and he was outraged at the sufferings which the Normans were inflicting on Apulia. With equal justice, he was apprehensive of the Norman threat to papal rights in Benevento, and he was involved even more deeply in the interests of the western emperor on whose support he so directly relied. The battle of Civitate was thus not only a Norman victory and a papal defeat; it was also a heavy reverse for the Empire. One chronicler indeed actually describes the battle as part of a war between Normans and Germans.[4] The dominant place of Swabian troops in Leo's army at the battle gave some colour to the description, and it was to be abundantly justified by the long-term ecclesiastical results of the engagement.

[1] R. L. Poole, 'Benedict IX and Gregory VI' (*Studies in Chronology and History*, pp. 185–219) – a notable study which modifies 'the famous story that in 1046 King Henry III of Germany went into Italy and held a synod at which three popes were deposed'. See also, G. B. Borino, in *Arch. R. Soc. Romana di Storia Patria*, XXXIX (1916).

[2] Poole, *op. cit.*, pp. 185–90.

[3] L. Duchesne, *op. cit.*, pp. 378–94; A. Fliche, *op. cit.*, I, pp. 129–58.

[4] Ann. Bari (Lupus), s.a. 1052, 1053.

After 1053 Leo was kept in honourable captivity by the Normans, but he always remained their bitter enemy, and in 1054 he cursed them on his death bed. His immediate successors were likewise all violently anti-Norman in sentiment.[1] But now papal policy was beginning to be dominated by Archdeacon Hildebrand and Cardinal Humbert of Silva Candida, and the party they led was above all things concerned to limit the imperial influence on the Church. These men had noted how rudely that influence had been shaken by the Normans at Civitate, and in 1056 they were presented with a new opportunity when the Emperor Henry III died leaving a boy as his successor. It was in these circumstances that at a synod held at Rome in April 1059, Pope Nicholas II issued his famous decree which attempted to destroy the emperor's power of appointing popes, by placing papal elections in the hands of the cardinal bishops, that is to say the bishops of the suburbican dioceses of Rome.[2] As a blow to the western empire it might in a sense be regarded as a counterpart to the Norman victory at Civitate six years before, and within four months the sequence was to be completed when in August 1059, at Melfi, the pope enfeoffed Richard of Capua and Robert Guiscard with the lands which they had seized in southern Italy. How close was the interconnexion between these events can be seen in the wording of the oaths which the Norman vassals of the pope now took to their overlord. Not only did they swear to support the general interests of the Holy See, but Robert Guiscard specifically promised:

> If you or your successors die before me, I will help to enforce the dominant wishes of the Cardinals and of the Roman clergy and laity in order that a pope may be chosen and established to the honour of St Peter.[3]

The interactions between papal and Norman policy from 1053 to 1059 had evidently produced an anti-imperial alliance which was to condition the relations between papacy and empire just at a time when these were approaching a crisis.

The detailed implications of that alliance were in fact immediately

---

[1] According to Leo of Ostia (II, c. 94), Stephen who 'had a horror of the Normans', actually wanted to use the treasure of Monte Cassino in order to hire mercenaries against them.

[2] The synod is fully described in Hefele-Leclerc, *Conciles*, IV (2), pp. 1139–79. On the various versions of the decree, see Fliche, *op. cit.*, I, pp. 214–316.

[3] For the council of Melfi, see Hefele-Leclerc, II (2), pp. 1180–1190. There are two versions of Guiscard's oath. The free translation here given is from the text supplied by the *Liber Censuum* of the Roman Church, ed. F. Fabre and L. Duchesne, 1910, p. 224.

to be revealed. In 1061 it was the Norman, Richard, prince of Capua, who, at the instigation of Desiderius, abbot of Monte Cassino, established Alexander II at Rome, and when in 1066 Richard quarrelled with the pope, William of Montreuil the 'Good Norman' took over the task of protection.[1] Alexander II, in turn, supported the Normans on many notable occasions. He backed the Norman venture in Spain in 1064 and the Norman expedition against England two years later. Similarly, his support of the Norman expeditions into Sicily from 1063 to 1072 was consistent, and it was a factor in the Norman success. But the anti-imperial implications of the pope's policy towards the Normans were also clearly recognized north of the Alps. As early as 1061, at a council held at Basle, supporters of the young King Henry IV refused to recognize Alexander II and set up Cadalus, bishop of Parma, as an anti-pope. Moreover, the eastern empire in its turn found cause for alarm, and Byzantium was induced to recognize Cadalus.[2] It might almost have seemed that the two empires were ready to ally against the papacy and the Normans, and, though this was obviously unlikely, the very fact that such negotiations had taken place showed how far the Norman alliance had assisted the papacy in its confrontation of the Western empire. The way was prepared for Gregory VII.

The career of Gregory VII has always been recognized as crucial in the history of the medieval papacy but comparatively few studies have been made of the influence exercised by the Normans upon him. Yet this was undoubtedly considerable, and it was hardly surprising that it should have been so. For when in 1073 Hildebrand became pope his relations with the Normans were already of long standing. As archdeacon, he had in 1059 advocated the alliance at Melfi, and he is reported to have brought about the reconciliation between Duke William of Normandy and the pope in respect of the former's marriage. Again, he is said to have urged Alexander II to favour the Norman designs upon England, and his later relations with William the Conqueror were to be as exceptional as were his relations with Robert Guiscard. Throughout his pontificate Gregory VII was always to be implicated with the Normans, and it needs only to be added that Norman influence affected most particularly just those parts of his policy that were to be of greatest consequence to the future – namely

---

[1] Benzo (Watterich, *Vitae*, I, p. 270); Amatus, VI, c. 8.
[2] *Ibid.*, and cf. Runciman, *Eastern Schism*, p. 57.

the development of papal hegemony in the West and the extension of papal claims towards the East.

The hostilities between Gregory VII and the Normans which occurred from 1074 to 1080, were thus not only of importance to the progress of the Norman conquests in the peninsula.[1] They also affected papal policy just at a time when the papacy was making a supreme effort to dominate the affairs of western Christendom. It is doubtful whether Gregory VII in 1074 would ever have made his bid to check the advance of Robert Guiscard in the peninsular had the pope not been strengthened at that time in his opposition to Henry by the success of the Saxon rebellion in the previous year. In 1075, again, Robert Guiscard in his turn was ready to exploit against the pope the recovery of Henry's fortunes. Tentative negotiations seem to have taken place between Guiscard and Henry IV in 1075 whilst the pope on his side looked even further afield for allies. At the height of his struggle with Robert Guiscard, Gregory VII appealed for assistance from Sweyn Estrithson whose son was in this very year engaged in attacking the Norman king of England.[2] Neither of these plans had, it is true, much chance of success. The Normans in Italy had cause to fear the success of an emperor whose rights in Italy they had seized with papal acquiescence; whilst Sweyn Estrithson, who was to die in the next year, was fully occupied with the affairs of northern Europe.

None the less, proposals such as these indicated how widespread were the implications of the relations between the Normans and the papacy at this time, and their significance was soon to be signally demonstrated. In 1077 within a few months of Gregory's most spectacular triumph over the Emperor at Canossa, the pope lost his last remaining ally in southern Italy when the Normans at last captured Salerno from the Lombards. This was, in fact, a blow from which Gregory was never fully to recover. For the rest of his life, he had to reckon with the Normans at every stage in his struggle with the Empire. In 1080, for example, it was without effect that he declared Henry IV deposed, and in the same year he was brought at Ceprano to his humiliating reconciliation with the Norman duke of Apulia. As a result Robert Guiscard was to sail to the East in 1081 with the papal blessing, and in 1084 he was to sack Rome as the pope's ally.

Papal policy as conducted by the most vigorous of medieval popes

---

[1] See above, pp. 59, 60.
[2] Jaffé, *Monumenta Gregoriana*, p. 199 (Reg., II, 75); A.S. Chron., 'E', s.a. 1075.

had been modified by Norman action, and the connexion persisted when both Gregory VII and Robert Guiscard were dead. Desiderius, abbot of Monte Cassino, who, after great controversy, became pope as Victor III had for long been associated with the Normans, and he was now glad to call on their aid. Clement III, as anti-pope, was now firmly installed at Rome, and it was only with the help of Jordan, the Norman prince of Capua, that Victor was brought to the city and there established after fierce fighting in the precincts of St Peter's itself.[1] Similar conditions marked the beginning of the next pontificate in 1088. Urban II who then succeeded is justly regarded as one of the most influential of the medieval popes, but during his whole pontificate he was either directly dependent upon the Normans, or strongly influenced by them.

Urban II was French; he had been elected outside Italy; and once more it was left to the Normans to conduct the pontiff to Rome in opposition to Clement III. The new pope seems indeed to have been compelled to spend nearly a year in southern Italy under the protection of the rival Norman princes Roger Borsa and Bohemund, and only after these had been reconciled could he be brought to Rome under escort of a Norman force.[2] Later, in 1091, when the supporters of Henry IV's anti-pope drove him once more from Rome it was again to the Normans that he turned. The emperor who had just defeated the troops of Matilda of Tuscany at Tricontai near Padua, was now at the height of his power, but once more the Norman support of the pope was to prove effective, and in 1093 Urban was again restored to St Peter's.[3] Two years later, the same alliance between the Normans and the papacy against the emperor was exemplified in the marriage of Constance, daughter of Roger of Sicily, to Conrad the rebelling son of Henry IV.[4] The interrelation is impressive, and its consequences are apparent. The emergence of Urban II in 1095 at the councils of Piacenza and Clermont as a dominant European figure, and as a prime mover in the First Crusade, would hardly have been possible apart from the earlier alliance between the papacy and the Normans, and it was in keeping with their past history that in the Crusade itself the Normans were to play a special part.

[1] *Vita* (by Leo and Peter) (Watterich, *op. cit.*, I, pp. 561, 562).
[2] *Cod. Dipl. Barese*, I, pp. 59–67.
[3] Bernoldus, *Chronicon* (Watterich, *op. cit.*, I, pp. 588, 589).
[4] Malaterra, IV, c. 23.

II

The close association of the Normans with the papacy between 1053 and 1096 involved them directly in what was to prove the most formative ecclesiastical development of the age. Modern scholars have been eager to emphasize – perhaps even to exaggerate – the importance of that Easter synod which Nicholas II with Norman support convoked in Rome in 1059. There the papal leadership in the reforming movement was clearly asserted against secular princes, and there too was promulgated the notable decree against lay investiture that was to be effectively developed and given precision by Gregory VII. All this, which was prepared by the theories propounded by Cardinal Humbert of Silva Candida in 1058, and later summarized in the *Dictatus Papae* of 1075, inaugurated, we are now told, 'a great revolution in world history'.[1] The judgement should not perhaps be accepted at its face value, but it is at least true that by attempting to emancipate the papacy from imperial control, and by asserting the freedom of canonical elections, Nicholas II in 1059 also enunciated principles which might affect the whole relationship between clergy and laity within the Church, and perhaps even the relationship between the Church and the world. Was it being claimed that the Church, far from seeking to withdraw from the sinful secular world, should now seek to dominate that world through the action of a divinely established hierarchy? Clearly, the issues involved were far-reaching, and most certainly they were – and remain – controversial.[2]

It is, therefore, against a very wide background that the Norman influence on papal policy during these years needs to be appraised. The questions before western Christendom were not to be solved by street-fighting in Rome, or by a scramble for territory in southern Italy. On the other hand, the advance by the papacy towards a position of overriding political authority in western Europe was of essential importance, and it was clearly dependent in large measure on the Normans. Moreover, every stage in the Norman progress entailed from the first a practical extension of papal power in the countries which were being subjected to the Norman allies of the papacy. It was an essential prerequisite of the papal political advance that the papacy should be able to base its claims to administrative authority on a recognized system of the law which possessed the sanction of antiquity, and which

[1] G. Tellenbach, *Church State and Society* (1940), p. 111.   [2] *Ibid.*, pp. viii, 188.

was itself of undoubted validity. And not the least influential effect o
the Norman achievement between 1050 and 1100 was the impetus it
gave to a wider acceptance of a recognized code of canon law.

The process was difficult. In the middle of the eleventh century
the law of the Church – canon law – was not embodied in a single code.
Rather, it was to be found in compilations of a vast number of conciliar
acts and papal decrees, some of which were false, but all of which were
believed to be genuine. Among these were the so-called 'False Decretals' which included the famous 'Donation of Constantine' con-
ferring secular sovereignty in the West upon the papacy. To make
proper use of this immense bulk of scattered material for the purposes
of appeal, or of legislation, was clearly impossible, and so from time to
time collections had been made by individuals in different provinces
of the Church. But these collections, though they were treated with
respect, were naturally often of only local or partial relevance, and
they might even on occasion be mutually contradictory. Here, then,
was a major problem confronting the Hildebrandine papacy and one
in which the Normans were to be directly involved. One of the most
important achievements of the papacy during the latter half of the
eleventh century was to win widespread acceptance of the principle
that canon law, far from being recorded merely in individual compilations of varying value, was in fact a body of law universally applicable,
with the authority of the papacy, throughout the Church. It was thus
of the first importance that during these same years the Normans
should have introduced canon law, as thus conceived, into all the
countries they conquered.[1]

Each advance of Robert Guiscard, for example, that was won at the
expense of the Greeks in Apulia, Calabria or Illyria contributed
directly to the establishment in these lands of the legal principles which
were being propounded from Rome, and one of the most noteworthy
features of the special relations that were achieved between Roger I of
Sicily and Urban II was the count's guarantee that all bishops and
clergy in his dominions should receive judgement for all offences by
canon law and before spiritual judges.[2] Similarly, one of the most
notable acts of William the Conqueror in England was embodied in
his famous writ which, in, or shortly after, 1072 ordered that spiritual
pleas should henceforth be tried by bishops and archdeacons in their

[1] Cf. Z. N. Brooke, *English Church and the Papacy*, pp. 32–41.
[2] P. Kehr. *Papsturkunden in Sizilien* (Göttingen, 1899), p. 310; Chalandon, *op. cit.*, I, p. 347.

own courts 'in accordance with the canons and episcopal laws'.[1] Moreover, the reception of canon law in England after the Norman conquest was effected in the first instance by a collection made by Lanfranc,[2] which contained not only the matter of the 'False Decretals' but also the decrees issued by Nicholas II in 1059 at the Council of Rome. This council Lanfranc had attended on the business of Duke William of Normandy, and there the legislation was passed which necessitated the concordat that was made five months later between the papacy and the Norman rulers of Apulia and Capua.

The interrelated effects of the Norman conquests on the establishment of canon law in western Christendom were matched by the results of those conquests upon the structure of ecclesiastical administration in the lands which came under Norman domination. The men who after 1070 were progressively introduced into the English bishoprics were not only Norman in sympathy; they were subjected more closely than their predecessors had been to the control of their metropolitan, and, under Lanfranc, they were active in reorganizing the Church in England. In their time, for example, the cathedrals later to be known as those of the 'Old Foundation' – namely Salisbury, London, Lincoln, York, Exeter, Hereford, Chichester and Wells – began to be served by chapters and dignitaries similar to those which had previously existed in the Norman cathedrals.[3] Even more important, however, was the transference of many English sees to the cities in which for the most part they still remain. Thus the sees of Dorchester, Lichfield, Selsey and Sherborne were moved respectively to Lincoln, Chester, Chichester and Salisbury whilst that of Elmham was transferred first to Thetford and then to Norwich. The episcopal structure of the Church in England had in fact been made by the Normans to assume much the same form as it was to retain until the Reformation.[4]

A similar development took place in Italy and Sicily where, as in England, the Norman conquests resulted, not only in the introduction into the Church of prelates with Norman sympathies, but also a drastic reorganization of bishoprics within the conquered countries. In Apulia, the Church underwent widespread changes with the decline of Byzantine power after the fall of Bari in 1071, and in Calabria, at the same

[1] Stubbs, *Select Charters* (1913 ed.), pp. 99–100.
[2] Brooke, *op. cit.*, pp. 64–71.
[3] Edwards, *English Secular Cathedrals*, pp. 12–17.
[4] Cf. Douglas, *William the Conqueror*, pp. 328–30.

time, the bishoprics were increased in number and largely regrouped in their provinces.[1] Thus Mileto achieved episcopal status, through a union of the former bishoprics of Tauriana and Vibona,[2] whilst the number of suffragans owing allegiance to Reggio was reduced from thirteen to five.[3] But it was in Sicily that the changes were most spectacular. The archbishopric of Palermo had been effectively reconstituted by May 1073, that is to say within eighteen months of the Norman capture of the city,[4] and the subsequent Norman advance – marked as has been seen by the foundation of the sees of Troina in 1081, and those of Agrigento and Mazzara, Messina, Catania and Syracuse, between 1087 and 1088 – was rounded off, in 1095, when the bishoprics of Troina and Messina were united.[5] Before 1100, in short, the Norman conquest of Sicily had resulted in the establishment of the second Sicilian church.

III

The combined effects of the Norman conquests during the latter half of the eleventh century upon western Christendom were in fact so widespread that the relationship between the papacy and the newly established Norman rulers became a matter of urgent concern. The attitude of William the Conqueror towards the papacy during his reign as king of the English has for instance always been recognized as of particular interest. Here the papacy was in a sense committed to the Norman cause. The conquest had been undertaken with papal support; and one of its first consequences had been the deposition of Stigand as archbishop of Canterbury and his replacement by Lanfranc, with papal approval. William as king had, in 1070, been blessed by papal legate and a long series of councils, held between 1070 and 1087 in Normandy and England, had with his sanction passed legislation designed to give effect to much of the reforming programme which was now being preached at Rome. During these same years, too, the

---

[1] Cf. L. Duchesne, 'Les évêques de Calabrie' (*Mélanges – Paul Fabre*).
[2] See the bulls of Gregory VII (Jaffé, *Monumenta Gregoriana*, p. 499 – Reg., VIII, 47), and Urban II (*Pat. Lat.*, 154). Vibona was near Monteleone di Calabria, Tauriana is to the south east of Nicotera.
[3] Cf. Leib, *Rome, Kiev et Byzance*, p. 134. The remaining suffragans of Reggio were Locre Controne, Nicotera Nicastro and Cassano.
[4] Ménager, in *Rev. Hist. Eccl.*, LIV, 1958, pp. 15, 18.
[5] Malaterra, III, c. 18, 19; IV, c. 7. Cf. Ménager, *loc. cit.* For the diplomatic evidence, see above pp. 121, 122 and below, pp. 143, 144.

papacy, in the turmoil of its developing struggle with the empire, stood in need of the support of the Norman king of the English.

William on his side had much to gain from the papacy. Papal support might give some legitimacy to his royal position, and it could help him to retain his new realm in face of the attacks which were directed upon it. Many of the problems which beset him had moreover strong ecclesiastical implications. Thus in the vexed question of the primacy of the see of Canterbury, which reached a crisis in 1070, the king was not only anxious to increase the authority of Lanfranc within the Church but he was probably apprehensive that, in the circumstance of the time, an independent archbishop of York might crown a rival king from Scandinavia who would receive widespread sympathy in the north. Again the fact that the bishops and abbots of England were now entering into the feudal structure of the realm by becoming tenants-in-chief of the king made the Normanization of the prelacy of England a matter of immediate political consequences to William. But all these matters could only be settled smoothly with the acquiescence of the pope. Papal approval was something therefore that the Conqueror was always reluctant to forfeit. Evidently, both parties stood to gain by their association.

On the other hand, the Conqueror came from a province where the duke had firm control over the Church, and in England he had acquired regalian rights which he was resolved to defend. Correspondingly Lanfranc, who had been brought up in Italy when papal prestige was low, had a keen sense of the independent responsibilities of a metropolitan archbishop. King and primate could thus agree in prosecuting an ecclesiastical policy that was strictly comparable with that which had been followed by the Emperor Henry III before 1056. The new Norman king of the English had, like the victors of Civitate, the highest respect for the papal office; and he would foster the reforms. But he considered it the responsibility of the secular ruler to provide good government to the Church in his dominions, to make proper ecclesiastical appointments for that purpose, and to resist any act that might divide the allegiance of his subjects. His attitude on these matters was indeed summed up in the 'customs' which he was later held to have established.[1] In the case of a disputed papal election no pope was to be recognized in England without the king's consent. No ecclesiastical council held in his kingdom might initiate legislation without his

[1] Eadmer, *Hist. Nov.*, p. 9.

permission. No papal letter was to be received by any of his feudal tenants without his knowledge; and, by implication, his permission would be needed before any papal legate came to his kingdom. William in fact was perfectly sincere in his concern for the welfare of the Church in Normandy and England, but he thought of himself as a co-operator with the pope, not as the pope's agent.

Clearly, there was here matter for controversy as well as co-operation, and it is interesting that the disputes between William I and the pope reached their climax between 1074 and 1080, that is to say precisely during those years when William was most beset in France and when Gregory VII was engaged in hostilities against the Normans in Italy.[1] Thus, after Gregory's accession, it became clear that the primacy of Canterbury recognized by an English council was not going to be confirmed at Rome, and during the following years William con-sistently rejected the papal demands for the regular attendance of Anglo-Norman prelates at Rome. He was equally firm in resisting Gregory's strange proposal in 1079 that the archbishop of Rouen should be subjected to the primatial authority of Lyons, and, as is well known, he repudiated the demand made or renewed by Gregory in 1080 that he should do homage to the pope for his English kingdom.[2] In all these disputes, however, neither side was ready to push matters to an open rupture. William used diplomacy as well as firmness, and Gregory more than once mitigated the actions of his legates. Moreover, after Gregory's acceptance of the settlement with Robert Guiscard in 1080 at Ceprano the pope could never again afford to antagonize the Norman king of the English. Speaking generally, the co-operation between William I and Gregory VII was far more important than such disputes as took place between them.

After 1087 the situation was, however, rapidly to deteriorate. William Rufus sought to maintain the 'customs' of his father, without the Con-queror's care for the Church, and unscrupulously invaded ecclesiastical rights. Thus after Lanfranc's death the see of Canterbury was left vacant for four years so that the king might enjoy its revenues. Further, when Anselm in due course became archbishop he showed himself, on his part very ready[3] to give full effect to a papal policy which was in fact itself becoming more intransigent. The burning question was now

[1] Douglas, *op. cit.*, p. 338.
[2] *English Historical Documents*, II, no. 10; Brooke, *op. cit.*, pp. 141, 142.
[3] On everything concerning Anselm in this context see R. W. Southern, *St Anselm and his Biographer* (1963).

that of the investiture of prelates by laymen, which involved the royal right to make ecclesiastical appointments – a right which no eleventh-century king could afford to lose. It was partly because of this that Saint Anselm, who was greater as a thinker than as a statesman, departed in exile to Italy, and there in 1098 first at the Council of Bari and then at Rome, he heard the papal case on lay investiture stated in the most immoderate fashion. It was declared shocking that prelates whose hands might re-create Christ at the altar should be defiled at their investiture through the touch of lay hands 'expert in obscenity and bloody with carnage'.[1] When such language could be used at Rome, and when there reigned in England a king who in moral character and in public policy represented the worst features of secular influence on the Church, it might well seem that the relations between the Anglo-Norman monarchy and the papacy must be broken. Yet this was not so. William Rufus never incurred the excommunication he expected and deserved, and Anselm could on occasion recognize the force of the Conqueror's 'customs'. There were wide political considerations underlying Anselm's charitable intervention at the Council of Bari in 1098 to prevent Urban II excommunicating William Rufus,[2] and the accord achieved between the Conqueror and the papacy was to survive the strains of the last decade of the eleventh century. It was soon to be tested afresh, but it is perhaps significant that in 1107 a compromise on the investitures question was to be reached in England eighteen years before it was attained in Germany. The king gave up the right to invest prelates with ring and staff, but they had to do homage for their temporalities.[3]

The history of the Anglo-Norman Church in this period is in this respect strictly comparable with that of the Church in the Norman lands of Italy and Sicily. The savage conflict between Gregory VII and Robert Guiscard from 1074 to 1080 was no more typical of the relations between the papacy and the Normans than was the tension that developed during those same years between William I and the pope. In general the arrangements made at Melfi in 1059, and modified in the Norman interests at Ceprano in 1080 were sustained. Co-operation between the papacy and the Normans of the south was never closer than during the last two decades of the eleventh century. In

---

[1] R .W. Southern, *St Anselm and his Biographer* p. 336; Eadmer, *Hist. Nov.*, p. 114.
[2] Eadmer, *Hist. Nov.*, p. 107.
[3] *Ibid.*, p. 186.

return for Norman support the papacy was ready, here also, to acquiesce in the Norman rulers exercising a wide control over ecclesiastical affairs. Thus it was at the instance of Robert Guiscard that Urse, bishop of Rapolla, was translated to Bari by Gregory VII, and thereafter he was to prove an active agent of the Normans in secular affairs. He conducted the Duke's daughter Matilda to Spain for her marriage with Raymond-Berengar II of Barcelona, and after Robert Guiscard's death he mediated between Bohemund and Count Roger.[1] With equal pliancy successive popes between 1077 and 1097 accommodated their supervision of the diocese of Salerno to the political exigencies of the Norman dukes of Apulia until, in 1098, Urban II granted primatial rights to the see expressly 'at the request' of Duke Roger Borsa.[2]

Even more direct was the intervention in ecclesiastical affairs made by Count Roger I in Sicily.[3] It was through his acts that the new sees were constituted, and to them he gave bishops of his own choice. The language of his charters displays, moreover, a keen sense of his ecclesiastical rights and responsibilities. 'In the course of my conquest of Sicily,' he says, 'I have established the Sicilian bishoprics.' Therefore he 'appoints' Gerland to Agrigento, and Stephen to Mazzara, and in uniting the sees of Troina and Messina, he speaks of what he has 'decided', what he 'has discovered', and what he has 'bestowed'.[4]

These assertions are explicit, and their importance should not be minimized. However, in nearly all these cases a papal bull was subsequently issued confirming the arrangements which had been made,[5] and on occasion there may have been previous consultations between the count and the pope, who are known to have met at Troina in 1088, at Mileto in 1091 and at Capua in 1098.[6] But the claim later made by

---

[1] Leib, op. cit., p. 54. The extended jurisdiction of the see of Bari in his time is indicated by a papal charter of 1089 (Cod. Dipl. Barese, I, no. 33).

[2] See the bull of Urban II, Pat. Lat., CLI, col. 507, no. 240.

[3] This has been discussed in detail in two remarkable articles. The former is E. Caspar, Die Grundungsurkunden der sicilischen Bistumer und die Kirchenpolitik Graf Rogers I (Innsbruck, 1902), which was reprinted as an appendix (pp. 582–634) to the same author's Roger II (1904). The other article to which reference should particularly be made is E. Jordan, 'La politique ecclesiastique de Roger I', Moyen Age, XXIII (1922), p. 237, and XXIV (1923), p. 32.

[4] The relevant charters, which survive for the most part only in sixteenth century copies, are printed in R. Starrabba, 'Contributo allo studio della diplomatica Siciliana dei tempi normanni –' (Archivio Storico Siciliano, n.s., XVIII, 1893). This material is commented on constructively by Caspar and E. Jordan in the articles cited above.

[5] Pat. Lat., CLI, col. 339, no. 59 (Catania); col. 370, no. 83 (Syracuse); col. 510, no. 242 (Agrigento); Pat. Lat., CLXIII, col. 45 (a confirmation by Paschal II for Mazzara). See also Jaffé–Loewenfeld, nos. 5460, 5497, 5710, 5841.

[6] Jordan, op. cit., XXXIII, pp. 258–60.

the papacy that Roger had acted simply as the pope's representative hardly accords with the facts of the situation which was in truth dominated by the 'Great Count'. It was his will that was in the first instance decisive. Beyond that, there was, none the less, every reason for co-operation between Roger and the pope. The count stood to gain by papal pronouncements that his Sicilian venture was a crusade, and the pope was fully conscious that Roger was in fact making the island once more a part of Christendom. There was thus sufficient unity of purpose to force a compromise in favour of the secular power. Urban might denounce lay investiture in unmeasured terms, but he normally confirmed without effective protest the episcopal arrangements which had been made in Sicily by that 'champion of the Christian faith the warrior Roger', 'a man excellent in counsel and valiant in war'.[1]

In July 1098, Urban II issued from Salerno his famous bull which conferred on Count Roger and his successors all or some of the powers of a papal legate in Calabria and Sicily. This bull,[2] which created the so-called 'Sicilian monarchy', was for centuries to cause fierce dispute among those parties whose interests were involved, and the long political controversy was not in fact ended until 1867 when another papal bull annulled the original act of 1098. It is therefore not surprising that the bull itself, about whose authenticity there is now no doubt, should have been very diversely interpreted by scholars. It has, for instance, been held on high authority that Count Roger and all his successors became by this bull exclusively possessed in Sicily of all the rights pertaining to a papal legate.[3] It has also been contended that the grant was limited to Roger and his son, and again that in the event of a legate being sent to Sicily *a latere* for a special purpose, the count would thereupon become his deputy.[4] It would, however, be unwise to minimize the content of this privilege, and in any case, even if the bull be interpreted in its narrowest sense, Count Roger undoubtedly acquired some legatine powers for himself and his son, and also an

---

[1] *Pat. Lat.*, CLI, col. 338, no. 58; col. 370, no. 93.

[2] The text of the bull is derived solely from Malaterra, IV, c. 29 (ad finem) but in view of a letter of Paschal II which refers to it (Jaffé–Loewenfeld, no. 6562) there can be no reasonable doubt of its authenticity. The long political controversy which it caused continued after the Middle Ages and reached a climax in the sixteenth century when the papal case was stated with force by Baronius against Philip II and Philip III of Spain who then held Sicily. In 1715 Clement XI declared the privilege void, and this was confirmed by the so-called abolition bull of Pius IX in 1867. See further of these matters: E. Curtis, *Roger of Sicily*, App. A.

[3] Caspar, *op. cit.*,; Chalandon, *op. cit.*, I, pp. 303–7.

[4] E. Jordan, *op. cit.*

VI   Cefalù Cathedral Apse

VII   West Front of St Stephen's, Caen

assurance that no papal legate should enter his dominions without his consent. At the same time it was solemnly agreed by the same instrument that the permission of the Norman ruler of Sicily was needed before any bishops from the lands he ruled could attend an ecclesiastical council summoned anywhere by the pope.

Once more, comparison between Norman Sicily and Norman England is suggested, and it is noteworthy that Anselm was in the company of Urban II and Count Roger in June 1098, that is to say within a year of his making his own claim to the privilege that the Pope should never appoint a legate to England other than the archbishop of Canterbury.[1] There is however a great difference between such a claim made for a metropolitan archbishop, and the privilege which in Sicily was given to a secular ruler; and in point of fact Anselm's case was rejected by the pope. Furthermore, despite a bull of Gregory VII which in 1083 conferred the *pallium* on Alcher, archbishop of Palermo, no definite arrangement of provinces under metropolitans and suffragans was completed in Sicily in the time of Roger I.[2] The true analogy is here between what occurred in Sicily under the 'Great Count' and the 'customs' which in England were established through the policy of William the Conqueror. For like Count Roger, the Conqueror had insisted that his consent was necessary before any legate could be sent to his realm, and he had risked a quarrel with the most intransigent of medieval popes by his consistent refusal to allow any prelate from his kingdom to attend the council of the pope without his sanction. In short, the Norman rulers of Sicily and Apulia, and the Norman rulers of England all received exceptional treatment from exceptional popes, and they all took to themselves exceptional privileges of a similar character.

That they were able to do this was one of the inevitable ecclesiastical consequences of the Norman conquests. The bishops whom Roger had placed in the Sicilian bishoprics he established were not likely to oppose the count's ecclesiastical policy even if their sees were immediately subjected to Rome, and similar conditions prevailed on the Italian mainland where prelates such as the archbishop of Bari and the archbishop of Salerno owed their position directly to the Norman dukes of Apulia. In England also the same considerations applied. When William

---

[1] Southern, *op. cit.*, p. 131.
[2] *Pat. Lat.*, CXLVIII, col. 702, no. 60. Cf. Jordan, *op. cit.*, XXXIII, pp. 270-1; XXIV, pp. 32-4.

of St Calais, bishop of Durham, who had rebelled against William Rufus, was brought to trial in 1088, he might cite the 'False Decretals' and appeal to Rome, but his plea was rejected by both the clerical and the lay members of the king's court.[1] And when in 1095 Anselm confronted William Rufus at the council of Rockingham every one of the bishops present supported the king against the archbishop.[2] It was natural that they should do so, for most of them had been appointed by William the Conqueror. Secular rulers so placed were in a strong position to maintain their control over the Church. It is significant that two of the best medieval representations of Christ-centred royalty are to be found in mosaics at Palermo and Monreale,[3] while perhaps the strongest medieval assertion of the ecclesiastical rights and responsibilities of kings was produced before the eleventh century had closed by a Norman writer living at Rouen or perhaps at York.[4]

Nothing would however be more misleading than to interpret the ecclesiastical policy of the great Norman rulers of this age in the light of controversies that developed at a later date. William the Conqueror, for example, had no thought of establishing anything resembling a national Church, and he would have been as shocked as any eleventh-century prelate at the thought that within a century of his death a dispute between the temporal and the ecclesiastical authorities in England would lead to the murder of an archbishop of Canterbury in his own cathedral. Similarly, the policy of Count Roger I of Sicily is not to be judged by reference to the secular and centralizing policy of his son, King Roger II, and still less in connexion with the government of Sicily by the Emperor Frederick II which might have served to destroy the whole medieval political system.[5] Neither William the Conqueror nor Count Roger I ever pursued a policy that could with accuracy be described as anti-papal. Both were fully conscious of Christendom as a political reality, and within Christendom both acknowledged the overriding authority of the pope.

It must be recalled also that all the greater Norman rulers of this age, though inspired by mundane motives, none the less normally pursued a policy towards the Church that could be defended for ecclesiastical reasons. William the Conqueror has been justly described as 'a ruler who was resolved of set purpose to raise the whole standard

---

[1] *English Historical Documents*, vol. II, no. 84.   [2] Eadmer, *Hist. Nov.*, pp. 53–7.
[3] See Plate IX.   [4] See below, pp. 171, 172.
[5] See A. Brackmann, 'The Beginning of the National State in medieval Germany, and the Norman monarchies' (*Medieval Germany*, ed. Barraclough, vol. II, pp. 281–99).

of ecclesiastical discipline in his dominions',[1] and if in truth he exercised too much influence on appointments within the Church, his nominations were usually good. In Italy, Robert Guiscard, unscrupulous and violent, was none the less a lavish benefactor of religious houses. And though his motives and his methods might be suspect, the man who was responsible for the foundation and enrichment of four such notable religious houses as S. Eufemia, Holy Trinity, Venosa, Holy Trinity, Mileto, and S. Maria della Mattina;[2] who contributed so directly to the rebuilding of the cathedral at Salerno, and who, together with his wife Sigelgaita and his son Roger Borsa made many lavish grants to La Cava,[3] can hardly be excluded from the ranks of the great ecclesiastical patrons of the age. Finally, Roger, the 'Great Count', was not only to stand friend to Greek monks in Sicily, but he was to found or endow the important Latin monasteries of St Bartholomew in Lipari, St Agata at Catania, and shortly before his death S. Maria 'Monialium' at Messina.[4] Certainly the new Sicilian bishoprics could not have been created without him, and the second Sicilian Church owed more to him than to any other single man.

Such facts must be given full weight when assessing the Norman influence on the politics of Christendom, and in particular in appraising the relations between the greater Norman rulers and the papacy. When due note has been taken of the six years' conflict between Gregory VII and Robert Guiscard, of the crudities of William Rufus, and of the acerbities which sometimes entered into the papal correspondence with King William and Count Roger, it remains true that the political fortunes of the papacy and the Normans were linked together and interdependent. The Norman conquests were achieved with papal approval, and the temporal power of the papacy was increased by Norman arms. This, moreover, was not only asserted at the Norman courts, it was also recognized at Rome. In July 1080 Robert Guiscard, so recently excommunicated, found himself specially commended by Gregory VII to the bishops of Apulia and Calabria, and two months later Gregory VII referred to the 'Glorious Duke Robert and his most

---

[1] Knowles, *Monastic Order*, p. 93.
[2] Ménager, 'Les fondations monastiques de Robert Guiscard', *Quellen und Forschungen*, XXXIX (1959), pp. 1–116.
[3] Guillaume, *La Cava*, App. 'D', nos. I–IV; 'E', nos. I–VII.
[4] For Lipari see Ughelli, *Italia Sacra*, I, p. 775 (with date 26 July 1088); Jaffé–Loewenfeld, no. 5448. For St Agata see Caspar, *Roger II*, p. 614. See also Ménager, *Messina*, pp. 12, 13, and no. 1; and White, *op. cit.*, pp. 77–85; 105–10.

noble wife Sigelgaita'.[1] Again, in 1080 the same pope could speak of William the Conqueror (who had just refused him homage) as a 'Jewel among princes'.[2] And despite rare misunderstandings, Roger the 'Great Count' worked for most of his career in close accord with successive popes. In 1076 Gregory VII saluted him as a Christian warrior,[3] and in 1098 Urban II formally expressed the debt of Christendom to his martial exploits against the Saracens.[4] Such utterances cannot be dismissed as the formal language of diplomatic courtesy. They reflected an alliance which had proved vital to both the parties concerned. The Norman achievement between 1050 and 1100 enlarged the bounds and helped to condition the structure, of western Christendom in the Middle Ages.

[1] Jaffé, *Monumenta Gregoriana*, pp. 435 and 437 (Reg. VII, nos. 6 and 8).
[2] *Ibid.*, p. 415 (Reg. VII, no. 23).
[3] *Ibid.*, p. 225 (Reg. III, no. 11).
[4] *Pat. Lat.*, CLI, cols. 329 and 370 (nos. 59 and 93).

Chapter 8

EAST AND WEST

I

The Norman impact upon the politics of Christendom between 1050 and 1100 was not confined to Latin Europe. It also modified the relations between western Christendom and its neighbours. It was no coincidence that the western Church should begin to show a more intransigent attitude towards the East at a time when it was itself achieving greater unity under papal leadership, and the support given to the papacy by the Normans needs no further emphasis. Apart from this, however, Norman policy between 1050 and 1100 helped to develop a schism between the eastern and western Churches. The Normans made a special contribution both to the progress of the First Crusade, and also to some of its most lamentable consequences. Thus they not only fostered two of the most important movements of this age: they helped to combine them.

So far-reaching were to be the results of the eastern schism and of the Crusades that it is tempting to believe they were inevitable. But in the earlier half of the eleventh century there was considerable goodwill not only (as was proper) through all the parts of the Christian world, but even between Christendom and Islam. The eastern patriarchates of Antioch, Alexandria and Jerusalem were, for example, evidently anxious not to be involved in any tensions that might grow between Rome and Constantinople, but rather to keep in cordial touch with both of them. The attempt made early in the century by Constantinople to modify the independence of Antioch was repelled without ill-feeling, and during a period when Rome was in political eclipse, the patriarch of Alexandria paid overt official respect to the papal office. Similarly, during these years the patriarchate of Jerusalem remained in touch both with Byzantium and the West.[1] In such conditions Christians could hope to move freely and with mutual respect throughout the Christian world. Pilgrims not only passed from the West to Constantinople and Jerusalem; they also came from the East to worship at the shrines of Rome. At

---

[1] Runciman, *Schism*, pp. 37, 69; Every, *Byzantine Patriarchate*, pp. 138, 157–9.

Constantinople too there were Latin churches for the use of western residents in the great city, and in southern Italy, Greek and Benedictine monasteries existed side by side. Greek monks such as St Nil of Rossano, when flying from Saracen raids on Calabria, were welcomed at Monte Cassino, while monks from that monastery carried their practice of the rule of St Benedict to Mount Athos and Mount Sinai.[1]

Tension between Christendom and Islam also seems to have lessened during the earlier half of the eleventh century. The Byzantine emperor, Romanus III (1028–34) entered into a treaty with the khalif of Cairo, and at Jerusalem the Christian shrines were made readily accessible by the Moslems.[2] Similarly, though there was perpetual warfare among the states of southern Spain after the death of Al Mansour at Cordova, in 1002, none the less a spirit of religious tolerance was here beginning to appear. Christian scholars were eager to take advantage of the flowering of Islamic culture which now occurred in the surviving Moslem states, and the rulers of those states relied for their protection on the subsidized armies of their Christian neighbours such as Leon, Castille and Aragon.[3] Doubtless such conditions could not last. But the transformation to which the Normans were so signally to contribute can be measured by some of the dynastic alliances of the period. At a later date, when the danger of a schism between the eastern and western Churches was impending, two of the greatest of western rulers, namely Henry I of France, and Henry IV of Germany, were to marry Russian princesses from the orthodox royal house of Kiev.[4] And it comes as something of a shock to be told[5] that scarcely more than a hundred years before the opening of the first Crusade, the Fatimite khalif al Aziz, reigning in Cairo, chose as his favourite wife a Christian girl whose brothers were patriarchs respectively of Alexandria and Antioch. Certainly as late as 1054, Byzantine was on very good terms with the Fatimite khalifs who ruled over Palestine.[6]

Such occurrences should not, however, mask the difficulties which lay in the way of maintaining peaceful relations between Christendom and Islam, or even between the western and eastern Churches. The men of the eleventh century were well aware of the enduring consequences of

---

[1] Leib, *Rome, Kiev et Byzance*, pp. 101, 103, 107–22; H. Bloch, *Monte Cassino, Byzantium and the West*, pp. 193–201.
[2] Cf. Runciman, *Schism*, p. 69.
[3] Menendez Pidal, *Cid and his Spain*, pp. 31–3.   [4] Leib, *op. cit.*, pp. 14, 167.
[5] C. Dawson, *Medieval Essays*, p. 121. But he cites no evidence.
[6] Runciman, *Schism*, p. 68.

the rise of Islam in the seventh century and of the Iconoclast controversy within the Church during the eighth. Wide divergencies both in
mental outlook and in the ordinary practices of worship had naturally
grown up in the various Christian communities,[1] whilst the great controversies about the nature of Christ which had rent Christendom for so
many centuries had not yet spent their force. The addition in the western
Church of the *Filioque* clause in the Nicene creed was felt as an outrage
in the East whilst the eastern use of leavened bread in the Eucharist was
deeply resented in the West.[2] The immense literature devoted to these
and kindred subjects during the eleventh century testifies to the extent
to which they inflamed passion. They involved the leaders of the Church
in bitter dispute, and they fired the emotions of ordinary men and
women who were deeply concerned (especially in the East) with any
change in a familiar liturgy which they had learned to reverence. These
disputes must not therefore be dismissed in this context as either trivial
or without importance. During the eleventh century they were powerful
incentives to political action.

In particular they were to affect the burning question of what (under
God) was the source of ultimate authority in the Church. Broadly
speaking the Church of Constantinople, whilst respecting the authority
of the emperor, asserted that it was for ecumenical councils to define
doctrine, and that the rule of the whole Church was vested in the five
patriarchates of Rome, Constantinople, Alexandria, Antioch and Jerusalem. Among these, it was added, Rome should be accorded no more
than a primacy of honour. Against this the papal doctrine was that it
had always lain with the papacy to apply the test of the *regula fidei*, and
that the eastern patriarchates, including that of Constantinople, were
in this sense ultimately subject to Rome.[3] These claims had in the past
often been categorically made, and had often been admitted. Frequently
ignored during the years when Byzantium, under the Macedonian
emperors, advanced to the peak of its power, while the papacy was the
sport of Roman factions or of German kings, they began to be restated
with ever more practical emphasis when the papacy, with Norman assistance, moved towards a position of greater political strength.

[1] The promotion of eunuchs to ecclesiastical office particularly in the case of priests serving
religious houses, was for instance a practice within the patriarchate of Constantinople that
was repellant to the West. See on this, H. Delahaye, in Baynes and Moss, *Byzantium*, p. 153.

[2] See the long article 'Filioque' by A. Palmieri, in the *Dictionaire de Theologie Catholique*. On
the question of unleavened bread see the article 'Azymes' by F. Cabrol in *Dictionaire d'Arché-
ologie chretienne et de liturgie.*

[3] Cf. Jugie, *Schisme byzantine*, pp. 219–34.

The implications of this question were of course very wide. If the Roman primacy were proclaimed in the West as an article of Faith, its denial might be a cause not only of schism but also of heresy. And Roman assertions of authority inevitably touched also on the allegiance of many dioceses, particularly those in *Magna Graecia*.[1] It was not to be forgotten that many sees in southern Italy had been lost to Rome through the annexions made by Constantinople at the time of the Iconoclast Controversy in the eighth century. Someday they might perhaps be restored. Nor could secular rulers afford to be indifferent to the issues that were involved. The rulers of Germany had for long exercised too close a control over the papacy for them to wish that papal prerogatives should be challenged by others, and in the East the situation was even more clearly defined. The emperor in the East was recognized throughout the empire as possessing ecclesiastical rights and duties far more exalted than those of any other secular ruler. He too therefore was directly concerned in any disputes between the eastern and western Churches, and in any ecclesiastical controversy that might follow hostilities within the Byzantine territories in southern Italy. He was in fact to face such disputes just at a time when his own empire was lethally menaced by Islam.

In this manner the Normans were again thrust into the very centre of political movements which were to affect the whole European future. They were to be actively involved in strengthening the papacy against the patriarchs of the East, and the emperors both of the East and the West. Their own conquests were to be made in southern Italy where lay the dioceses most immediately concerned with the rival claims of Rome and Byzantium. Their boundless ambitions would in due course impel them to attack the eastern empire at a time when Rome was challenging the patriarchate of Constantinople. And during these same years they would conduct a war in Sicily that could be proclaimed as a Christian endeavour against the Moslems. In the developing tension between Rome and Constantinople, and in the growing hostility between Christendom and Islam, the Normans during the latter half of the eleventh century exercised a powerful and sometimes a determining influence.

II

The support which had been given to the first Norman adventurers into Italy by Pope Benedict VIII at the time of the revolt of Meles of Bari

[1] Leib, *op. cit.*, pp. 122–43.

against the Greeks was very probably connected with disputes between Rome and Byzantium over the bishoprics of Apulia. The defeat of the Normans and their allies at Canne in 1018 helped however to stabilize the situation, and in 1025 the patriarch of Constantinople with the support of the Emperor Basil II proposed to Pope John XIX, who was a brother of the count of Tusculum, that there should be a settlement of all the outstanding differences between Rome and Constantinople. He therefore suggested that, 'with the consent of the Pope, the Church of Constantinople in her own sphere, as Rome in the world at large, might be called and accounted universal'.[1] The formula, if careful and vague, was in all the political circumstances not ungenerous, and it might even have been accepted by John XIX had there not existed north of the Alps a strong party that was rigid in stressing the prerogatives of the papal office. In a notable letter the pope was urged to act resolutely as a 'Universal Bishop', and was reminded that 'although the Roman Empire . . . is now ruled in diverse places by many sceptres, the power to bind and to loose in Heaven and Earth belongs alone to the *magisterium* of Peter'.[2] The letter was in truth remarkable and its authorship was likewise noteworthy. For it was written by William of Volpiano, Abbot of St Benigne of Dijon, and abbot also of Fécamp where for some twenty years he had been fostering the revival of the Norman Church.

After the accession of Leo IX in 1049 the papal claims were asserted with renewed vigour and once more the Normans were constructively involved in the controversies that ensued. Here as in so much else, Leo was inspired by Cardinal Humbert of Silva Candida who was emerging not only as the most proponent of papal supremacy in the west, but also as the most passionate advocate of papal rights in the east. It was, for instance, probably on his advice that Leo made many visits to the dioceses of southern Italy at this time, and convoked in 1050 councils at Salerno and Siponto. More significant still was the astonishing appointment of Humbert as archbishop of Sicily, for Sicily was in Moslem hands and its church had been taken not from Rome but from Byzantium. During these years too, and particularly after the cession of Benevento to the pope in 1050, Leo began his opposition to the Normans, and since their progress had been made at the expense of Greeks it was natural

[1] Rodulf Glaber, IV, i, p. 92. The Latin must be quoted: quatenus cum consensu Romani pontifiis liceret Ecceslaism Constantinopolitam in suo orbe, sicut Romana in universo universalem dici et haberi. This tactful and enigmatic statement is difficult to render into English, and is itself a translation of a Greek text now lost.

[2] Rodulf Glaber (ed. Prou) IV, 1, iii, p. 93.

that the pope's policy should have received the approval of Argyrus, the imperial governor of Bari.

But this approach to the papacy by the Greek administration in southern Italy was promptly opposed by one of the most forceful patriarchs who ever reigned at Constantinople. Michael Cerularius, who had succeeded to his office in 1043, was as intransigent as Humbert, and he was utterly opposed to any conciliation in respect of the papal claims. On the contrary, he was resolved to enforce a uniform Greek observance on the churches of Apulia and Calabria, and he caused to be circulated in southern Italy an uncompromising challenge to the papal authority. Finally he closed the Latin churches in Constantinople. The pope was bound to take counter measures, and thus it was that the defeat both of Leo and Argyrus by the Normans in 1053 brought the relations between Rome and Constantinople to a new crisis. The pope was actually a prisoner of the Normans when, in 1054, his famous legation carried the papal protest to Constantinople, and since its leader was Humbert of Silva Candida the confrontation with Cerularius was inevitably violent and disastrous. Neither of the two men were capable of compromise, and the Roman mission did not end before Humbert had placed upon the high altar of Santa Sophia a solemn excommunication of the Patriarch of Constantinople. Before Humbert had returned to Italy the pope who had sent him to Byzantium had died.[1]

The events of 1054, traditionally described as the 'Schism of Cerularius' are no longer regarded as marking a definitive break between the western and eastern Churches,[2] but they undoubtedly increased the feelings of bitterness between them, and these were soon to be further exacerbated by Norman policy. After the death of Leo IX, the influence of Humbert continued to grow, and together with Hildebrand he sponsored the alliance between the papacy and the Normans in order to secure the pope's independence from Germany. The wide implications in this respect of the arrangements made at Melfi in 1059 have already been noted, but it must here be added how directly they were to affect the relations between Rome and Constantinople. By becoming vassals of the pope, Richard of Capua and Robert Guiscard not only committed themselves to free the papacy from German control, they also became

---

[1] Runciman, *Eastern Schism*, pp. 41–54, 77; Jugie, *op. cit.*, pp. 187–219; Michel, *Humbert and Kerularius*, II, pp. 432–554.

[2] *Ibid.*, it may be added that on 7 December 1965 Pope Paul VI and the Patriarch Ahenogoras lifted the excommunications which had been severally imposed by Humbert and Michael Cerularius in 1054.

pledged to restore to the papacy the regalian rights she had lost to Constantinople. And in due course even Guiscard's designs against the eastern empire could be co-ordinated with papal aspirations to recover for St Peter the provinces of Illyria and Greece which had once received their metropolitans from Rome.[1]

Thus after 1059 the Norman conquests were made progressively to subserve the restoration of the Latin rite and the extension of papal jurisdiction in southern Italy. How hardly these conquests bore on the established institutions of the Greek Church can be seen, for instance, in the monastic policy which was consistently pursued by Robert Guiscard and his son Roger Borsa. The monasteries which Guiscard endowed were often enriched by gifts of what had previously belonged to Basilian houses. His great Benedictine foundation of S. Eufemia in Calabria in 1062 was based upon the restoration of the ruined Greek abbey of the Parrigiani, and Greek endowments must surely have passed to the notable abbey of S. Maria Mattina in the Val di Crati which he and Sigelgaita set up in 1065.[2] Some of the Greek abbeys which survived were despoiled for the sake of Latin monasteries. Thus estates of Santa Anastasia at Folicastro, and S. Nicola at Bisignano were given to Monte Cassino, while the Benedictine monasteries of Holy Trinity Venosa, La Cava and Holy Trinity Mileto all obtained lands from several Greek houses.[3] Further to the north in Apulia many Greek abbeys such as those of Monopoli and Lesina were subjected to the rule of prelates who followed the Latin discipline.[4]

Even more influential in this respect was the policy adopted by the Normans towards the secular church. It would seem that already in 1059 at the synod of Melfi a new Latin archbishopric was decreed for Cozenza, and in 1067 Alexander II, with the backing of Richard of Capua, refused the title of archbishop to the Greek Eustacius of Oria.[5] About this time too, a significant development took place in the region which lay between Potenza and Guiscard's own stronghold of Melfi. There, in time past, an attempt had been made to establish suffragan bishoprics subject to the Greek metropolitan of Otranto. Now, a new province was to be created under the control of a Latin metropolitan

---

[1] H. Gregoire in Baynes and Moss, *op. cit.*, pp. 123, 124; Every, *op. cit.*, p. 175.

[2] L. R. Ménager, 'La Byzantisation de l'Italie méridionale' (*Rev. Histoire ecclesiastique*, liv, p. 29; F. Lenormant, *La Grade Gréce*, III, p. 40; Gay, *L'Italie Méridionale*, p. 593.

[3] Ménager, *op. cit.*, pp. liv, 29; Chalandon, *op. cit.*, II, p. 588. St Nicholas of Morbano was among the Greek houses subjected to Venosa while Basilian monasteries at Gerace, Stilo and Squillace were placed under Mileto.

[4] Leib, *op. cit.*, p. 109.   [5] Gay, *op. cit.*, pp. 548, 549.

who was established at the ancient cathedral city of Acerenza within thirty miles of Melfi itself.[1] In view of the close inter connexion between secular and ecclesiastical politics in southern Italy in this period it is hardly surprising that the capture of Bari by the Normans in 1071 should have inflicted upon the patriarchate of Constantinople a loss comparable with that which was then sustained by the eastern empire. The metropolitan see of Bari itself now reverted unequivocally to the Roman allegiance, and, as has been seen, archbishops of the Latin rite were appointed to Trani, Siponto and Taranto. Even at Otranto itself a Latin archbishop was appointed in the place of the Greek metropolitan who in 1071 was absent at Constantinople, and in 1081–2 Latin prelates were installed at Mileto and Reggio.[2]

These changes were far-reaching, but, of course their full effect was only gradually disclosed. It is possible that some Greek bishops continued to officiate for a while along the littoral between Bari and Brindisi, and except in the Val de Crati, Greek resistance to the Latin rite was prolonged in Calabria.[3] Not until the period 1093–6, were Latin prelates established at Cosenza, Bisignano and Squillace.[4] At Rossano in 1093 a revolt took place in favour of restoring the Greek rite,[5] and at Bova Gerace and Cotrona the clergy continued to use the Greek liturgy although they were under Latin bishops.[6] During the last decade of the eleventh century both the Greek and the Latin liturgies were used at Nardo and Gallipoli, and even as late as 1099, Bohemund of Taranto, then prince of Antioch and at the height of his quarrel with the eastern empire was apparently among the benefactors of the Basilian monastery of S. Nicolas of Casole near Otranto.[7] Evidently Greek ecclesiastical traditions died hard in Calabria and southern Apulia.[8] None the less the changes wrought by the Normans in southern Italy at the expense of Constantinople and for the benefit of Rome were very great.

In Sicily, too, the papacy was to profit by Norman action though in

---

[1] Gay, *op. cit.*, p. 549; Lieb, *op. cit.*, p. 123, n. 4; for a similar development at Troia, see Jaffé–Loewenfeld, no. 4727.

[2] Gay, *op. cit.*, p. 551; Ménager, *op. cit.*, p. 27.

[3] Ménager, *loc. cit.*   [4] Leib, *op. cit.*, p. 126, 131; Jaffé–Loewenfeld, no. 5198.

[5] Malaterra, IV, c. 21.   [6] Leib, *op. cit.*, pp. 125, 130.

[7] Ch. Diehl, *S. Nicolas di Casole*, pp. 173, 179.

[8] The last Greek archbishop of Rossano reigned there from 1348 to 1364, and the Greek liturgy persisted at Gallipoli until 1513 (R. Weiss, *Proc. Brit. Acad.*, XXXVII (1951), pp. 30–1). The Greek rite persisted at Gerace and Oppido until 1480, and at Bova until 1573 (Ménager, *op. cit.*, p. 27). The convent of S. Adrian in San Demetrio seems to have used the Greek ritual as late as 1691, and in 1911 a traveller found that Greek was freely spoken in many districts of Aspromonte (N. Douglas, *Old Calabrai*, pp. 192, 284).

circumstances wholly different from those prevailing on the mainland. In southern Italy the Norman conquests had been made for the most part in regions where the Greek Church was flourishing. In Sicily that Church had been almost ruined by the Saracens before the Normans arrived. In the north-east of the island, in the neighbourhood of Messina and in the Val Demone, there survived scattered Christian communities, and, after the capture of Palermo a Greek bishop was found in a suburb of the great city. But speaking generally, an organized Christian Church had ceased to exist in Sicily, and Count Roger was certainly not disposed to discourage any Greek Christians who might be hostile to the Saracens. The 'Great Count' may even have encouraged, particularly after 1080, a migration of Greek monks back to Sicily from the mainland where they must have felt the lash of Guiscard's policy.[1] In this way can perhaps be explained his establishment as early as 1080-1 of the Greek houses of St Nicolas of Butana in the Val Demone, and of St Michael at Troina, whilst some four years later he restored the monastery of St Michael the Archangel at Brolo near Messina.[2] Certainly, after he had become master of Sicily he continued to show himself a lavish benefactor of Greek houses, particularly in the north of the island; and in the last year of his life he established the monastery of St Philip the Great, and the convent of St Saviour at Messina.[3]

The Great Count's patronage of Greek monasteries is indeed remarkable, but it derived from the special circumstances of the Sicilian conquest, and it should not be regarded as running counter to the Norman support of Rome against Constantinople. Roger's own policy on the mainland was often more strictly Latin in effect as when he gave the Greek monastery of S. Opolo near Mileto to the abbey of S. Filippo at Gerace, and he had been responsible for the foundation of at least four great Benedictine houses in Sicily and the adjoining islands.[4] Most important of all was the fact that the new bishoprics, which were established as the result of his Sicilian conquest, were all assigned to the Latin allegiance.[5] Roger's wars in Sicily were directed against the

[1] Ménager (*op. cit.*, p. 22), shows that about this time many Basilian houses in southern Italy were deserted: the monks probably returned to Sicily.

[2] L. T. White, *Latin Monasticism in Norman Sicily*, pp. 41, 42, 191, n. 2.

[3] White (*op. cit.*, pp. 41-3) gives a list of these, but this apparently needs some correction. See further on this matter, Ménager, *op. cit.*, p. 23, n. 2.

[4] For Lipari see Ughelli, *Italia Sacra*, I, 775 (with date 26 July 1088; Jaffé Reg. no. 5448. For S. Agata, see Malaterra, IV, c. 7; Caspar, *Roger II*, App., p. 614. See further White, *op. cit.*, pp. 77-85, 105-10.

[5] See above, pp. 121, 139, 143, 144.

Saracens not the Greeks, but his conquests restored the Sicilian Church not to Constantinople but to Rome.

III

The capture of Palermo in January 1072 had regained for Christendom the greatest Moslem city in the central Mediterranean, and this occurred within a few months of the shattering defeat sustained by the eastern empire at Manzikert at the hands of the Seljuk Turks. After 1072 therefore, Norman ecclesiastical policy developed in a world which was rapidly changing. The accession of Gregory VII in 1073 gave to the west a pope who would be resolute in asserting his rights against all rivals, and eight years later the eastern empire received in Alexis I a leader whose competence was vastly superior to that of his immediate predecessors. And if the two chief branches of Christendom were thus brought into more direct confrontation, so also could a transformation be seen in Islam. The Seljuk Turks, who under Togrul Beg in 1055 had displaced the Abbassid rulers of Baghdad, were far less tolerant than their predecessors, and this gave an additional poignancy both to their successes against Byzantium, and more particularly to their occupation of Palestine. The capture of Jerusalem by Aziz-ibn-Abag, an obscure Turkish commander, in 1071[1] – the year of Bari and Manzikert – seems at first to have passed with little comment in the West, but soon the whole of Syria was overrun, including Antioch, in 1085, and Christian Europe began to be profoundly moved by the loss to pilgrims of the Holy Places. In the West also a similar development was taking place. It was an event of European importance when the tolerant and sophisticated Moslem states of Spain called to their assistance the Almorovid rulers who had fought their way northwards from the Senegal across the Sahara to Algiers.[2] For these dark fanatical warriors from the desert had little use for culture or compromise. They waged a total and a ruthless war.

The years (1071–85) during which Robert Guiscard consolidated his position against the Greeks in Apulia and Calabria, thus saw a heightening of the tension between Rome and Constantinople; whilst the corresponding period (1072–91) when Roger won Sicily from the

---

[1] Runciman, *Crusades*, I, p. 75. It should be noted however that Jerusalem was taken from the Turks by the Khalif of Egypt (Munro, *Kingdom of the Crusaders*, p. 54) in 1098 that is to say a year before it was captured and sacked by the Crusaders.

[2] Menendez Pidal, *op. cit.*, pp. 211–15.

Saracens witnessed a mounting hostility between the Cross and the Crescent. Gregory VII in his turn was very conscious from the beginning of his reign that the two problems were interlocked, and in 1074 he produced a spectacular plan by which he hoped they might both be solved. This was nothing less than a proposal that the pope should lead in person an army of western knights to rescue the eastern empire from the Turks, and that after this had been achieved the pope should preside over an ecumenical council which should finally settle the differences between the two Churches. Gregory, therefore, addressed a series of letters to the princes of western Europe appealing for their armed support for his expedition to the East.[1] In view of subsequent events the whole plan must be adjudged as of exceptional interest. But it is only with considerable qualification that it can be described as projecting a Crusade. It will be noted moreover that the pope seems throughout to have had Constantinople, not Jerusalem, as his objective, while his over-riding purpose was the re-union of the Churches under papal rule.

The plan was doomed to failure. It is doubtful whether either the Emperor Michael VII or the patriarch of Constantinople would have given it support, and Gregory was becoming too deeply involved with German politics to spare energy for eastern adventures. But the final collapse of the project was due to the Normans. It was precisely during these years that Gregory was engaged in hostilities against the Normans, and indeed in his letters to rulers in the West the pope had stressed that the subjugation of the Normans in Italy must be the prelude to the expedition to the East.[2] The whole situation was in fact to be transformed with startling rapidity by Norman action.[3] In 1077 Guiscard took Salerno. In 1078 Michael VII was deposed; and his successor Nicephorus III immediately repudiated the marriage contract between Michael's son and Guiscard's daughter. In the same year Gregory, disapproving of the revolution in Constantinople, excommunicated Nicephorus; and in 1080 the pope in Italy was compelled to accept Guiscard's terms in the settlement at Ceprano. Finally, as will be recalled, it was with the pope's support that in 1081 Guiscard opened his campaign against the Emperor Alexis I who in turn had been excommunicated by Gregory.[4]

---

[1] Jaffé, *Monumenta Gregoriana*, pp. 64, 65, 69, 111, 150, 151 (*Reg.* I, pp. 46, 49; II, pp. 3, 137). Erdmann, *Enstehung des Kreuzzugsgedankens*, pp. 149–53.
[2] Jaffé, *Mon. Greg.*, p. 65.
[3] See above, pp. 50–62.
[4] Jaffé, *Mon. Greg.*, p. 330 (*Reg. VI*, 5b); *Alexiad*, I, 12; Malaterra, III, c. 13.

These events, and the war which followed them, marked a disastrous deterioration in the relations between the Churches. The emperor, who was widely regarded by eastern Christians as the divinely appointed protector of the faith, had been cut off from communion with the Latin Church, and at the same time, western knights under Robert Guiscard and Bohemund had invaded imperial territory with the pope's approval. How seriously this was taken at Constantinople can be gauged by the fact that Alexis actually hired Turkish mercenaries to withstand these Christian invaders of his empire. Deep and enduring was the bitterness caused. Far from being the defender of the eastern empire, Gregory VII was denounced as its enemy, and the Normans were regarded with suspicion and as implacable foes. Anna Comnena, for example, describes Hildebrand with indignation and loathing, and a nearly contemporary account written in the East about the translation of the relics of St Nicholas of Myra to Bari in 1087 speaks of the Normans with positive hatred.[1] The Norman alliance had in fact destroyed any chance that Gregory VII may ever have had of reuniting the Churches, and the wars waged by Guiscard and Bohemund between 1081 and 1083 fore-shadowed the lamentable divergencies between eastern and western policy which occurred during the First Crusade.

The special influence which the Normans were to exercise on the Crusading movement had in fact been indicated before the death of Robert Guiscard in 1085, but during the following decade the political situation in which they had become so inextricably involved itself underwent considerable modification. Western Christendom despite its divisions was becoming more conscious of common aspirations and more amenable to papal direction. In the East Alexis I had consolidated his position at home; and in 1091, he had finally defeated the barbarian Pechenegs who for more than a century had threatened the northern frontiers of the empire.[2] At the same time the strength of Islam was being impaired. Sicily had been lost to the Normans by 1091, and in 1092 the death of Malik Shah, khalif of Baghdad, plunged the Moslem world into confusion. The warfare that ensued could reasonably be expected to weaken such resistance as Christian warriors might encounter n the lands he had ruled.[3]

---

[1] *Alexiad*, I, 13; Leib, *op. cit.*, p. 63. [2] Setton and Baldwin, *Crusades*, I, p. 291.
[3] Stevenson, *Crusaders in the East*, pp. 24, 25; H. A. R. Gibb, ed., *Damascus Chronicle*, pp. 21, 22. Tutush, brother of Malik Shah, who ruled in Syria was killed in 1095. He was succeeded at Aleppo by his son Ridiwan, and at Damascus by his son Duqaq. Both were to play a part in the First Crusade.

VIII West Front of St Nicholas', Bari

IX   Coronation of King Roger II by Jesus Christ

Even more remarkable was the manner in which, during these years, the religious cleavage between the Cross and the Crescent was being embittered. In Spain, for instance, apart from expeditions from the north such as that of the Normans against Barbastro in 1064, the wars among the Christian and Moslem states had for some fifty years been little inflamed by religious passion.[1] But when the Almorovids from Africa defeated Alphonso VI of Leon and Galicia at Sagvajas, near Badajoz, in 1086, they celebrated their victory with religious rites conducted over a pile of decapitated Christian heads, and when in 1094 the Cid came into conflict with them at Cuarte, the two armies advanced against each other (we are told) with shouts respectively of 'Santiago' and 'Mahomet'.[2] Such enthusiasms had not been wholly absent in the warfare between Count Roger and Ibn al Werd from 1076 to 1085, but they were rarer in Sicily than in Spain, and more significant in this respect was the expedition successfully launched in 1087 against Moslem Medhia, near Tunis, by men from Pisa and Genoa under the leadership of a papal legate.[3] All these events were indicative of the changing temper of the age, and they took place during years when the loss of the Holy Places in Palestine was increasingly being made to inflame the passions of western men.

It is against this background that the papal policy associated with Urban II must be viewed. It was he who, as will be recalled, had been brought to Rome in 1088 by Jordan, prince of Capua, and who was sustained by the Normans during the early years of his pontificate. The precise influence of the launching of the First Crusade exercised by the councils which Urban summoned at Piacenza and Clermont in 1096 has been much debated,[4] but undoubtedly it was very great. Yet the papal policy was only slowly disclosed. It seems possible that Alexis I, who was now faring better against the Turks, sent an appeal for mercenaries to the council at Piacenza,[5] and the pope's exhortations at that council appear to have been directed mainly, if not exclusively, to urging warriors from the West to go to the assistance of the eastern empire. Urban's policy at this stage did not therefore differ materially from that which had been proclaimed by Gregory VII before his treaty with

[1] Menendez Pidal, op. cit., p. 86.   [2] Ibid., 221, 354.

[3] Erdmann, op. cit., pp. 272, 273.

[4] The literature is listed in Setton and Baldwin, Crusades, I, p. 221. Here may be mentioned L. Rousset, Origines – de la Première Croisade, pp. 43–68; F. Duncalf, 'The Pope's Plan for the First Crusade' in Essays – D. C. Munro, pp. 44–5.

[5] See D. C. Munro in, Amer. Hist. Rev., XXVII, pp. 731–3. But note the judicious commentary in Ostrogorski, Byzantine State, trans. Hussey, p. 321.

Robert Guiscard in 1080. The rescue of Byzantium rather than Jerusalem, and doubtless also the reunion of the Churches, seems still to have dominated the pope's policy. But nine months later, at Clermont, the pope's famous sermon brought the restoration of Jerusalem into the forefront of his appeal.

> Let the Holy Sepulchre of the Lord our Saviour which is possessed by unclean nations especially move you. And remember also the Holy Places which are now treated with ignominy and polluted with filthiness – Reflect that the Almighty may have established you in your position for this very purpose that through you He might restore Jerusalem from such abasement.[1]

Urban well knew the outraged emotions of those whom he addressed. He was, also, according to all accounts, a great orator; and he certainly appreciated to the full the value of religious propaganda. But there is no reason to believe that he was not himself perfectly sincere in the sentiments he expressed, and in the indignation he expressed.

The Normans, who had for more than thirty years been assiduously exploiting the notion of the Holy War, must have felt particularly attuned to such an appeal, and in fact the Norman contribution to the First Crusade was outstanding. Among the nine principal leaders in that Crusade were a son and a son-in-law of William the Conqueror, two sons of one of his tenants-in-chief in England, and a son and a grandson of Robert Guiscard.[2] But while the Norman participation in the Crusade was so notable, support for it did not come uniformly from all the Norman lands. Thus Norman ecclesiastical writers were keenly interested in the Crusade, and in the share of the Normans in it, but a council held at Rouen in 1096[3] could repeat the reforming decrees of the Council of Clermont without reference to Urban's speech. In England as a result of Urban's preaching there was 'a very great commotion among the people'[4] and sailors from England were soon to distinguish themselves off the coast of Syria. But William Rufus, who had prevented any prelates from England from attending the Council of

---

[1] Fulcher, I, c. 1; Robert the Monk, I, c. 1 and 2; Translation in Krey, *First Crusade*, pp. 24–40. See also D. C. Munro, in *Amer. Hist. Rev.*, XI (1960), pp. 231 et seq. and Runciman, *Crusades*, I, p. 108.

[2] Robert, duke of Normandy; Stephen, Count of Blois, husband of Adela, daughter of William the Conqueror; Godfrey and Baldwin sons of Eustace, count of Boulogne; Bohemund; and Tancred.

[3] Bessin, *Concilia*, pp. 77–9.

[4] A.S. Chron., 'E', s.a. 1096. 'The Welshman' adds William of Malmesbury (*Gesta Regum*, II, p. 399) – 'left his hunting; the Scotsman his native lice; the Dane his drinking and the Norwegian his raw fish'.

Clermont, was too secular in temperament to allow his policy to be deflected to the Christian east, and Norman England was among those countries in the West that were least affected by the Crusade. Similarly, though Count Roger had recently won back from Islam a province of Christendom, he was not anxious to imperil his conquest of Sicily by undertaking new adventures in the East.

The Norman response to Urban's exhortation came in the first instance from men who hitherto had been comparatively unsuccessful. Robert, duke of Normandy, defending his Duchy precariously against his brother, the king of England, was eager for the undertaking, and the papal legate, Geronto, abbot of S. Beniqne of Dijon, was able to arrange that he should receive money for the purpose by placing his duchy in pawn to William Rufus. A distinguished Norman company joined him at once, including not only Odo, bishop of Bayeux, but also representatives of such notable Norman families as those of Montgomery and Grandmesnil, Gournay and Saint-Valery. They proceeded southwards through Burgundy, crossed the Alps by the Great St. Bernard, and then having passed through Lucca, they entered Rome. They were repulsed from St Peter's by followers of the anti-pope, Clement III, so they moved southwards to Monte Cassino where they sought the blessing of St. Benedict.[1] Thus at last they reached Bari; and there they learnt that a still more important Norman contingent under Bohemund, the son of Robert Guiscard, had already crossed the Adriatic and was making its way towards Constantinople.[2]

Bohemund took the Crusaders' oath as early as June 1096, and his decision was to be of major consequence. On the Crusade he had certain advantages over all the other leaders. He alone among them had experience of warfare east of the Adriatic through his campaigns in 1081–1083, and his followers formed a notably united band of trained warriors recruited from some of the most prominent Norman families of south Italy.[3] Their slow progress across northern Greece towards Byzantium during the autumn and winter of 1096–7 was thus watched with great interest and some apprehension. For Bohemund's relations with the eastern emperor were bound to be delicate and dangerous. In 1083 he had failed to take Constantinople by force of arms. It was therefore an

---

1 Cf. C. W. David, *Robert Curthose*, pp. 91–7. The admirable list he gives of Robert's companions of the Crusade apparently needs a little correction (Jamison, *Essays – M. K. Pope*.
2 *Gesta*, I, c. 4; Ann. Bari, s.a. 1096.
3 Above, pp. 65, 66.

occasion of critical importance when he entered the city on 9 April 1097[1] as an ally of the emperor. And in the next month he was joined there by Duke Robert of Normandy who had spent the winter in Apulia and then made a more rapid transit of Greece and Thrace.

The important negotiations which took place between Bohemund and Alexis during April and May 1097 may today be studied only in accounts that are coloured by prejudice, and in reports that may even have been falsified by deliberate forgery. It is certain, however, that Bohemund was persuaded to take an oath of fealty to the emperor, and that at the same time he demanded and was refused a high position at the imperial court.[2] It is possible also, though by no means certain, that in return for his oath Bohemund was granted the privilege of retaining for himself under the lordship of the emperor such land as he might win from the Turks in the fertile territory which lay between Antioch and Aleppo.[3] However this may be, there can be little doubt that Bohemund's own personal ambitions were now taking shape, and that his main pre-occupation was with the methods whereby they might be fulfilled. At the same time his increasing importance among the Crusading leaders placed him in a strong position to influence at every point the relations between the Crusaders and the emperor.

In the event, he was lamentably to exacerbate them. There was of course always a cleavage between the aims of the western knights who were concerned to recover the shrines, and those of the emperor whose primary purpose was to protect his empire. But Bohemund not only shared the views of his fellow westerners: he had now resolved to win Antioch for himself; and during 1098 his plans against Alexis prospered. In February the defection of the emperor's representative Taticius (which was perhaps engineered by Bohemund himself) gave the Crusaders a feeling that they were being deserted,[4] and this seemed to be confirmed when in June, Alexis, then advancing to the relief of Antioch, took the disastrous decision of turning back from the city and leaving the crusaders to their fate.[5] Thereafter Bohemund claimed not only that

---

[1] *Gesta*, II, c. 6; *Alexiad*, X, c. 11; Hagenmeyer, *Chronologie*, p. 64.

[2] Runciman, *Crusades*, I, p. 158.

[3] The passage in the *Gesta* describing the Emperor's grant to Bohemund is now generally considered to be a forgery inserted into the narrative by Bohemund who used the *Gesta* for propaganda purposes during his visit to western Europe in 1106, 1107. (See A. C. Krey, in *Essays – D. C. Munro*, pp. 57–9.) Miss Jamison puts forward another hypothesis (*Proc. Brit. Acad.*, XXIV, pp. 279–80), and she has shown that the passage did not refer merely to Antioch itself but to the neighbouring territory. (*Essays—M. K. Pope*, pp. 195–206.)

[4] *Gesta*, VI, c. 16; *Alexiad* XI, c. 4.   [5] *Gesta*, IX, c. 27; *Alexiad*, XI, c. 6.

he had been betrayed but that he had thereby been freed from his allegiance to the Emperor. The news of the retreat of Alexis did not reach Antioch until after the victory over Kerbogha, but Bohemund was able to use it to justify his subsequent acts when, despite the opposition of Raymond of Toulouse, he took final possession of Antioch, and allowed the rest of the Crusade to proceed to Jerusalem without him.

Bohemund well knew that this act would never be forgiven by Alexis, and that he would now have to defend his newly won principality not only against the Turks but against the Greeks. And this he was firmly resolved to do. Henceforth the emperor would be regarded by him not as a Christian ally against Islam but as an enemy whose possessions would be a legitimate object of attack. In particular, his attention was directed towards the neighbouring port of Latakia which had already been wrested from the Turks by other crusaders from the Norman lands. In March 1098 this port had been captured by English sailors under Edgar Atheling, and a few weeks later it was handed over to Robert, duke of Normandy, who in turn after a short interval restored it to the eastern emperor.[1] Bohemund was well aware that this outlet to the sea possessed by a man whom he now feared as an enemy might in the future be a menace to his own power. But for the moment he had every reason to be content with what he had achieved.

The wide implications of these events were indeed immediately to be disclosed. On 1 August 1098 there died Adhémar bishop of Le Puy, Urban's legate with the army, and early in the next month the secular leaders of the Crusade addressed to the pope a letter[2] which was certainly inspired by Bohemund, and may even have been compiled at his direction. In this the military exploits of Bohemund at Antioch were formally recorded, and the pope was urged to come at once in person to the city where St Peter had been bishop.

> We have driven out the Turks and the pagans, but we have not been able to conquer the heretics: the Greeks the Armenians the Syrians and the Jacobites. Come then our beloved Father and Chief... Seated on the Chair that was established by Blessed Peter, you will find yourself in the midst of your obedient sons. Your authority and our valour will extirpate and utterly destroy all heresy of every kind.[3]

The change in papal policy here demanded is startling. No longer should the prime object of the Crusade be the rescue of the eastern

[1] C. W. David, *Robert Curthose*, App. 'E'. See also the criticism in Runciman, *Crusades*, I, pp. 255, 256.   [2] Hagenmeyer, *Die Kreuzzugsbriefe aus den Jahren 1088–1110*, pp. 161–5. [3] *Ibid.*, pp. 164, 165.

empire and the reunion of the Churches. Rather it should now be the capture of Jerusalem coupled with an attack on the heretical subjects of the eastern emperor.

The manner in which the Normans had thus altered the character of the Crusade, and associated the attack against Islam with the question of the schism, could hardly be better illustrated than by reference to what occurred in southern Italy during this summer and autumn of 1098. On 5 July of that year Urban II issued from Salerno his famous bull which conferred special ecclesiastical privileges upon Roger of Sicily in return for the count's having rescued the islands by Norman arms from the Saracens. The pope then proceeded slowly towards Bari where he had convoked a council. Just before it opened he received the letter from Bohemund and his fellows urging the pope to action against the heretics of the eastern Church. Then, at the council itself, Anselm, the exiled archbishop of Canterbury, on the pope's command, argued at length from the Latin side the theological points at issue between Rome and Constantinople. Finally, before the council rose, the establishment of the new Latin churches in Apulia, Calabria and Sicily was recognized and their allegiance to Rome was confirmed.[1]

The tragic conclusion of these related developments was already foreshadowed in the situation which had been created by the Normans. Count Roger had wrested Sicily from the Saracens, and Bohemund had captured Antioch from the Turks. But in both cases the eastern empire had been deprived of territories it had formerly possessed, and in both cases Constantinople had been compelled to watch ecclesiastical provinces being restored by the Normans to the Roman jurisdiction.[2] The establishment at Antioch of a Norman prince who was at once bitterly hostile to Byzantium and also a vassal of the papacy was bound, in its turn, to entail ecclesiastical as well as secular consequences, and Bohemund immediately sought to curtail the powers of the Patriarch John who was recognized at Constantinople. Even before the end of 1099 prelates of the Latin rite had been introduced into the sees of Tarsus, Artah Mamistra and Edessa, and though these bishoprics all pertained to the patriarchate of Antioch, the newly appointed prelates were compelled to go to Jerusalem for consecration by Daimbert of Pisa, the papal legate.[3] The next year the decisive step was taken when Bohemund secured the election of Bernard of Valence as Latin patriarch

---

[1] Malaterra, IV, c. 29; Eadmer, *Hist. Novorum*, pp. 105–7; Hagenmeyer, *op. cit.*, p. 369.
[2] Runciman, *Crusades*, I, pp. 299–305.   [3] Ralph of Caen, ch. CXL.

of Antioch.[1] This brought the whole ecclesiastical question to a new crisis. For the appointment as patriarch of Antioch of a prelate owing allegiance to Rome challenged the whole conception of the patriarchate current in the East. And with the existence at Antioch of two lines of patriarchs, one supported by Rome and the other by Constantinople, the schism between the Churches was brought a stage nearer completion.

A breach had been opened between East and West, and it was soon to be further enlarged. In 1100 Bohemund was taken prisoner by the Turks, and after his release in 1103 he returned to the West leaving his nephew Tancred as regent in Antioch. Everywhere, in Italy and France, he was treated as a hero, and people (we are told) flocked to gaze at him 'as if he were Christ himself'. Everywhere, too, with the support of the new pope, Paschal II, he denounced the treachery of Alexis, and appealed for help against Byzantium.[2] The Greeks, not the Turks, were now to be considered as the chief objects of attack from the Christian west, and the consequences were to be profound. Just as the appointment of Bernard of Valence as patriarch in Antioch in 1100 had marked a stage in the schism between the Churches, so also was a turning point reached in the Crusading movement on that day in 1106 when Bohemund, just wedded to a daughter of the king of France, stood up in the cathedral of Our Lady at Chartres, and, with the sanction of the pope, called on the warriors of the West to join in a crusade against the emperor of the East.[3]

Bohemund's expedition against the eastern empire, undertaken in 1107 with the papal blessing and in co-operation with a papal legate, was to be repelled by Alexis with the aid of Turkish mercenaries.[4] But the damage which the Normans had done to the eastern empire was not to be easily repaired. When in 1108 Bohemund surrendered to Alexis and submitted to the so-called Treaty of Devol,[5] the Norman state under his nephew Tancred was approaching the zenith of its power and Cilicia would soon be added to it. Thus although Bohemund himself retired to Apulia where he ended his days in 1111, there was never any question of Antioch under Tancred being regained by Constantinople.[6] At the same time, Norman control over Sicily, and the narrows

[1] Cahen, *Syrie du Nord*, pp. 309, 310.   [2] Ord. Vit., IV, pp. 142–4; 211–13.
[3] Ord. Vit., IV, p. 213.   [4] *Alexiad*, bk. XIII; Runciman, *Crusades*, II, pp. 48–51.
[5] The terms of Bohemund's submission (*Alexiad* XIII c. 12) included both a recognition of the Emperor's sovereignty over Antioch, and also the suppression of the Latin patriarchate. Neither of these concessions was enforced.
[6] Runciman, *Crusades*, II, pp. 51–5.

of the Mediterranean, would soon entail the dominance of western European and Italian fleets over those of Byzantium throughout the inland sea.

Moreover the very fact that Bohemund's attack on the eastern empire in 1107 had been hailed throughout the West as a Crusade undertaken for a holy purpose, indicated how complex and how powerful had been the Norman influence on ecclesiastical politics during the previous fifty years. The Normans had helped to establish the Hildebrandine papacy and to promote the ecclesiastical unity of the West. They had won back Sicily from Islam, and been largely responsible for the military successes of the First Crusade. But Norman policy had divided Christendom. The Norman sword had torn the Seamless Robe.

Chapter 9

SECULAR DOMINION

I

The general influence exercised by the Normans upon Christendom was matched by the particular effects of their rule over the countries they conquered. The results of Norman secular government in these states have, however, been very diversely judged. It is not long since a prominent German scholar declared that it was 'above all in England and south Italy that the new conception of the State exerted its greatest influence during the eleventh and twelfth centuries' and that in consequence 'it was the Normans who reshaped the life of Europe both politically and intellectually, and who set the development of European civilization on a new course'.[1] These are large claims, and they are not lightly to be dismissed, but today in many quarters they would be vigorously challenged. The successors of François Lenormant and Jules Gay have demonstrated how important was the Greek influence on southern Italy both before and after the Norman conquests, and since the days of Michele Amari, a long series of writers have been concerned to show how vital were both the Arabic and the Greek contributions to the government of Sicily in the Middle Ages.

In England, similarly, there has in recent years been a strong tendency among some scholars to minimize the results of the Norman impact upon English development. 'In face of the deeper currents of continuity,' we are now told, 'the Norman Conquest and its immediate consequences were but ripples on a troubled surface.'[2] By contrast, two important lectures delivered in 1966 were concerned to emphasize the important contributions made by the Normans to English political and artistic growth, and a prominent legal historian has lately declared that the Norman Conquest 'was not an episode but the most decisive event

---

[1] Brackmann, trans. Barraclough (*Medieval Germany*, II, 288).

[2] The important work of F. Barlow also tends towards this interpretation. A learned though less balanced argument in the same direction will be found in H. G. Richardson and G. Sayles, *Governance of Medieval England*, 1963, chs. V and VI.

169

in English history with the most enduring consequences'.[1] A detached inquirer might well be excused if he felt bewildered by these conflicting voices, but he may be reassured by the judicious moderation of Sir Frank Stenton. That great scholar brought about an enhanced appreciation of the Anglo-Saxon achievement, but he also declared that 'sooner or later every aspect of English life was changed by the Norman Conquest'.[2]

It is no part of the purpose of the present study to enter into this debate which (especially in England) has become charged with emotion. It may however be relevant to inquire whether common factors can be discerned in such secular influence as the Normans exercised (for good or ill) over all the lands they ruled. Obvious contrasts might at once be suggested by the various titles which the Norman rulers assumed during this period, and the manner in which these were acquired deserves some notice. Richard of Aversa seems to have taken the title of 'prince' from the Lombard dynasty which he supplanted at Capua in 1058 and the earliest diploma in which he is so styled probably comes from that year.[3] Again, while William, Dreux and Humphrey, sons of Tancred of Hauteville, all called themselves 'counts' in Italy there is insufficient evidence to show that they were ever recognized as 'dukes',[4] and Robert Guiscard who was perhaps the first Norman to assume the full style of 'duke of Apulia and Calabria' undoubtedly adopted the title from Byzantine usage. About 1051 Argyrus had been nominated 'duke' by the eastern emperor in order that his authority might over-ride both that of the *catepan* who was at Bari, and that of the *strategoi* in Calabria.[5] As 'duke' therefore, Robert Guiscard, at the same time as he renounced any dependence on Constantinople, could assert supremacy over all the inhabitants of Apulia and Calabria whether they were Norman or Italian or Greek.

In both these cases, however, it was the papal sanction accorded in 1059 both to the Norman 'prince' and to the Norman 'duke' which gave permanence to these arrangements, and the same events certainly inspired Bohemund when, forty years later, following the Capuan example,

[1] R. A. Brown, 'The Norman Conquest' (R. Hist. Soc., *Trans.*, Ser. 5, XVII (1966), pp. 109–30); G. Zarnecki, '1066 and architectural sculpture', *Proc. Brit. Acad.*, LII (1966), pp. 86–104; G. W. Keeton, *Norman Conquest and the Common Law* (1966), p. 54. Dr Brown's conclusions have subsequently been amplified in his *Normans and the Norman Conquest* (1969).

[2] *Anglo-Saxon England*, p. 677.

[3] Chalandon, *Domination normande*, I, p. 146.

[4] L. R. Ménager, *Quellen und Forschungen*, XXXIX, p. 39.

[5] L. R. Ménager, *Messina*, pp. 30-6.

he assumed the title of 'prince' at Antioch. By this act he meant to assert his independence both from the eastern emperor, and also from any ruler who might later be established at Jerusalem; and like his Norman predecessors in Italy he speedily had his title confirmed by papal authority.[1] It would, however, be unwise to give further precision to what these titles implied. Robert Guiscard certainly claimed as 'duke', rights over the lands he ruled as wide as those exercised by Richard of Capua as 'prince', and in Sicily Roger I wielded the same authority as 'count' or sometimes as 'consul'.[2] During Guiscard's lifetime Roger I was subject to his elder brother, and after 1085 he was to pay overt deference to Roger Borsa. But during the last ten years of his life Roger I certainly enjoyed as 'count' an independent and unrestrained dominion over Sicily and much of Calabria, and this authority became so firmly based that it could serve as the foundation of the royal power established after 1130 by his great son Roger II.

On the other hand, during the eleventh century a clear distinction must be made between the titular position attained by all the other Norman rulers, and that which was acquired by William the Conqueror (styled duke and count in Normandy), when in 1066 he became 'king'. The impact of the Conqueror's coronation as king was felt through all the Norman lands. After 1066 William enjoyed the semi-sacred authority accorded among secular rulers at the time to kings, and to kings alone. He was saluted with the specifically royal *laudes*, and in these litanies, Our Lady, St Michael and St Raphael were invoked on his behalf. As king, therefore, he was recognized in the liturgy of the Church as one of the few divinely appointed secular rulers of western Christendom.[3] And as such, throughout the intensely self-conscious Norman world of the eleventh century, he was accorded a unique prestige.

The coronation of William the Conqueror as king thus gave an added impetus to the religious propaganda that everywhere accompanied the establishment of the Norman governments. Its significance should not however be misconceived. The glorification of Christ-centred royalty was waning in western Europe during the latter half of the eleventh century, and henceforth there would be few pictorial representations of secular rulers in mystical communion with the Godhead such as were made about 975 of Otto II in the Aachen Gospels, or of the Emperor

---

[1] Guillaume, *La Cava*, App., nos. D II, III, IV.

[2] *Ibid.*, no. D I. Roger Borsa contented himself with the style of 'duke' by divine favour, the son and heir of Duke Robert.

[3] Cf. Douglas, *William the Conqueror*, pp. 154, 249, 250, 261, 262.

Henry II about 1020 in the Monte Cassino Gospel Book.[1] None the less the self-asserted participation of the Normans in the Holy War, and their close association with the papacy, enabled them to keep the idea alive albeit in a modified form. Even Robert Guiscard could be given a place in the liturgy of the Church of Bari, and the Christian mission of Roger I was loudly proclaimed by the Great Count himself, and admitted by Pope Urban II.[2]

Such assertions implied a dependence upon the papacy which would not have been admitted in this connexion by tenth century rulers. The papacy was indeed beginning to claim that dynastic change might be ratified (as against hereditary right) by ecclesiastical consecration, and there was here the basis of a great controversy in the future. None the less, reverting to the eleventh century, it may be recalled that the ecclesiastical rights exercised both by William the Conqueror and Count Roger I were exceptional and famous. Nor in the whole political literature of the period is there any more vigorous assertion of the spiritual character of kingship than is contained in the *Tractates* which were anonymously written about 1100 by a Norman resident in the north. In these famous treatises[3] the power of the king is exalted. By unction he has become sacramentally transformed: he is a *christus Domini*; he has become a *sanctus*; and there may even be found in his office a reflexion of the authority of God Himself. These *Tractates* may well represent the sentiments of an earlier age, but they were none the less well attuned to Norman sentiments at the close of the eleventh century, and the ideas they propounded were soon given magnificent pictorial illustration. A perfect reflexion at a later date of the doctrine of the Norman tractates of 1100 is to be found in the splendid mosaic in the Martorana Church at Palermo which depicts Roger II, the first Norman king of Sicily, receiving his kingdom directly from the hands of Christ Himself.[4] And this notion which had been adumbrated in England in the time of William the Conqueror, and suggested in the charters of Roger, the 'Great Count', was to be kept notably alive in the Norman Sicilian kingdom. Roger II ceased to regard himself as 'responsible to God alone – a sharp sword held in the hands of God for the punishment of the wicked',[5] while his grandson, King William II of Sicily, is displayed

---

[1] E. H. Kantorowicz, *King's Two Bodies*, pp. 61–78; H. Bloch, *Monte Cassino, Byzantium and the West* (Dumbarton Oaks Papers, No. 3, pp. 177–86).

[2] See above, pp. 106, 107.

[3] Mon. Germ. Hist. *Libelli de Lite*, III, pp. 642, 687. Cf. Kantorowicz, *op. cit.*, pp. 45–60.

[4] Plate IX. [5] E. Jamison, *Apulia*, p. 265.

at Monreale (like his grandfather at Palermo) receiving his kingdom from Christ.

II

The foundation of the Norman states in the latter half of the eleventh century was not only marked by the establishment of rulers such as William the Conqueror, Robert Guiscard, Count Roger I and Bohemund. It also entailed the intrusion into the conquered lands of new aristocracies recruited directly or indirectly from Normandy itself. It was these aristocracies which effected the Norman dominance over the subjugated countries, and their relations with the greater Norman rulers provided the enduring basis of Norman government.

The establishment of these aristocracies proved everywhere the most catastrophic consequence of the Norman conquests, and nowhere could the effects be better illustrated than in England. In 1086 there was drawn up the Domesday Survey, and the changes in the upper ranks of society which were revealed in that record are little short of astonishing. The Old English nobility, recently so wealthy and so powerful, had, within two decades of the battle of Hastings, almost passed away. In 1086 the survivors of the overmighty Anglo-Saxon aristocracy of the Confessor's reign possessed only some 8 per cent of the land of England, and much of this was held from alien overlords by services which were themselves alien and unfamiliar.[1] Between 1066 and 1086 in short, the Old English nobility had been supplanted by a new aristocracy. Some of its members came from Flanders and Brittany, but the vast majority derived from Normandy, and their rewards were immense. In 1086, only twenty years after the battle of Hastings, about a fifth of the land of England was held by the Norman king, and about half by his greater followers, whilst among these wealth and power were concentrated in the hands of a limited number of men and families who had been most actively associated between 1050 and 1066 in the political consolidation of Normandy during William's reign as duke.[2] This tenurial transformation in England deserves some emphasis. Much is rightly said, and more will here be added, about the use made by the Normans of existing institutions. But if this immense transference of landed property within two decades, involving more than half the land of England,

[1] F. M. Stenton, in R. Hist. Soc., *Trans.*, Ser. 5, XXXI (1944), pp. 1–17; Corbett, in *Cambridge Medieval History*, vol. IV, ch. XV.
[2] Douglas, *William the Conqueror*, pp. 268–71.

cannot be regarded as constituting a revolutionary change effected by the Normans, then some new meaning must be attached to the term.

No eleventh century record such as Domesday Book survives to illustrate with the same precision the aristocratic changes which the Normans effected in south Italy and Sicily, but there is no question that the process was the same there as in England. In the middle of the twelfth century there was drawn up for the reigning Norman king of Sicily an elaborate list of feudal tenures which is now known under the title of the *Catalogus Baronum*.[1] This relates to the Apulian duchy from the Abruzzi in the north to the region of Otranto in the south, and the survey extends westward towards Salerno. It records a very large number of fiefs held both in chief and by sub-tenants, and their holders were predominantly Norman. Evidently the greater landholders existing in this region before the Normans came had been dispossessed and there is every reason to believe that this process began in the eleventh century, and was far advanced before its close. The chronicles also describes the manner in which estates were seized by the numerous connexions of the house of Hauteville and by such families as those of Échauffour, Grand-mesnil, Ridel, Laigle and many others. Nor can it be doubted that these were typical of most of the associates of the prince of Capua and of the duke of Apulia and Calabria. In Sicily, as will be seen, Robert Guiscard and Roger, the 'Great Count', systematically endowed their followers in the regions which were successively conquered between 1072 and 1091. And the greater fiefs in the Principality of Antioch were given to men who for the most part belonged to Norman families in South Italy who had come on Crusade in the company of Bohemund of Taranto.[2]

These new aristocracies were, moreover, not only Norman in composition, they were also feudal in structure. They were composed of men who held their lands in return for military service of a particular type. The more important men among them held their estates directly from their rulers, and were charged with the provision of a specified number of knights; whilst the sub-tenants were obliged either to serve themselves in this capacity or to contribute to this service by others. The complexities of feudal organization between 1060 and 1130 were intricate, and are not here to be discussed, but it may be remarked that nowhere during this period were the basic institutions of military feudalism

[1] This is printed in Del Re, *Cronisti e Scrittori*, 1868, I, pp. 571–615. A critical edition by Miss Evelyn Jamison is eagerly awaited. Meanwhile students may greatfully ponder the remarks of G. H. Haskins, in *Eng. Hist. Rev.*, XXVI (1911), pp. 655–65.
[2] Cahen, *Syrie du Nord*, esp. pp. 535, 536.

more efficiently developed at this period than in the Norman lands.[1] Naturally there were differences in regions so widely separated. Thus the number of knights owed for service by the greater tenants was proportionately higher in England than in Normandy or Italy,[2] whilst the institution of the 'money fief' by which the tenant received money in place of land from his lord played a larger part in earlier days in Syria than in England.[3] Again, the payments known as the 'feudal incidents' owed by vassals to their lords, were regularized earlier in England than in Italy, Sicily or Antioch.[4]

The special situation in southern Italy deserves some note in this respect.[5] In England and Sicily and Antioch the Norman conquests had been completed under strong and unified command. But in Apulia the first conquests had been separately made by the leaders of small bands, many of whom had served under the Lombard and Greek rulers whom the Normans were subsequently to supplant. Only slowly, therefore, as the conquests proceeded was any central authority set up. The result was on the one hand a rapid multiplication of very small fiefs, and on the other hand the establishment of a few very large lordships whose autonomy was only very gradually to be qualified. The case of the feudal *comtés* set up by the Normans in Italy is particularly noteworthy. Eleventh-century Normandy had its counts; so also had Norman Sicily; and Norman England had its earls. But all of these men were subjected to higher authority. In Italy, however, not only were there numerous counts, but for long these claimed, and sometimes exercised, virtual independence. Towards the Abruzzi there were, for instance, the comital families of Loritello and later of Molise. To the south of Naples there were the counts of the 'Principate' while to the north of Salerno there was the *comté* of Avellino to be held by descendants of Richard of Capua. Again, in the region of Bari there were the *comtés* of Conversano and Montescalgioso held by two of the four sons-in-law of Robert Guiscard. It is a formidable list, and it could be extended by the addition of many more names.[6]

---

[1] Compare Stenton, *English Feudalism*, pp. 7–40, with C. Cahen, *Régime féodale de l'Italie méridionale*, pp. 35–96.

[2] Douglas, *op. cit.*, pp. 273–83.

[3] Cahen, *Syrie du Nord*, p. 529; La Monte, *Feudal Monarchy*, p. 143. Cf. B. D. Lyon, in *Eng. Hist. Rev.*, LVI (1941), pp. 161–93.

[4] Compare Pollock and Maitland, *Hist. of English Law*, 2nd ed. I, pp. 296–536; Haskins, *op. cit.*, p. 661; Chalandon, *op. cit.*, II, pp. 573–9; Cahen, *op. cit.*, pp. 522–4.

[5] Cahen, *Régime féodale*, esp. pp. 55–62.

[6] A long list of these *comtés* in the twelfth century is given in Chalandon (*op. cit.*, II, p. 567). The comital houses of Acerra, Alife, Gravina, Bova, Squillace and Policastro may with some

These comital dynasties, which had sometimes acquired earlier Lombard jurisdictions but which more often had won new and enlarged *comtés* for themselves, played an important part in the feudal development of Apulia and Calabria. Indeed, the fact that some of the more important of them were closely connected with the house of Hauteville itself[1] was a factor in the establishment of Norman power in the south. Thus the first count of the 'principate' south of Naples was William, the full-brother of Robert Guiscard, and of his sons one, named Robert, succeeded to his father's *comté*[2] while another, named Tancred, pursued his fortunes into Sicily, and was in due course rewarded with the lands of the *comté* of Syracuse.[3] Again the, *comté* of Loritello in northern Apulia was first held by Geoffrey, a half-brother of Robert Guiscard, and then passed to his son, Robert, who so prospered that he could style himself 'counts of counts', whilst his brother, Ralph, became count of Catanzarro, the most important *comté* in Calabria.[4] Such connexions, which could be widely illustrated, have far more than a merely genealogical significance. They not only illustrate the process by which the Norman dominion was extended in Italy. They also show why comital families such as these, ever increasing in power and perpetually at war with each other, remained a constant source of turbulence in southern Italy, even after the Norman ducal government had been set up at Bari.

The slow establishment of central authority in Apulia was also responsible for the fact that the Church in Norman Italy never became feudalized to the same extent as did the Church in Norman England. Such monasteries as Monte Cassino and La Cava had immense estates, but though their abbots under Norman rule were expected to give feudal counsel and to pay feudal dues that might be heavy, they were not burdened with military service. When in 1060 the monastery of Monte Cassino gave privileges to its *milites*, and subsequently increased its enfeoffments, the abbot was acting for precisely the same reasons as impelled the abbot of Abingdon a few years later to increase his

---

coincidence be referred back to the eleventh century. There seems however, to have been only two local *comtés* in eleventh century Sicily – those of Paterno and Syracuse.

[1] In addition to the connexions already mentioned two of the daughters of Roger I were to marry respectively Rannulf, Count of Alife, and Ralph Maccabees, Count of Montescaglioso.

[2] Ménager, *Quellen und Forschungen*, XXXIX, pp. 65–82.

[3] Thus Tancred received the lands of the *comté* of Syracuse after the death in 1091 from Jordan, the illegitimate son of Roger I. He was a benefactor of the bishopric of Syracuse and of St Agatha at Catania. He was a constant member of the court of the 'Great Count'. (Ménager, *Messina*, p. 59.)

[4] Ménager, *Messina*, p. 72.

establishment of household knights.[1] He wished to make provision for a private force that might defend the abbey and its lands during a period of disorder. But the abbot of Monte Cassino did not, like the abbot of Abingdon, have to provide a service of thirty knights for his secular overlord.

In general, however, it is the similar character of Norman feudalism wherever it was established, and not the differences within it, that must challenge attention. It has been suggested for instance that the Normans, earlier than most others in Europe, established the principle that the amount of service owed should be clearly determined before the grant of the fief;[2] and certainly nowhere in the feudal world did the notion of liege-homage play a more important part than in the Norman lands. By liege-homage, a man who might hold from several lords owed to the chief of these allegiance of an absolute and particular king, and the notion was later to be exploited to the benefit of the feudal monarchies. Consequently, it is of interest that liege-homage appears very early not only in Norman England, Sicily and Antioch,[3] but also in Norman Apulia where its development might well have been delayed. Since in 1075 a 'patrician' of Bari could actually describe himself as *ligius* to a lord,[4] it is evident that strict notions of feudal practice were already recognized in Apulia at that time, and a charter by Bohemund for St Nicholas of Bari, which is ascribed to the year 1090, is completely feudal in tone.[5] It has been noted how striking are the similarities between the feudal practices revealed in the *Catalogus Baronum* as long established in Italy and those which are known to have existed in Norman England.[6] And if in the Latin kingdom of Jerusalem feudal institutions were to be more French than Norman, in the principality of Antioch those institutions were more Norman than French.[7]

Feudal arrangements of a special kind were in fact made everywhere by the Normans almost immediately after their conquests. In England, the allocations of quotas of knights owed by the greater tenants – the

---

[1] R. Palmarocchi, *L'abbaye di Monte Cassino*, 1913, pp. 185, 186; *Chron. Mon. Abingdon*, II, p. 3. Cp. Douglas, 'Some early surveys from the Abbey of Abingdon' (*Eng. Hist. Rev.* (1929), pp. 618–22).

[2] Cahen, *op. cit.*, pp. 66, 67; *Syrie du Nord*, p. 530.

[3] Stenton, *English Feudalism*, pp. 29–31; Cahen, *Syrie du Nord*, pp. 527, 528.

[4] *Cod. Dipl. Barese*, V, no. 1.

[5] *Ibid.*, V, no. 15. This charter may, however, be inflated in its present form.

[6] Haskins, *op. cit.*, pp. 655–65.

[7] La Monte, *Feudal Monarchy*, p. 149; Cahen, *Syrie du Nord*, pp. 435, 436; *Régime féodale*, pp. 91, 92.

servitia debita as they were called – were first made by William the Conqueror himself. There is evidence of this in 1072, and again in 1077, and most of the details of the scheme were apparently worked out before 1087. In the principality of Antioch feudal institutions 'relatively simple as in Normandy, Sicily and England' were imposed at an early date and 'probably go back to the conquest itself'.[1] In south Italy it was at first hard for Richard of Capua and Robert Guiscard to enforce superiority over the other Norman leaders. But fiefs are known to have been established in south Italy at an early date.[2] As charters dated in the year 1087 reveal, it was, at that time, necessary for vassals of the prince of Capua and the duke of Apulia to obtain the consent of their feudal overlords before making gifts to the Church.[3]

In Sicily the development was even more rapid. There, Robert Guiscard and Roger I had no rivals of their own race, and so, rather in the manner of William the Conqueror in England, they could invest their followers with land at their discretion and dictate the terms on which it was to be held. Already by 1077 Robert Guiscard is said to have created several very large fiefs in the north of the island, but after his death the 'Great Count' abolished these, and out of them made a distribution of smaller fiefs to many of his knights. Moreover an emphatic statement by Geoffrey Malaterra[4] indicates that this distribution was made wholly or in part at a formal assembly held shortly after the completion of the Sicilian conquest, and a remarkable Greek charter for the bishopric of Catania suggests that this assembly over feudal distribution took place at Mazzara in 1093.[5] At all events before the death of Count Roger I the feudal structure of Norman Sicily had become based on a number of small fiefs held in the north together with some very large fiefs which had been created by the 'Great Count' in the centre and to the south east of the island.[6] Many of these large lordships were held by the Church, but a *comté* of Syracuse was created by Roger I for his nephew Tancred who did not survive him, and another *comté* based on Paterno was given into the hands of the husband of Roger's

[1] Cahen, *Syrie du Nord*, p. 527.
[2] Chalandon, *op. cit.*, II, p. 511; *Codice Diplomatico – Aversa* (ed. Gallo), pp. 35, 37; Cahen, *Régime féodale*, p. 71.
[3] Chalandon, *op. cit.*, II, p. 521, citing the archives of La Cava.
[4] Malaterra, IV, c. 15. Cf. Amari, *op. cit.*, III, pp. 306, 326, followed by C. Waern, *Mediæval Sicily*, pp. 32, 33, and by Garufi, *Centimento e Catasto*, p. 12.
[5] S. Cusa, *I Diplomi Greci e Arabi di Sicilia* (1868), II, pp. 541 and 696. And see further, below pp. 186, 187.
[6] Chalandon, I, p. 347; Amari, *op. cit.*, III, pp. 307, 308.

sister who had married into the powerful family of the Aleramici.[1] In Sicily, the feudal organization effected by the Normans had certainly taken shape before the end of the eleventh century.

The overriding unity of Norman feudal arrangements (despite differences in detail among them), and the early date at which these arrangements were made, must be taken into account in estimating how far, if at all, the feudal institutions of the Normans had been anticipated in the earlier social development of the countries they conquered. Vassalage and commendation of man to lord had long been familiar to Europe and to England. The conditional character of land-holding known as the benefice, and the political rights pertaining to magnates by way of the 'immunity' were features of the social structure of all parts of the former empire of Charlemagne. Also in the tenth century there had risen to power in the eastern empire great landed families, and these, particularly in frontier provinces such as southern Italy, were beginning to claim political authority over their dependents in connexion with the need to defend the empire against the constant assaults of the Saracens.[2] It has likewise been asserted that in Worcestershire,[3] as also in Calabria[4] dependent tenures already existing on ecclesiastical lands needed little change to make them conform to later Norman arrangements. Normans, indeed, seem to have followed Lombards as the greater tenants of the abbey of Monte Cassino even as Normans undertook the obligations of their Saxon predecessors on the estates of the abbey of Bury St Edmunds.[5] The relevance of such conditions to the general question of the origins of military feudalism in the Norman lands is of course debatable, but in recent years there has been a tendency to consider that Anglo-Norman aristocratic feudalism as a whole was evolved gradually and smoothly out of the Anglo-Saxon past.[6]

On the other hand, it is not easy to discover anything convincingly analogous either to the fief or to the *servitium debitum* in the England of Edward the Confessor or in Byzantine Apulia or in the Lombard states

---

[1] Amari, *loc. cit.*; Cahen, *Régime féodale*, p. 60.

[2] Diehl., *Hist. of the Byzantine Empire*, pp. 102, 108–10; Cf. Lenormant, *Grande Grèce*, II, pp. 403–10.

[3] M. Hollings in *Eng. Hist. Rev.*, LXIII (1948), pp. 453 et seq.

[4] E. Pontieri, *Tra i Normanni nel Italia* (1948), pp. 49–79.

[5] Palmarocchi, *op. cit.*, pp. 82–5; Douglas, *Feudal Documents*, pp. cxiv–cxvi.

[6] The most emphatic recent statements in this sense will be found in K. John, *Land Tenure in Early England* (1960), and in H. G. Richardson and G. Sayles, *Governance of Medieval England* (1963).

of the south.[1] And the heavily armed warrior trained to fight on horse-back who was the essential product of Norman feudal arrangements was, to say the least, a rarity in pre-Norman England and pre-Norman Italy, while he was non-existent in pre-Norman Sicily. The transition here seems to have been abrupt. The fact that mounted knights were not used against the Normans at Civitate or at Hastings is in itself highly significant. And it might be added that if in their feudal arrange-ments the Normans had slavishly followed the customs of the peoples they conquered, then it would be difficult to explain how they erected so similar an aristocratic structure in England, in Italy, in Sicily and in Syria where they worked under such divergent conditions.

Feudal tenure involved not only military service but also suit of court, and in all the Norman states the immediate tenant of the ruler formed a court which met regularly to implement his policy and to support his acts. The court which surrounded William the Conqueror was famous, and its composition during the later years of his reign as king is attested by a long series of charters.[2] Most of the greater Norman families from both sides of the Channel here made their appearance though with varying frequency. Such names as those of Beaumont and Montgomery, Fitz-Gilbert and Warenne are constantly recorded together with many prominent ecclesiastics such as Lanfranc, the archbishop of Canterbury, and also the king's half-brothers Robert, count of Mortain, and Odo, bishop of Bayeux. These were in every respect most impressive assem-blies, and they were comparable with those which after 1130 Roger II is known to have convoked as king of Sicily.

Evidence is lacking to indicate with any precision the composition of the courts of Robert Guiscard when duke of Apulia at an earlier date, for his charters are disappointingly meagre in the information they supply on this point. But the meetings of the court of his brother Roger, the 'Great Count', are specifically described by chroniclers such as Geoffrey Malaterra, and charters reveal that the court of duke Roger Borsa could include men such as Robert, count of the Principate, Robert, count of Loritello, with Ralph his brother, Roger from Barne-ville in the Cotentin, William of Grandmesnil, Romanus, bishop of Rossano, and Berengar, abbot of Venosa.[3] Passing eastward the picture

---

[1] The Lombard *gastaldi* in the earlier half of the eleventh century are to be considered as local officials (who were frequently disobedient) and not as vassals (who were often rebellious).

[2] Davis, *Regesta*, I, *passim*. Cf. Douglas, *William the Conqueror*, pp. 284–88.

[3] Chalandon, *op. cit.*, II, pp. 626, 627; citing charter testimony from the archives of La Cava. Cf. P. Guillaume, *La Cava* (1877), App., nos. E I–VII.

is similar though less detailed. The reign of Bohemund I at Antioch was too short to produce charters that might adequately reflect the composition of his court. But it must have been of a similar nature, for the court which later surrounded Tancred contained representatives of many eleventh-century Norman families.[1]

The most essential political relationship in the government of the Norman world was that between the Norman rulers and their courts. It was concerned with all the functions of government, and with the overriding supervision of justice and finance. It symbolized and enforced the Norman secular dominion. For this reason a close co-operation between the ruler and his court was imperative if Norman dominance was to survive. It was therefore a most outstanding characteristic of the Norman states that during the first period of their history the Norman monarch was everywhere able to dominate and control his courts; to associate his magnates with his acts; and to convince them that their interests were identical with his own. Such for instance was the situation at the court of William the Conqueror where 'no man dared do anything contrary to his will',[2] and similar conditions prevailed in Italy and Sicily. The prestige of Robert Guiscard was enormous, and in his distribution of Sicilian lands, Roger the 'Great Count' took care that his own possessions vastly exceeded those of any of his followers. He became indeed, before his death, one of the wealthiest princes in Europe. Even in Syria a parallel development took place. It is well known that in the Latin kingdom of Jerusalem the power of the feudal court was to hamper the growth of the monarchy. But in Norman Antioch things were different. The imprisonment of Bohemund I in 1100 gave the court a perilous opportunity in appointing a regent. But it chose Tancred who would have been his uncle's nominee. Both Bohemund and Tancred always dominated the courts over which they presided.[3]

III

Before the twelfth century was far advanced, monarchies established by the Normans controlled the best organized kingdoms of Europe, and a Norman prince ruled the strongest of the Crusading states. This success was however not due merely to the facts of conquest or even to the establishment of notable rulers supported by strong feudal aristocracies.

---

[1] Cahen, *Syrie du Nord*, p. 535.   [2] A.S. Chron., 'E', s.a. 1087.
[3] La Monte, *op. cit.*, p. 197; Cahen, *Syrie du Nord*, pp. 229, 436–443.

It derived also from a particular administrative policy which was everywhere adopted by the Normans. In all the states they governed, the Normans at this time were concerned to give fresh vitality to the administrative institutions which they found in the conquered lands, and to develop these constructively to their own advantage. Thus it was that the Norman conquests between 1050 and 1100, which destroyed much, were none the less almost as important for what they preserved as for what they created.

The Norman genius for adaptation was given greater scope in that it was displayed in countries which had themselves been made subject to diverse influences from the past. In England, Anglo-Saxon traditions had in many regions been heavily overlaid by usages from Scandinavia, and affected also (though to a lesser degree) by influences from western Europe. In like manner, southern Italy continued for long to cherish loyalties to the Lombard and still more to the Greek past, whilst the Sicily which the Normans conquered was a mosaic of languages, religions and races. Equally composite was the principality that Bohemund came to rule at Antioch. There the strongest element in governmental practice was undoubtedly Byzantine since the eastern empire had controlled Antioch until some twelve years before the Norman conquest. But in the countryside Moslem customs were firmly established, and after 1099, as before, the peasantry continued their traditional life under the immediate jurisdiction as heretofore of *cadis* of their own race and faith.[1]

Tolerance is not the first quality one would predicate in early Norman rulers, but these men seem to have been ready to admit wide divergencies among their subjects and to combine them to their own profit. The case of the Jews may be relevantly cited in this respect. Before 1066 a colony of Jews was established in Rouen but only after the Norman conquest were Jewish communities settled in England where they first appear in London.[2] In the East the situation was different, since the Crusading movement had been lamentably marked by persecutions of Jews, particularly in Germany; and ill treatment of the Jews continued in Syria after the Latin states had been set up.[3] None the less there is evidence for a continuous Jewish community in Norman Antioch where it was noted for its glass-making. But it was in the central Mediterranean zone that the Normans were brought most directly

---

[1] Runciman, *Crusades*, II, pp. 295-7.
[2] H. G. Richardson, *English Jewry and the Angevin Kings*, ch. I.   [3] Runciman, *loc. cit.*

into contact with the Jews, and relations between them do not seem to have been unduly strained. A charter issued by Robert Guiscard after his seizure of Bari concerned the Jews in that city, and the ghettoes of Rossano and Catanzarro long remained famous.[1] More notable still were the relations between Roger I and the Jews. Jews formed a prominent section of the varied population which gathered at Mileto under the 'Great Count' and in his time, as in that of his son, Palermo housed one of the biggest Jewish colonies in the whole of western Europe.[2]

The reliance of the Normans on the institutions of those they conquered was everywhere shown from the very beginning of their rule. William the Conqueror, always concerned to stress that he was the legitimate successor of Edward the Confessor following an usurpation, was able to make full use of royal powers which would otherwise have been denied him. In like manner Robert Guiscard immediately after his establishment as duke of Apulia began to depend upon Greek officials and Byzantine practice, and the same was true at a later date of Bohemund and Tancred at Antioch. More notably still, Roger, the 'Great Count', lost no time in Sicily in creating a composite administration to which Moslems, Greeks and Normans were all to contribute. Particular local traditions were likewise everywhere utilized. The Norman land settlement to the west of the Welsh border was based on different principles to those they applied on the English side, and after King Roger II had united all the Norman lands in Italy to his Sicilian kingdom, he was careful not to make any wholesale transference of the administrative practices of Sicily and Calabria into Apulia or Capua.[3]

Evidence for the early exploitation of this policy could in fact easily be adduced from all the Norman states. In 1075, four years after the fall of Bari, Robert Guiscard is to be found closely associated with a certain Maurelianus, the same who was styled *ligius*, and who as 'patrician and catepan' was clearly carrying on a Byzantine system of administration under the Norman duke.[4] Six years later, when Bohemund was in control of the city William 'Flammengus', the *catepan*, was active in its administration. He declared that he had been appointed to that office by 'my excellent and glorious Lord, Bohemund who was inspired by God',

[1] *Cod. Dipl. Barese*, I, no. 27. See also the charter of Sigelgaita, *ibid.*, no. 28. Cf. Lenormant, *Grande Grèce*, I, pp. 340–56; II, p. 278; N. Douglas, *Old Calabria*, p. 294.
[2] Lenormant, *op. cit.*, III, pp. 316–21 (for Mileto). Benjamin of Tudela states that after a century of Norman domination there were 1500 Jews in Palermo.
[3] J. G. Edwards, 'The Normans and the Welsh March' *Proc. Brit. Acad.*, XLII (1956), pp. 153–79; E. Jamison, *Apulia*, pp. 238–58.
[4] *Cod. Dipl. Barese*, V, no. 1 and no. 12.

and in another charter Bohemund himself formally authorized the same William as *catepan* to act for him in all matters of sales and exchanges within the city of Bari.[1] Again, in 1096, in a notable charter[2] Duke Roger Borsa gave administrative instruction to 'all his justices, counts, catepans *turmarchs* and *vicomtes*'. The process in Apulia was moreover matched in Calabria. There, before the advent of the Normans, the powers exercised in Apulia by the *catepan* were normally wielded by the *strategos*. Consequently it is of considerable interest to observe that Roger the 'Great Count', not only continued to employ *strategoi* of his choice in Calabria, but also introduced them on his own account into Messina after his capture of that city from the Moslems.[3] Similarly, even as the eastern emperor had on occasion appointed 'dukes' to govern provinces so also did Bohemund I and Tancred set up 'dukes' to administer the towns of Antioch, Lattakieh and Jabala, and the Normans who filled these offices made plentiful use of subordinates who had been trained in the traditions of Byzantine administration.[4] It is also possible to see an eleventh century counterpart to the same policy even in England. William the Conqueror from the start of his reign made use both of the office of sheriff, and of the courts which the sheriffs controlled; and he speedily ensured that the sheriffdoms were placed in the hands of Normans.

The character of early Norman administration was reflected also in the documents which it issued. The early Norman rulers in southern Italy 'modelled their Latin acts upon those of the Lombard principalities, and their Greek charters upon those of Apulia and Calabria, and when an organized chancery was established in the twelfth century it imitated Byzantine and Papal usage'.[5] In England, there was a similar reliance on earlier traditions. No diplomatic form has attracted more attention for instance than the short writ in the vernacular which was being produced in England in the time of Edward the Confessor, and the frequency with which these were issued has been held to suggest an organized royal *scriptorium* which certainly did not exist in Normandy before the Norman Conquest. But after 1066 the Norman monarchy in England continued without interruption to produce writs which at first were scarcely distinguishable from those of Edward the Confessor.

---

[1] *Cod. Dipl. Barese*, V, nos. 20, 21, 22.
[2] Guillaume, *La Cava*, App. no. E II.
[3] Ménager, *Messina*, pp. 27–40.
[4] Cahen, *Syrie du Nord*, pp. 457–60.
[5] Haskins, in *Eng. Hist. Rev.*, XXVI (1911), p. 44.

The writs, however, gradually came to be couched in Latin, and the royal *scriptorium* which now contained both Norman and English clerks came to be presided over by a Chancellor who was likewise a Norman. Moreover, the function of the writ itself was extended. The writs of the Confessor had normally recorded grants of land or right. The later writs of the Conqueror more usually embodied commands or prohibitions. The writ, which in form had derived from the Anglo-Saxon past, had thus been made the chief means of expressing the administrative will of the Norman kings of England.[1] These writs, though much more efficient and concise, could in this sense be compared with the later *mandata* which, in the twelfth century, gave effect to the government of the Norman kings of Sicily.[2]

The manner in which the diverse races in Sicily were harmoniously subjected to the single political rule of King Roger II has frequently attracted the admiring comments of historians. But these conditions could hardly have been achieved apart from the administrative acts in the eleventh century of Robert Guiscard and Count Roger I. In the whole story of the Norman conquests there are few episodes more remarkable than the conduct of the terrible Duke of Apulia in the early months of 1072. Palermo had just fallen, but Robert Guiscard, we are told, released his Greek prisoners and offered them amnesty. Then having returned to Reggio 'he left at Palermo a knight of his own race whom he placed over the Saracens as *Emir*'.[3] There was thus to be no interruption of Moslem administrative practice, and as late as 1086 there was still an emir (now styled admiral) of Palermo under Norman rule.[4] Before the end of the eleventh century the admiral of Palermo had enlarged his jurisdiction and become emir over all the dominions in Sicily and Calabria which were subject to the 'Great Count'. As such he was ultimately responsible for fiscal administration, and under the count exercised an overriding supervision over the administration of justice. His powers were soon to be distributed among several officials. But the importance of these early admirals (or emirs) is evident, and the significance of their position is further enhanced by the fact that most of the early holders of this powerful Moslem office under Norman rule

---

[1] For the writ see in general F. E. Harmer, *Anglo-Saxon Writs* (1952); Bishop and Chaplais, *English Royal Writs* (1957).

[2] Haskins, *op. cit.*, pp. 445-7.

[3] William of Apulia, III, v, pp. 340-5.

[4] He was styled *Petrus Bidonis Amirati Palermi*, in a charter of Roger I of that date (P. Guillaume, *La Cava*, App. no. E II).

were (like the first Admiral Eugenius at the end of the eleventh century) themselves of Greek descent.[1]

Conditions in Sicily were in many respects exceptional but eleventh-century parallels might none the less be sought in Apulia, Antioch and England. Nothing, for instance, is more remarkable than the manner in which William the Conqueror took over the system of taxation which he found operative in England, and used it to exact yet heavier 'gelds' from his new subjects. In like manner, both in Apulia and Syria the new rulers utilized Byzantine methods of assessing and collecting taxes; whilst in Sicily the Normans took from their Arab predecessors the centralized financial bureau of the *diwan* which was itself to undergo reorganization at their hands, and which was to exercise local control by visitations of its members rather in the same way as in England the sheriffs were later to be called to annual account.[2] Again, during the earlier half of the twelfth century, the small Arabic local units of the *iklim* seem to have been used by the Normans in Sicily in a manner reminiscent of the policy adopted by Henry I and his greater subjects towards the *hundreds* in England.[3]

In the absence of exhaustive examination it would be rash to press these analogies too closely, but the comparisons suggested might perhaps point the way towards the solution of some of the more intractable problems of early Anglo-Norman history. It is, for instance, impossible to believe that the Domesday Survey could have been carried out apart from the work of men trained in the administration of the shires which were there described. But, even so, a more difficult question remains. Domesday Book records the possessions which had already been previously allotted to members of the new aristocracy. These men had not been given their lands haphazard. In shire after shire they had acquired the carefully defined, and often scattered, estates of one or more Saxon predecessors whose obligations they also took over. How could such a complicated allotment have taken place if there had not been some Saxon records (perhaps fiscal in character) which described the possessions and the liabilities of the greater landowners in Anglo-Saxon England?

No such comprehensive records are known to have survived, and so the question is somewhat rhetorical. But a partial answer to it might be

---

[1] See E. Jamison, *Admiral Eugenius of Sicily* (1961), pp. 33–6.
[2] E. Jamison, *op. cit.*, pp. 49 et seq.; Chalandon, *op. cit.*, II, pp. 644–50; Haskins, *op. cit.*, p. 652; Amari, *op. cit.*, III, pp. 324, 326.
[3] Chalandon, I, p. 348.

suggested, however tentatively, by reference to Italy and Sicily. A charter issued by Roger Borsa in 1087,[1] indicates that the Norman government at Bari made plentiful use of Byzantine fiscal registers known as *Quaterniones*, and the Sicilian testimony is in this respect yet more challenging. There, Roger I utilized existing records, and in a very significant manner. Thus in the Greek charter[2] which he issued in 1095 for the bishopric of Catania (which he refounded) it is indicated that when fiefs were bestowed by the 'Great Count' on his followers the recipients received a description of the estates that had been granted together with a list (*platea*) of the dependent peasantry. These *plateae* were rolls, written sometimes in Greek and sometimes in Arabic,[3] and they were compiled out of the public records preserved in the diwan. Moreover, the Catania charter (which contains a copy of one such record) clearly associates it with similar lists which were evidently made when, in 1093, Roger completed at Mazzara, his great distribution of the fiefs of northern Sicily.[4] The original *plateae* of 1093 seem all to have been lost, and that for Catania in the charter of 1095 is the earliest to have survived. But references in later charters suggest that such descriptive documents were compiled in connexion with grants by the 'Great Count' to the sees of Messina, Mileto and Palermo and to a monastery at Stilo.[5] It might even be supposed that Roger I utilized the records he found in the land he conquered to make a survey of the economic and military resources of his new dominions comparable to that which William the Conqueror had effected in England in 1086. In any case the Sicilian analogy with what took place in England in connexion with the establishment of the Anglo-Norman aristocracy as recorded in Domesday Book is very striking.

This is not to suggest that between 1050 and 1100 there was any deliberate transference of institutions from one Norman state to another or detailed imitations of administrative practice between them. But throughout the whole self-conscious Norman world at that time a similar temper prevailed. It might perhaps be illustrated from a new angle by the manner in which the lesser Norman notables so frequently gave to their own official subordinates high-sounding titles derived from

---

[1] Cited by Chalandon, *op. cit.*, II, p. 530 from the Archives of La Cava.

[2] S. Cusa, *I Diplomi Greci e Arabi di Sicilia* (Palermo, 1868) II, pp. 541, 696.

[3] Garufi, *Censimento e Catasto*, pp. 21–3.

[4] See above, pp. 178, 179. The Catania schedule of 1095 declares the 'Great Count' in his charter 'was made by my order when I was at Messina, and it was based upon the lists (*plateae*) of my lands, and of the lands of my enfeoffed men which were compiled at Mazzara two years ago'.   [5] Garufi, *op. cit.*, p. 7.

their new subjects. Thus even as Bohemund, mindful of imperial practice, set up 'dukes' to preside over cities, so also did smaller Norman counts and lords in Apulia appoint *catepans* to act as their administrative deputies,[1] and in like fashion many of the Norman magnates in England appointed their own baronial 'sheriffs'. These may seem small matters. But a similar attitude was adopted by those who controlled the Norman situation. In 1065 Richard of Capua bestowed an estate to be held 'according to the legal customs of the Lombards'[2] and about 1094 Roger the 'Great Count' made a grant to the bishop of Messina, the extant of which was to be defined 'according to the earlier divisions of the Saracens'.[3] Similarly, throughout the great trials respecting land and rights which marked the reign of William the Conqueror in England, Anglo-Saxon custom was regularly appealed to and applied.[4] Evidently before the eleventh century had closed, the Normans had everywhere come fully to appreciate how much they had to gain from the administrative experience of those whom they had beaten in battle.

IV

It would, however, be wrong to conclude that in the sphere of government the Normans were themselves unoriginal or uncreative. Some idea of the magnitude of the problems which they faced, and the special opportunities which they seized, can be obtained by reference to the multitudinous communities where they ruled. Here a contemplation of the greater Norman capitals is particularly revealing, Bari for instance was a natural bridge between east and west where men came from Constantinople, Durazzo and Ragusa to mingle with others from Venice and even from Russia.[5] From Bari, too, western venturers might start on enterprises not only to Byzantium but also to Jerusalem and to that other Norman capital of Antioch where under the rule of Bohemund and Tancred, Frankish knights shared with officials of Byzantine training in the government of the Moslems of northern Syria. And scarcely less remarkable in this respect was Mileto[6] which in the time of

---

[1] Ménager, *Messina*, p. 33. Catepans were established in this way at Barletta, Brindisi, Conversano, Monopoli Canne, and elsewhere.

[2] Gattola, *Hist. Abb. Cassinensis*, p. 164. 'Secundum legem Langobardorum'. Cf. Cahen, *Régime féodale*, p. 36.

[3] Pirro *Sicilia Sacra*, p. 384: 'cum omni tenemoneto et pertinentiis secundum anticas divitiones Sarecenorum'. Cf. Amari, *op. cit.*, III, p. 326; Garufi, *op. cit.*, p. 15.

[4] Cf. Douglas, *op. cit.*, pp. 306-8.   [5] Leib, *op. cit.*, p. 53.

[6] An excellent account of Mileto in the time of Roger I is given by F. Lenormant, *Grande Grèce* III, pp. 280 et seq. See also Leib, *op. cit.*, pp. 127, 128.

the 'Great Count' witnessed a great concourse of merchants and travellers from the sea-ports of western Italy, from north of the Alps, from the eastern empire and from the Moslem south. Here the Norman ruler kept his own guard of Saracen troops; Greek monasteries flourished; and the Latin Church, officially patronized by Roger, was represented by visits of St Bruno from Cologne, of St Anselm from Canterbury and in 1097 of Pope Urban II himself.

London, too, under William the Conqueror was a meeting point of many peoples, cultures and interests.[1] Here the Latin link forged by the Norman Conquest became associated with that earlier expansion from Scandinavia which, having involved England had passed on to Iceland, Greenland and America. Indeed a man from Rouen who had followed William across the Channel might readily meet in Norman London someone who was familiar with the Christian capitals of Rome and Constantinople, or even someone who had sighted the coast of Labrador. And all alike were submitted to the Norman duke who in England had become a king. But the final symbol of Norman administrative dominion should perhaps be sought in Palermo which between 1050 and 1100 was a city much larger and wealthier than London. In its streets during the last quarter of the eleventh century three tongues could be heard, and three languages were used in official documents. Clerics of the Roman and Byzantine allegiance mingled together, and merchants came to the city not only from the Latin West and the Christian East, but also from all parts of the Moslem world. There too under the shadow of Monte Pellegrino, Arab *emirs*, Greek *strategoi* and Norman justiciars co-operated under Roger the son of Tancred of Hauteville in the government of a teeming population of Moslems, Jews, Greeks, Lombards and Latins.

To impose upon communities so heterogeneous and so diverse, a unified and stable government was in itself a notable administrative achievement. If the Normans most properly utilized the governmental institutions existing in the countries they conquered, their purpose was not only to preserve but also to develop. In this they excelled. Thus the Old English writ was not only used; it was also applied more widely and effectively.[2] Similarly, while the Norman *duana* in Sicily derived from the Arab *diwan* it was at the start, unlike the Moslem institution, a branch of the omnicompetent feudal curia, and it was to

[1] Cf. R. W. Chambers in *Harpsfield's Life of More* (Early English Text Soc. CLXXXVI (1932), p. lxxvi). [2] Bishop and Chaplais, *op. cit.*, pp. xiv, xv.

develop on original lines. It is possible, again, that in Norman Apulia, itinerant justices went, as in England, from the central *curia* to conduct trials in the provinces, and if this in fact occurred, it was a departure from Byzantine practice.[1] In England, likewise, the Normans not only preserved the institutions of the shrievalty and the earldom; they also transformed them. The sheriffs who were now recruited from the foremost families of the Norman aristocracy, grew in importance, and in respect of the power they exercised, they came to resemble the greater *vicomtes* of pre-Conquest Normandy. Conversely, the earls who under Edward the Confessor had controlled the greater part of England were now, like the earlier Norman counts, confined to frontier districts such as those on the Welsh border.[2]

No complete estimate of the Norman achievement in secular dominion could be adequate without a more detailed examination both of the feudal arrangements which they made, and of the administrative institutions which they operated. Judged by results, however, the policy they everywhere adopted between 1050 and 1100 may be confidently pronounced as having been highly successful. The government of Roger, the 'Great Count', in Sicily and Calabria was original in conception, and it established, with great efficiency, the Norman rule over a disparate dominion, and over many diverse peoples. Again, of the principality of Antioch it has been said that 'had it not been for constant wars ... and the substitution of a French for a Norman dynasty, Antioch might have developed a government as efficient as that of Sicily'.[3] In the north, too, the Anglo-Norman realm of William the Conqueror was, under his rule, one of the most powerful states in Europe.

Nor should it be forgotten that out of the Norman states of the eleventh century there were to grow within sixty years two great empires, the one stretching from the Tweed to the Pyrenees, and the other linking the whole of southern Italy, now at last politically united, not only with Sicily, but also with the North African territories from Bone to Tripoli. It is, of course, true that King Henry II was the son of a count of Anjou, but he owed his position as King of the English to the fact that his mother was a grand-daughter of William the Conqueror. It is likewise true that Roger II, a southerner by upbringing, never

[1] Haskins, *op. cit.*, pp. 649–51.
[2] Douglas, *op. cit.*, pp. 294–9, 301–8.
[3] Runciman, *Crusades*, II, p. 308. The feudal institutions of Norman Antioch should be compared in the first instance not with those of Jerusalem but with those of South Italy and Sicily (Cahen, *Syrie du Nord*, pp. 435–9, 530–7).

visited the Norman duchy from which his father came. None the less, the so-called 'Angevin Empire'[1] would have been impossible without the Norman conquest of England in the eleventh century; and the splendid Sicilian kingdom of Roger the Great derived directly from the acts and the policy of Roger, the 'Great Count', who died in 1101. Even the administration of these two great empires, which both in the north and in the south, offered such wide recognition to provincial customs and titles[2] might be held to reflect the administrative practices that had been adopted by the Normans in the conquered lands during the latter half of the eleventh century.

Certainly, between 1050 and 1100 Norman government was everywhere based on the same principles. In all the lands subjected to the Normans, a feudal aristocracy acting under the control of strong leaders sustained the Norman supremacy, whilst at the same time the Normans adapted their administration to the various traditions of those they ruled. For this reason the later constitutional growth of all the countries which the Normans conquered was in each case to be individual, but in each case it was stimulated and modified by Norman action. The Normans were in one sense the pupils of their subjects, but their remarkable success in secular government was due to the political capacity of the Normans themselves.

[1] In the opinion of C. H. Haskins (*Normans in European History* (ed. 1959), p. 85): 'the phrase is a misnomer since it leads one to suppose that the Angevin counts were its creators, which was in no sense the case. The centre of the empire was Normandy; its founders were the Norman Dukes.'

[2] King Roger II of Sicily, was prince of Capua, duke of Naples and duke of Apulia. King Henry II was duke of Aquitaine, count of Maine, count of Britanny and so forth. Both kings were anxious to apply the provincial customs of say Poitou, Touraine or Calabria.

Chapter 10

SCHOLARS AND ARTISTS

I

Despite the preoccupation of the Normans with the problems of politics, the results of their conquests cannot be appraised without some reference to that 'renaissance' of art scholarship and letters which overtook western Europe in the twelfth century.[1] Then (as will be recalled) philosophical method was transformed, and legal studies entered on a new phase. Then, too, new styles of architecture were evolved, new secular poetry was written, and a new interest in physical science was awakened. At the same time new monastic orders were established, and new methods of devotion became popular. Finally, before the century had closed, the intellectual curiosity of the age was reflected in the rise of the medieval universities. So varied in fact were these endeavours that it would be difficult to describe them under a single formula. Today, however, it is being stressed, with ever increasing emphasis, that the foundations of the 'twelfth-century renaissance' were laid before ever the twelfth century began.[2] In other words, that renaissance, in all its manifestations, might never have taken place, and would certainly have assumed a different form, had it not been for the notable preparatory work that was done between 1050 and 1100. But these were precisely the decades during which the Normans were modifying the structure of Europe, so that it seems pertinent to inquire whether during these years also there was a connexion between the political and the cultural history of Europe.

To associate the endeavours of the poets and scholars, the writers and the artists of western Europe during this productive age with the armed successes of a warrior people might seem to be futile or at best capricious, the more especially as comparatively few Normans made any personal contribution to literature or scholarship during this

---

[1] Cf. Haskins, *Renaissance of the Twelfth Century* (1927), Preface.
[2] *Ibid.*, pp. 16, 20–9; R. W. Southern, 'The Place of England in the Twelfth century Renaissance', *History*, XLV (1960), pp. 201–16; Knowles, *Historian and Character*, pp. 16, 17.

X   Durham Cathedral Nave

XI   Capella Palatina, Palermo

period. John, abbot of Fécamp until 1079, whose moving prayers still grace the Roman missal,[1] came from Ravenna, and the two great scholar archbishops whom the Normans gave to Canterbury in the eleventh century – Lanfranc and Anselm – were both of Italian birth. Similarly, Desiderius, who as abbot of Monte Cassino from 1058 to 1087 contributed perhaps more than any other single man to the cultural revival in southern Italy during the Norman occupation, was himself a Lombard, and so also was his friend, the equally distinguished Alfanus I, archbishop of Salerno, who was the close associate of Robert Guiscard. The situation in Sicily was somewhat different. But it might be noted that the writer Gerland – who under the patronage of Roger, the 'Great Count', advanced towards beatification by way of a hermitage on Mount Etna and the bishopric of Agrigento – derived not from Normandy but from Besançon.[2]

It would of course be possible to cite Norman names in connexion with the cultural productions of this period, but except in the sphere of architecture, the Norman influence on the revival was, in general, indirect. It was not however negligible. All scholars are agreed that the 'renaissance' of the twelfth century was due to a resuscitation of three distinct traditions. In the first place there was a revived interest in the great writers of Roman antiquity, which also enabled the chief exponents of this culture to express themselves in a Latin which for grace and accuracy was hardly to be matched again until the sixteenth century.[3] Secondly, there was an enhanced concern with Greek traditions radiating from eastern Christendom, and chiefly from Byzantium. And thirdly, there were Saracenic influences, chiefly concerned in the first place with mathematics and science, which emanated from the Moslem world. The relative importance of these three factors in producing the twelfth century revival in the West is debatable, as is also the date and the manner in which these external influences were brought to bear on western Christendom. But of their combined operation there is no question. And it is equally certain that nowhere were conditions more favourable for an intermingling of Latin, Greek, and Moslem ideas than in those lands in the south which during the latter half of the eleventh century were conquered by the Normans.

---

[1] They are there ascribed to St Ambrose (Knowles, *Monastic Order*, p. 86).
[2] Malaterra, IV, c. 7.
[3] Knowles, *Historian and Character*, pp. 18, 19.

II

To estimate what may have been the cultural consequences of the Norman conquests it is appropriate therefore to turn in the first instance to southern Italy. It was there that the Normans were first established, and it was there too that during the same decades the great abbey of Monte Cassino, the home of St Benedict, advanced to pre-eminence as a cultural centre unsurpassed in importance in western Europe.[1] At first, of course, the two movements were wholly distinct. The earliest Norman marauders in Italy had little interest in things of the mind, whilst the political concerns of the abbey were with the two empires whose rivalries were convulsing southern Italy. Thus western influence was exercised on Monte Cassino by visiting emperors from north of the Alps such as Henry II, but at the same time the abbey received benefactions both from the emperors at Constantinople and from their representatives at Bari.[2] In these circumstances the Norman intrusion into the peninsular was naturally regarded with horror at Monte Cassino, and in 1053, Abbot Richerus, who was a German, gave full support to Leo IX in his war against the invaders.[3] Even after the papal defeat at Civitate the same anti-Norman policy was pursued at the abbey particularly by the German Frederick of Lorraine who was abbot from 1056 until he became pope as Stephen X in 1057.[4] Indeed until that year it might be said that with few intermissions the interests of Monte Cassino and those of the Normans in southern Italy had been directly opposed.[5]

In 1058, however, an abbot was elected whose reign was to mark the beginning of a new era. This was Desiderius (Dauferus), a member of the Lombard ducal house of Capua, and under his rule the external policy of Monte Cassino was dramatically reversed. In 1058 Desiderius placed the abbey's interests at Capua under the protection of the victorious Richard of Aversa, and offered his personal friendship to the Normans.[6] Normans were then re-established as major tenants on

---

[1] On Monte Cassino between 1050 and 1100 see E. A. Loew (Lowe) *The Benevantan Script* (1914); H. Bloch, in *Dumbarton Oaks Papers* No. 3 (1945); R. Palmarocchi, *L'abbazia di Monte Cassino e la Conquista normannica* (1933). There are also many important papers relating to this subject in *Casinensia* (2 vols., Monte Cassino, 1929).   [2] H. Bloch, *op. cit.*, pp. 168–73.

[3] Chalandon, *Domination normande*, I, p. 146. Cf. Jaffé–Loewenfeld no. 4164.

[4] L. Duchesne, *L'État pontificale*, pp. 393–4; Lowe, *op. cit.*, pp. 10–16.

[5] According to Leo of Ostia (II c. 71) Abbot Richerus had ejected many of the Norman tenants of the abbey.

[6] Leo of Ostia, III, cc. 8 and 9; Amatus, III, cc. 49–53; IV, c. 3; cf. M. Schipa in *Casinensia*, I, p. 159.

the estates of the abbey,[1] and the abbot became a strong supporter not only of Richard of Aversa who was now at Capua but also of Robert Guiscard in Apulia. Abbot Desiderius was also largely influential in bringing about the momentous alliance between the papacy and the Normans. In March 1059 he was made Vicar Apostolic in southern Italy by Nicholas II, and at about the same time the seigneurial rights of the abbey were confirmed by Richard of Capua with the express approval of the pope.[2] Then, in June, was held the famous synod of Melfi where both Richard and Robert were recognized as papal vassals in their new dominions.

The friendship of Desiderius for the Normans was in fact to continue for the whole of his life. In 1076, for example, at a crisis in the Norman fortunes, he effected, in the pope's despite, the reconciliation between Richard of Capua and Robert Guiscard which precipitated the Norman capture of Salerno, and it was with Norman support that Desiderius in 1087 succeeded Hildebrand as Pope Victor III. The Normans on their part repaid their debt to the abbey with lavish benefactions.[3] Both Robert Guiscard and his Lombard wife, Sigelgaita, made great gifts to the monastery, and the latter was eventually brought there for burial. It was only after 1091, when the death of Jordan, the Norman prince of Capua, robbed Monte Cassino of its greatest protector, that the fortunes of the abbey began at last to wane, and its contributions to art and learning started to decline.[4] The close association of Desiderius with the Normans deserves considerable emphasis because it was during the period of his rule that Monte Cassino reached the peak of its cultural achievement, and the abbot, who was himself personally responsible for much that was then accomplished, could hardly have acted with such success apart from the assistance of his chief temporal supporters.

The Norman rulers may thus claim some share in what was then achieved, and assuredly the production of Monte Cassino at this time was noteworthy. There were, for instance, the beautiful manuscripts wherein was displayed the famous 'Beneventan script' in its perfection.[5] Again, the assiduous study of the Roman past which was pursued in the abbey led to a vigorous cultivation of Latin letters, as well as to the production of original work written in Latin. Thus Leo of Ostia,

---

[1] Cahen, *Régime féodale*, pp. 129, 133; Palmarocchi, *op. cit.*, pp. 82–6.
[2] Palmarocchi, *op. cit.*, p. 210.
[3] Amatus, VIII, c. 35; Peter the Deacon, IV, c. 8.
[4] Palmarocchi, *op. cit.*, p. 158.   [5] Lowe, *op. cit.*, *passim*.

later cardinal, and Alfanus, later archbishop, produced their best literary work as monks at Monte Cassino, the former compiling one of the most attractive of medieval chronicles, and the latter establishing himself as the most notable Latin poet of the eleventh century in Italy. Under Abbot Desiderius, too, there was assembled at the abbey at this time a remarkable library of copies of classical texts to which we owe much of our knowledge of Apuleius, and most of our slender acquaintance with Varro. Moreover, the text of the first five chapters of the *Histories* of Tacitus, and that of chapters XI to XVI of his *Annals* depends on a single manuscript compiled in this period at Monte Cassino.[1]

The interests of Monte Cassino during this period were not however confined to Latin letters, since the abbey continued to be strongly subjected to Greek influence.[2] Desiderius was politically allied to the Normans against the eastern empire, but his abbey continued to be artistically indebted to Byzantium. This was particularly evident in the great new basilica which the abbot decided to construct. In 1066, for instance, massive bronze doors, made at Constantinople on the model of those already existing at Amalfi, came to Monte Cassino, and the transformation of the abbey church thereafter proceeded apace. And if the external structure of the basilica was western, its interior decoration reflected predominantly the work of Byzantine artists who had been brought to Monte Cassino specially for the purpose. Most of their work has perished but their skill, we are told, was most notable in the fashioning of 'silver, bronze, glass, ivory, wood and alabaster, and their mosaics in particular attracted the enthusiastic admiration of contemporaries.[3]

At length the whole church was completed, and its dedication by Pope Alexander II on 10 October 1071 – six months after the capture of Bari by the Normans – was one of the most spectacular events of the time.[4] Besides the pope, there were present, Archdeacon Hildebrand and the cardinal bishops of Ostia, Portus, Tusculum, together with a large number of prelates such as the archbishops of Capua and Salerno.

[1] Lowe, *op. cit.*, pp. 10–21, and in *Casinensia*, I, pp. 256–72.

[2] H. Bloch, *op. cit.*, pp. 192–5. Five years after the fall of Bari the monastery received a diploma from the eastern emperor, Michael VII.

[3] Leo of Ostia, III, c. 27.

[4] It was commemorated not only by Leo of Ostia (*loc. cit*) but also by Alphanus of Salerno in two poems (*Pat. Lat.*, vol. 147, cols. 1234–8). The bull of Alexander II (Jaffé–Loewenfeld no. 4689) records the names of many of those who were present.

Nor was this all. It was symbolic of the special position attained by the abbey of Monte Cassino that there should now come to the monastery of St Benedict, prelates of the Greek rite such as the archbishops of Trani and Taranto, Siponto and Oria. And it was equally significant that on this occasion Desiderius, the friend of the Normans, should have been supported by a great concourse of Norman magnates from all over southern Italy, with the notable exception of Robert Guiscard and Count Roger who were even then engaged against the Saracens outside Palermo.

The cultural activities sustained during these years at Monte Cassino were to be of concern both to the papacy and to its Norman allies in several unexpected ways. Thus Desiderius caused to be copied the registers (now lost) of the fifth-century popes, and one of his monks was in turn to make his own contribution to papal official documents. This was Alberic 'of Monte Cassino', who was largely responsible for reviving an ancient form of rhymical Latin prose – the *cursus*.[1] He came in due course to Rome to serve under Pope Urban II, and his pupil, John of Gaeta, subsequently chancellor of the papal court (and eventually himself Pope Gelasius II), introduced the *cursus* into the papal chancery so that the *cursus Romanae curiae* as it was called, came to be a test of the authenticity of papal documents. Students of medieval records thus have cause to be interested in Alberic, but he was himself more concerned with the direct study of Latin literature. He was particularly interested in Virgil, Ovid and the *Pharsalia* of Lucan, and he also engaged in theological controversy and composed lives of saints.[2] And the same overriding interest in the Latin past was to be found in another contemporary monk at Monte Cassino, who was intimately connected with the Normans, and whose work has been so often cited in these pages. The importance of the historical narrative of Amatus 'of Monte Cassino' might easily obscure the fact that its author was a typical product of Monte Cassino culture. The man who composed the earliest history of the Normans in Italy seems in his turn to have had a considerable acquaintance with the classical learning of his day. At all events a poem which Amatus composed in honour of St Peter and St Paul contains references to Cicero, Ovid, Livy, Virgil and the inevitable Lucan.[3]

---

[1] On the *cursus* see R. L. Poole, *Papal Chancery*, pp. 76–97.
[2] Haskins, in *Casinensia*, I, pp. 115–24; M. Willard in Haskins, *Anniversary Essays*, pp. 351–364; Poole, *loc. cit.*
[3] F. Torraca in *Casinensia*, I, pp. 161–71.

The Norman implication with the cultural revival in southern Italy during the latter half of the eleventh century was exhibited not only at Monte Cassino through Abbot Desiderius, but also at Salerno through Archbishop Alfanus I. It was in 1058 that this remarkable man became archbishop of Salerno. He had already established himself in high repute as a writer of Latin poetry, and he was soon to become a most notable patron of the arts and sciences. His versatility was considerable, and his outlook unrestricted. Like his fellows at Monte Cassino (where he had been a monk) he had been nurtured in the Latin tradition, but in 1063 he travelled to Jerusalem and Constantinople, and he could appreciate the Byzantine legacy to culture sufficiently well to compare the mosaics in the new church of Desiderius at Monte Cassino with those in *Santa Sophia*. He was always a strong supporter of the reviving papacy, and he wrote some notable verses for Archdeacon Hildebrand which prophetically envisaged a new Roman empire subject to St Peter.[1]

Alfanus was in fact to be closely associated in his later career both with the papacy and with the Normans. In 1077 he stood friend to Robert Guiscard after the Norman duke of Apulia had captured Salerno. And it was at his instigation and with the encouragement of Gregory VII, that the Norman duke began the rebuilding at Salerno of the great new cathedral which should worthily house those relics of St Matthew that had come to the city in the tenth century.[2] The consecration of that cathedral was in fact to be one of the last acts of Pope Gregory VII when many years later he came to Salerno to die in exile under the protection of the Normans. In style it was reminiscent of the basilica built by Desiderius. Doubtless through the intervention of Alfanus, it too was adorned with bronze doors of Byzantine workmanship, and while the external structure reflected western skills, the interior was embellished with mosaics of Greek inspiration.[3] Robert Guiscard's great cathedral at Salerno was in truth symbolic and the strange contribution which the Normans made to the artistic revival in southern Italy during the eleventh century.

Archbishop Alfanus I of Salerno died in 1085 – the same year that

[1] *Pat. Lat.*, 147, cols. 1234–8.

[2] Bertaux, *L'art dans l'Italie méridionale* (1904), pp. 190, 191, 213–15; H. Bloch, *op. cit.*, p. 215; M. Schipa in Casinensia, I, pp. 159–60; P. Capparoni in *Casinensia*, p. 151. After the death of Robert Guiscard relics of St Matthew were brought from Salerno to Monte Cassino at the instance of Sigelgaita who at about the same time conferred on the abbey the lordship of Cetraro in Calabria.

[3] Bertaux, *op. cit.*, pp. 191, 425, 504.

saw the passing both of Hildebrand and Robert Guiscard. His literary work was considerable, and his elegant verse reflected a respectable knowledge of classical antiquity. But this Lombard prelate whose fortunes were so curiously intertwined with those of the Normans, was important also for the contribution he made, both as scholar and patron, to the development of medical knowledge in the West. Here his Greek connexions stood him in good stead. He translated from the Greek the medico-philosophical treatise which Nemesius bishop of Emea in Syria composed 'on the nature of man' towards the end of the fourth century; and Alfanus himself wrote two medical essays, one of which depended on a Byzantine physician named Philaretus, while the other was constructively derived from Galen.[1] It is impossible, in short, to dissociate Archbishop Alfanus I from the development of the medical school at Salerno, and the growth in the city that was captured by Robert Guiscard in 1077[2] of what has been called the earliest of the medieval universities.

It was Alfanus, moreover, who was responsible for bringing to Italy a widely travelled Moslem physician who became known to the West as Constantine 'the African'. This man was taught Latin and installed by Alfanus as a monk at Monte Cassino.[3] It is possible, though uncertain that, as has been alleged,[4] this Constantine also served for a time in the household of Robert Guiscard, but he undoubtedly resided for some years at Salerno, and he produced a number of medical works, mostly in the form of translations.[5] The most important of these, entitled *Pantecne*, was dedicated to Abbot Desiderius, and it is of interest to note how the ethical rules of Hippocrates were here set down in Latin by this Arab scholar and made to harmonize with the *Rule* of St Benedict.[6] Assuredly, Constantine 'the African' is a romantic figure, but his true significance in the development of western medicine has been diversely judged. Certainly, medical studies were cultivated at Salerno under Greek influence long before he ever came there, and the treatises of Alfanus himself were pre-Constantinian in spirit, and wholly

---

[1] Haskins, *Renaissance*, pp. 322, 323; *Medieval Science*, p. 142; P. Capparoni, in *Casinensia*, pp. 152–60. In the twelfth century the work of Nemesius was to be translated again by Burgundius of Pisa (H. Bloch, *op. cit.*, p. 220), but the enduring importance of the work of Alfanus in this respect is illustrated by the fact that one of his medical treatises was in the Library of Christ Church Canterbury about 1300.

[2] Cf. H. Rashdall, *Medieval Universities*, I, ch. III.

[3] L. Thorndike, *History of Magic and Experimental Science* (1923), I, ch. xxxi; Courtois, 'Gregoire VII et l'Afrique du Nord', *Révue historique* (1945).

[4] Thorndike, *loc. cit.*   [5] H. Bloch, *op. cit.*, p. 221.   [6] *Ibid.*

without trace of any Saracenic influence.[1] None the less it might be rash to discount too ruthlessly the influence of Constantine on Salerno, or of the monastery of Monte Cassino which was linked to Salerno through Alfanus.[2] At least one of the translations of Constantine was made from the works of the Arab doctor Ali ben Abas, and this was later to be improved and enlarged by Stephen of Antioch in the time of Tancred, the nephew of Bohemund. Moreover, a pupil of Constantine, named John 'Afflacius', was later to work constructively at Salerno where he produced treatises on urology and fevers.[3]

It might seem reasonable to conclude therefore, that Constantine 'the African' may have been the first to enable the medical school at Salerno to take some advantage of Moslem experience at the same time as they kept alive their own earlier Greek traditions. More certain is it that the medical school at Salerno which developed into the earliest of the medieval universities owed much to Alfanus at the time of the archbishop's close association with Robert Guiscard. Between 1077 when Guiscard captured the city and the deaths of Alfanus and Constantine, which occurred respectively in 1085 and 1087, the Salernitan medical school began to take definite shape. Later the university was said to have owed its origin to four founders: a Latin, a Greek, a Moslem and a Jew. That, of course, was pure myth. But the legend aptly reflected the actual conditions which prevailed in the great cities of southern Italy when they were under the rule of Robert Guiscard, Jordan of Capua, Roger Borsa and Roger the 'Great Count' – and not least in Salerno under Normans. Nowhere else in western Europe during the latter half of the eleventh century was there such a mingling of the races save in Norman Sicily.

II

Conditions in Sicily during the last quarter of the eleventh century may be compared with those in southern Italy. Apulia and Calabria had been part of the Byzantine empire until the Norman conquest, whereas Sicily was under Moslem rule for more than a century before the coming of the Normans. As a result, while in southern Italy a large

[1] P. Capparoni, in *Casinensia*, I, p. 156.

[2] Charles Singer (*History* (1925), pp. 244, 245) was inclined to minimize the importance of Constantine, and so also did Rashdall who was equally sceptical about the influence here of Monte Cassino. But it may be noted that in the new edition of Rashdall's book (1936) this chapter (I, ch. iii) has been heavily revised by his editors.

[3] Haskins, *Medieval Science*, pp. 155–90.

Greek-speaking population carried on the traditions of an earlier culture into the age of Robert Guiscard and Roger Borsa, in Sicily strong Moslem as well as Greek elements survived. Moreover, the Norman conquest of the island was not completed until 1091 so that Norman influence began to be exercised at a later date than on the mainland, and indeed, its effects were not fully revealed until the twelfth century. None the less, Palermo and the northern Sicilian sea-board were under Norman rule from 1072 onwards, and the acts of the 'Great Count' in Sicily were to prove of high consequence to the future. Sicily was the natural meeting point between east and west. It was therefore peculiarly adapted for a fusion of Latin, Greek and Moslem cultures, a place where translations from Arabic and Greek might be expected, and where original works in those tongues might be composed. All this would, however, obviously depend on the type of secular rule that was established in the island.

From the start, the policy of Roger, the 'Great Count', in Sicily, though doubtless inspired by diverse motives, was precisely calculated to provide the conditions wherein might flourish in propitious circumstances the later cosmopolitan culture of the island. It is true that at the start the Norman conquest led to a considerable exodus of Arabic scholars and men of letters who left Palermo for Morocco, and more particularly for Spain; and there were laments by Islamic writers for what was thus lost to Sicily.[1] But Roger I showed from the first a remarkable tolerance towards his Moslem subjects, and employed many of them as officials or as soldiers. As a consequence, Arabic letters never ceased to be cultivated in Norman Sicily though at first on a diminished scale; and soon the court of King Roger II was to be celebrated in the verses of Abd-ar-Rahman, of Trapani, while the geography of Sicily was entertainingly described by his contemporary Edrisi.[2]

Even more productive however was the 'Great Count's' patronage of Greek culture. His motive here may have been to ensure the support of all his Christian subjects in an island whose population was still largely Moslem. But as a result, Byzantine influence upon the intellectual and artistic development of Sicily was to be dominant through much of the twelfth century. Only gradually was it to be supplanted by the Latin culture which followed the restoration to the Roman allegiance

---

[1] E.g. Ibn el Athir (trans. Amari, *Bibliotheca* I, pp. 553 et seq.). As late as 1950 aristocrats of true or pretended Sicilian origin were enjoying prestige in Morocco. (Setton and Baldwin *Crusades*, I, p. 65.)

[2] Amari, *Storia dei Mussulmani in Sicilia*, III, pp. 458, 471.

of those bishoprics which Roger I set up before his death in 1101. In short, the tolerant and enthusiastic patronage of Moslem, Greek and Latin culture that was characteristic of the reign of King Roger II between 1130 and 1154 was largely a development from the acts of his father.

The consequences for western Europe were to be pervasive. It is true that Greek erudition was transmitted to Latin Christendom in the twelfth century more through Norman Italy than through Norman Sicily, and it is also true that the most important single channel through which Moslem learning reached the West at this time was Spain. But the special contribution made by Norman Sicily to the 'renaissance' of the twelfth century needs no emphasis. Here there was not only an association with the Moslem east, but also immediate contact with Greek science and philosophy which was known at Toledo only through the medium of Arabic translators. Thus in the middle of the twelfth century Aristippus, archdeacon of Catania, was making Latin translations of the *Meno* and the *Phaedo* of Plato, and he was followed in such work by Eugenius the Emir who, in the intervals of serving the Norman monarchy as an administrator, composed Greek verses and translated from the Arabic the *Optics* of Ptolemy.[1] Many other names could of course be added, such as Nilus Doxopatres, a Greek monk who composed in favour of Rome a treatise on the five patriarchates,[2] or Theophanos Keramenes, perhaps from Taormina, who won a high if undeserved reputation for his sermons.[3]

The full effects of this activity were only felt in the middle of the twelfth century, but they had already been prefigured at an earlier date. It is not to be forgotten that the father of King Roger II was born in the Cotentin, and that he himself was baptized in Mileto by St Bruno in the presence of a Norman godfather named Lanvinus who subsequently achieved beatification.[4] Certainly, before the death of Count Roger I in 1101, a varied company of scholars and artists had gathered in his courts at Mileto, Messina and Palermo where Greek, Arabic and Latin were all written. There, for example, Geoffrey Malaterra compiled his notable chronicle, while John, archdeacon of Bari, composed a life of the Greek St Nicholas of Myra which so fired the imagination of

[1] Haskins, *Renaissance*, pp. 292–4
[2] He tactlessly based the case for the primacy of Rome on the fact that Rome was once the seat of the empire!
[3] Caspar, *Roger II*, pp. 459, 460.
[4] Lenormant, *Grande Grèce*, III, p. 305.

Ordericus Vitalis, then a boy at Shrewsbury, that in old age he commented upon it in his Norman history.[1] Evidently the achievements of Sicilian culture were constructively prepared before the eleventh century had closed.

IV

The individual character of that culture has been made familiar by the magnificent architectural monuments which it produced. Of these the most famous is of course the cathedral of Monreale. The exterior is marked by romanesque towers while the eastern apse embodies an oriental design of interlacing arches inlaid with lava. Inside, the walls are covered with mosaics which evidently came from a Byzantine workshop but which also reflect Arabic influence. And the same blend extends to the cloisters with their pointed Saracenic arches, their Islamic fountain, and their coloured columns with romanesque capitals. Monreale fittingly houses the tombs of two Norman kings of Sicily – William I and William II – and one of its most famous mosaics appropriately depicts the latter offering the resplendent church to the Queen of Heaven. But the cathedral itself is too well known to need further description, and it is scarcely necessary to add that the same stylistic variety is to be found in the wonderful cathedral of Cefalù, which, from the top of its own hill, looks down on the blue Sicilian sea. There, a romanesque west front admits to a nave supported by classical columns, and the whole church is dominated by its apse which shines with Byzantine mosaics complete with Greek inscriptions. There, unforgettably, a youthful Christ *Pantocrator*, of dominating size, blesses the world, and below is Our Lady as a young woman supported in adoration by seraphim and saints.[2]

It is, however, naturally in Palermo itself that the monuments of Sicilo-Norman architecture are most numerous. The famous *Capella Palatina* built in the residence of the Norman rulers is perhaps the brightest jewel of Sicilian building during the Norman period, and here the same blending of styles is to be found.[3] The basilican nave may derive from western models, the pointed arches may reflect Saracenic influence, the interior glows with mosaics of Byzantine inspiration whilst the roof is decorated with designs suggesting a Mohammedan heaven

[1] Ord. Vit., III, pp. 205, 218.   [2] Plate VI.
[3] See in particular O. Demus, *Mosaics of Norman Sicily* (1950), pp. 3–19, 91–141 and the Plates.

populated by djinns rather than cherubim, and houris rather than angels. It was a unique achievement, but the same spirit was displayed in churches elsewhere in the city – in San Cataldo for example with its three coloured domes, or in the Martorana which the Greek emir George of Antioch erected to the glory of the Virgin in or before 1143.[1]

To this short and summary list would have to be added San Giovanni degli Eremiti with its cluster of domes, and its romanesque cloisters, the more especially as this church was probably erected on the site of a mosque, and was certainly constructed with the aid of Arab craftsmen working under Norman directions. Nor was this blending of diverse techniques confined even to ecclesiastical edifices, for it can be found also in the secular buildings which about this time were erected outside the walls of Palermo. The large *Cuba* for instance looks from the outside not unlike a Norman keep, but the little Cuba is a Moslem pavilion. Similarly, the palace of the Ziza presents a square stone front almost reminiscent of a fortress but within there still remains a Saracenic hall complete with fountain and mosaics.[2] And it was here that at least one of the Norman rulers of Sicily, following earlier example, entertained his harem of Arab girls. Such apparently was the religious zeal of these ladies that (as was alleged) when from time to time Christian girls were added to their company, these were usually persuaded by their companions to embrace the faith of Islam.[3]

Some of the most characteristic examples of this unique type oi architecture, such as the cathedral of Monreale, come from the latter part of the twelfth century, but others were built at an earlier date. There is documentary evidence of the existence of the new cathedral at Cefalù as early as 1131; the *Capella Palatina*, was begun in, or shortly after, that year, and the Martorana was started during the next decade. There can, moreover, be no doubt that all these derived from a programme of building which had been initiated some time before. The palace at Palermo contained a chapel from the beginnings of the Norman occupation, and while there is some doubt whether this was decorated by mosaics (as has been stated)[4] it is possible that this may have been the case. Little has survived of the edifices erected by Roger, the

---

[1] Demus, *op. cit.*, pp. 25–85. See also Plate XII.

[2] *Ibid.*, pp. 178–80.

[3] The information comes from the twelfth century Arabic chronicler Ali al Husayn ibn Jubair, whose work is translated into Italian by Amari (*Bibliotheca*, vol. I), and in part into English by C. Waern, *Medieval Sicily*, pp. 6off.

[4] Demus, *op. cit.*, p. 25.

'Great Count', but he is known to have contributed to the structure of the cathedrals at Catania and Syracuse, and to have begun work on the cathedral at Messina. He was responsible also, for the restoration of many derelict Greek monasteries and for the construction of some new Latin houses.[1]

Finally there is an attractive tradition that the 'Great Count', in company with his brother Robert Guiscard, began to erect the charming church of San Giovanni now styled 'dei Lepprosi' outside the walls of medieval Palermo before their capture of the city in 1072. In any case, this is one of the earliest Norman buildings in Sicily and it invites contemplation. For in its basilican form, and with its little square sanctuary surmounted by a red oriental dome,[2] this unpretentious church now situated in a suburb of Palermo may be said to stand at the beginning of a continuous architectural development which, itself so eclectic in its inspiration and so individual in its products, was not to be completed until, after two or three generations, it had created such masterpieces as the Capella Palatina, San Giovanni degli Eremiti, of the great cathedrals of Cefalù and Monreale.

The architectural achievements of Norman Sicily in the time of King Roger II may thus be legitimately related not only to the acts of his father but also to what took place in Apulia and Calabria during the period of the Norman conquests. Between 1050 and 1100 southern Italy witnessed much ecclesiastical building which reached its climax with the consecration of the new church at Monte Cassino in 1071, and which was reflected in the cathedral that Robert Guiscard and Alfanus I began to construct at Salerno after 1077. The cathedral of Capua had been enlarged by the Norman Hervey who became archbishop there in 1068, and the Normans also contributed to the structure of the cathedrals at Aversa and Acerenza.[3] The ancient abbey of La Cava likewise received new romanesque cloisters about this time, and Robert Guiscard erected not only his abbey of St Eufemia, but also that of Venosa to which in due course his body was brought from Cephallonia for burial.[4] At Bari, both the cathedral and more particularly the abbey of St Nicholas received notable additions during these years, and at a slightly later date the large basilica of Gerace in Calabria with its three naves and its classical columns was constructed. Already, moreover, Count

---

[1] Cp. Jordan in *Moyen Age*, vols. XXIII and XXIV.
[2] See Plate IV.   [3] Bertaux, *op. cit.*, pp. 318, 326–30.
[4] Ménager, *Quellen und Forschungen*, XXXIX (1959), pp. 1–116.

Roger had caused to arise outside Mileto the great monastery which he dedicated to the Holy Trinity and to St Michael.[1] The twenty granite pillars of Gerace were taken from the ancient Locri, and the columns of Mileto are said to have been brought from the ancient Hipponion which is the modern Monteleone.[2]

Evidently, the Normans were responsible for much ecclesiastical building in Apulia and Calabria during the latter half of the eleventh century. The significance of this should not however be misconceived. The dominant architectural styles of southern Italy at this time were not Norman but Byzantine or Lombard. Thus the essential distinction between Sicily and the mainland in this respect was not that in Italy the Normans were more original, but that they borrowed in different degrees from different traditions. At Troia, for instance, it would seem that influence was exercised by craftsmen from as far north as Pisa, and Lombard work has been detected as far south as Cefalú.[3] Sicily was naturally more directly subject to Moslem influence than either Apulia or Calabria, but both on the island and on the mainland the architectural debt to Byzantium was overwhelming.

It is none the less easy to dogmatize too freely on such matters.[4] Before discounting any direct influence by Norman craftsmen on Italian architecture during these years, it may be useful to recall how widespread has been the destruction of the churches which the Normans built. The great Norman abbeys of St Eufemia and Mileto were, for instance, almost annihilated in the earthquake of 1783,[5] and though the surviving romanesque work at Venosa has been held to be French rather than Norman[6] we cannot be sure that Norman artists who were influencing the architecture of northern France at this time made no contribution to Italian building. Indeed, in one case it seems certain that they did so. Many hands contributed to the erection of the church of St Nicholas at Bari which was begun about 1084, and some of these were surely Norman. No one can contemplate the facade of this remarkable church without being reminded of the west front of St Stephen's at Caen,[7] and experts have been led to think that there are

---

[1] Bertaux, op. cit., pp. 317, 335–7, 367, 448–71. Cf. Lenormant, op. cit., III, p. 286.

[2] Douglas, Old Calabria, pp. 141, 142.

[3] Bertaux, op. cit., pp. 352–8.

[4] Compare the remarks of Gally Knight (Normans in Sicily, pp. 327–55), with those of Bertaux, op. cit., pp. 376–99.

[5] Lenormant, Grande Grèce, III, pp. 323 et seq.; Bertaux op. cit., p. 326. The cathedrals of Squillace and Nicastro were destroyed at the same time.

[6] Bertaux, op. cit., p. 330.   [7] See Plates VII and VIII.

features within the nave which suggest direct imitation from Normandy. But to the ordinary observer it is one of the lateral doorways which may be most convincing. This is surmounted by a stone frieze on which is carved a long succession of mounted warriors vigorously in action. Alike in posture and in equipment these might almost have been taken from the Bayeux Tapestry.[1]

V

The character of the cultural development of south Italy and Sicily during the period of the Norman conquest invites a comparison with the changes that during the same period took place in the intellectual and artistic interests of England. It must, however, be remarked at once how different were the conditions prevailing in the north. England and Normandy, as near neighbours, had already been exercising considerable influence on each other before the establishment of the Norman monarchy, and though England between 1042 and 1066 was vexed with much disorder, she enjoyed a measure of political unity that was unknown in Apulia or Calabria, and which was not matched in Moslem Sicily. Even more striking was the fact that before 1066 England had hardly been touched by those intellectual movements which were so deeply affecting all the other Norman lands. Even after the Norman Conquest these interests extended only gradually across the Channel.[2]

The isolation of pre-Conquest England in this respect needs, however, to be defined. It did not imply artistic sterility or excessive provincialism. Between 1042 and 1066 merchants and pilgrims from England visited many lands. Anglo-Saxon illuminated manuscripts, particularly those of the Winchester school, were famed for their beauty and some of them passed overseas to influence the work of continental *Scriptoria* not least in Normandy.[3] The productions of England at this time in metal work and in many of the minor arts were likewise widely appreciated. Latin scholarship had it is true declined since the days of Bede, but the language and its grammar continued to be studied; and while, during the reign of Edward the Confessor few contributions seem to have been made to Anglo-Saxon verse, the vernacular continued to

---

[1] Bertaux, *op. cit.*, pp. 335–9; 476; and Figs. 139 and 206.

[2] Cf. R. W. Southern, 'The Place of England in the Twelfth Century Renaissance' (*History*, XLV (1960), pp. 201–16). I am particularly indebted to this article.

[3] Tolhurst, 'An examination of two Anglo-Saxon MSS of the Winchester School', *Archaeologia*, LXXXIII (1933), pp. 27–49; D. Whitelock in *The Norman Conquest* ed. C. T. Chevalier (1966), pp. 40, 41.

be used effectively in legal documents, in homilies and in historical prose.[1] The cultural achievements of Anglo-Saxon England which in the past may have been underrated, and which perhaps are now over-praised,[2] are assuredly not to be ignored.

Nevertheless when all this is said, it remains true that the Confessor's England was isolated from the main stream which on the continent was flowing so strongly towards the 'renaissance' of the twelfth century. It was not merely that England possessed no great cathedral schools to vie with those which in France were developing new philosophical methods and giving a new turn to systematic theology. It was also that the monasteries of England (despite their great past and their great future) looked back to earlier traditions and not forward to new in-tellectual progress. They drew their inspiration from the past, and were concerned at this time above all with the 'laborious transmission of an attenuated legacy that had been exploited for five hundred years'.[3] The Confessor's England, in short, not only had no Chartres; she had no Le Bec and no contemporary Monte Cassino. And the results were notable. 'The more one reflects on the eleventh century' remarks Professor Southern 'the more one sees how essential was the material and intel-lectual foundation then laid for the achievements of the succeeding century', and 'of all this preparation which was well under way by 1066, Anglo-Saxon England shows not a single trace.'[4]

It is against this background that any comparison between the cul-tural consequences of the Norman conquests in the north and the south would have to be made. The new learning which was already spreading over the West came to England in the wake of the Normans, and the chief agents in bringing it across the Channel were the two new arch-bishops, Lanfranc and Anselm, whom the Normans brought from Le Bec to Canterbury. Before his coming to England, Lanfranc had con-ducted a famous dispute over the doctrines of Berengar by means of a logical discipline which was acceptable to all the dissentients in that

[1] R. W. Chambers, in *Nicholas Harpsfield's Life of More* (Early English Text Soc., CLXXXVI.

[2] We are now actually told on high authority that 'everyone would agree . . . that the Anglo-Saxons were far ahead of contemporary European kingdoms in cultural and admin-istrative achievements'. (*Columbia Law Review*, LXVII (1967), p. 1343.) Whatever may be the value of this judgment, such unanimity certainly does not exist. Compare for instance R. R. Darlington 'The Norman Conquest' (Creighton Lecture, 1963) with the lectures given by R. A. Brown and G. Zarnecki to the Royal Historical Society and the British Academy in 1966.

[3] M. D. Knowles, *Monastic Order* (1940), p. 94.

[4] Southern, *op. cit.*, p. 202.

XII   Church of San Cataldo, Palermo

XIII　Mausoleum of Bohemund at Canosa

XIV　Tomb of Robert, son of William the Conqueror, in Gloucester Cathedral

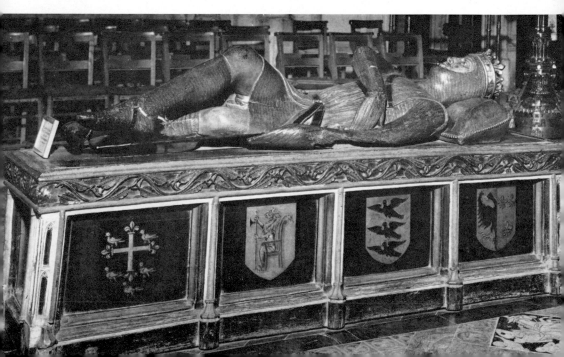

controversy, but which was then unknown in contemporary England. And Anselm, the greatest thinker of his age, imparted to England his formative teaching as a scholar and as a doctor of the Church. Such men inevitably influenced all those in England with whom they came in contact. But, even so, the cathedral schools in England and the formal theology which they sponsored lagged far behind those of northern France until the very end of the twelfth century.[1] It is not surprising therefore that for all these reasons English scholars after the Norman conquest were progressively inspired to travel abroad in order to make first-hand contact with the new movements of thought and with the men by whom they were propagated.

In particular were they attracted to those lands where the blend of Greek, Moslem and Latin cultures (a blend unknown to the Confessor's England) was most evident – countries such as Spain, for example, or lands such as southern Italy and Sicily under the rule of the Normans. The case of Adelard of Bath[2] is typical of this. Adelard was born about 1085 and England was his *patria*. But early in life he migrated to France where he studied at Tours and at Laon. Then he passed on to Apulia, Calabria and Sicily. It is possible that he also visited Antioch, then under Tancred, and it is almost certain that he studied for a time in Spain. His travels, and particularly those through Norman-dominated lands were highly productive, and he seems to have been largely responsible for the introduction into the West of Euclidian mathematics and Moslem astronomy. His interests in fact ranged from Platonic philosophy to applied chemistry and he exemplified the fusion of Greek and Arabic influence which was to operate on western Christendom during the twelfth century.

It was thus fitting that Adelard should have dedicated one of his books to William, bishop of Syracuse who was himself probably a Norman, for as a result of his travels he brought to England something of the cosmopolitan culture which, between 1050 and 1100, had been developed in the Norman lands of the south. And it was under these same influences that in due course England was to take her own share in the revival of the twelfth century. Salernitan medicine, for instance, may not have been scientific in the modern sense, but it was far in advance of the magical practices prescribed in the Anglo-Saxon leechdoms, and there is some reason to believe that its influence may have percolated into England within half a century of the capture of Salerno

[1] *Ibid.*
[2] Haskins, *Medieval Science*, pp. 20–42.

by Robert Guiscard.[1] More important, however, was the sustained endeavour made throughout the twelfth century to introduce Arabic science into England, and more particularly Arabic mathematics and astronomy. England was, in fact, eventually to play an outstanding part in bringing a knowledge of much of Greek and Arabic science to western Christendom. Again, while England's contribution to formal theology and philosophy might be regarded as subordinate, yet in the person of John of Salisbury England was to give to Europe one of the most complete types of a twelfth century humanism. It was typical of the new conditions which had been established that John of Salisbury should have studied under the great masters of France, and particularly those of Chartres, and that in his own words he should have 'ten times passed the chain of the Alps' and have 'twice traversed Apulia'. His career of course belongs to a later epoch, but it would hardly have been possible apart from the events which overtook England during the latter half of the eleventh century.

The Normans certainly ensured that England should be subjected to new cultural influences from the continent at a time when western Europe was experiencing a revival. None the less, many of the special interests of pre-Conquest England were to survive into the age of the Normans and beyond. For example it is of course true that as a result of the Norman conquest Anglo-Saxon vernacular prose received a blow from which it was never to recover. But the continuity of English prose was in some sense sustained, even if tenuously.[2] As for the vexed question of the relation of modern English literature to Anglo-Saxon, and the extent to which the Norman conquest affected the development between them, it is difficult to venture an opinion. One balanced judgement, however, is here perhaps pertinent. 'Those who ignore the relation of English to Anglo-Saxon as "a merely philological fact",' wrote C. S. Lewis, 'betray a shocking insensibility to the very mode in which literature exists.' On the other hand, 'changes in language soon made Anglo-Saxon unintelligible even in England', and, in respect of the subject matter of later medieval literature, we are told that 'for one reference to Wade or Weland we meet fifty to Hector, Aeneas, Alexander or Caesar.[3] Far greater than the debt of these writers to the old northern paganism, it would appear, was their debt to the classics.

[1] Charles Singer in introduction to the new edition of Cokayne, *Leechdoms* (1961), p. xxxix.
[2] R. W. Chambers, *op. cit.*
[3] C. S. Lewis, *The Discarded Image* (1961), pp. 6, 7, 8.

The special character of the literary influence exercised by the Normans upon England might perhaps in part be illustrated by reference to one particular branch of literary composition. Despite the continuation of the Anglo-Saxon chronicle in one of its versions down to 1154, historical writing in the vernacular languished in England after the Norman conquest. On the other hand, under the Normans, there occurred a great revival in England of historical writing in Latin, and this took a distinctive form. The notable chronicles of William of Malmesbury, and Ordericus Vitalis, the works of Eadmer and Simeon of Durham, were written in the language common to western Christendom, but all these writers, some of whom had at least one English parent, showed a keen interest in the past history of England. They wrote of a country whose political outlook had been recently changed by events in which they were proud to have had a share. But they wrote also about a country which they regarded as their own. William of Malmesbury, who avowedly aspired to revive the tradition of Bede, spent much of his energy in exploring Anglo-Saxon antiquities, and though Ordericus Vitalis, the son of a Norman father, left Shrewsbury for Normandy a the age of ten, he could still in old age, when a monk at St Évroul, describe himself as *Anglicanus*.[1]

The blend of Norman innovation with Saxon tradition could also be watched in devotional practices and in liturgical observance, and as in the south, so also in the north, the Normans seem often to have been concerned to foster the particular artistic skills of their new subjects. The Bayeux Tapestry could itself be cited as an example of this. That wonderful work was commissioned by Bishop Odo of Bayeux the half-brother of William the Conqueror, and the great artist who was responsible for its designs may himself have been a Norman. But the work was executed, as it seems, in England and perhaps at Canterbury.[2] The development of ecclesiastical sculpture in England during these years would likewise seem to have followed similar lines. In the latter half of the eleventh century romanesque sculpture in Normandy, attractive in itself, was notable in particular for the manner in which it was integrated with the architectural structures it adorned. It was, moreover, directly influenced by Norman contacts with other lands – with Spain, for instance, and more especially with southern Italy. In contemporary

[1] R. R. Darlington, Anglo-Norman Historians (1947); Douglas, *English Historical Documents*, II, pp. 101, 102.
[2] F. Wormald in *The Bayeux Tapestry*, ed. F. M. Stenton (1957), pp. 25–7; E. Maclagan, *The Bayeux Tapestry* (King Penguin Books, 1943).

England, by contrast, such sculpture tended to be two-dimensional in spirit, and applied to the walls of churches irrespective of their architectural needs. But it reflected also the traditional excellence of the Winchester school of manuscript illumination, and it was to have a great influence on the future growth of ecclesiastical sculpture both in England and in Normandy. Certainly the Normans encouraged the native English sculptors, and employed them both in the Kingdom and in the Duchy, not only in parish churches but also in great cathedrals such as Ely.[1]

VI

The employment by the Normans of Anglo-Saxon craftsmen to decorate their churches recalls the use they made of Byzantine and Saracen artists elsewhere and it is of particular interest because it was through their ecclesiastical buildings that the Normans made their most enduring mark upon the English countryside. Yet here too a distinction must be made between the north and the south of Europe. The condition of architecture in pre-Conquest England has been very diversely judged,[2] but whatever may have been the (undisclosed) potentialities of Anglo-Saxon architecture in the middle of the eleventh century, its actual productions were markedly inferior alike in scope and execution to the romanesque architecture which was already arising in northern France, and more particularly in Normandy. Such at all events appears to have been the opinion in eleventh century England itself. When Edward the Confessor decided to erect his great new abbey at Westminster he took for his model not any building in the kingdom he ruled but the abbey of Jumièges which had just been completed in Normandy.[3]

It was, therefore, with some confidence that the new Norman prelates in England could embark on their programme of building. But the zeal which they brought to their task, and the energy with which they carried it through, were little short of astonishing. Attention has been properly called to the 'veritable fury of building which possessed the Norman churchmen of the first and second generation after the Conquest',[4] and there were few of the greater cathedrals and abbey churches of England that were not affected. Lanfranc at Canterbury set an example, whilst Walchelin, Bishop of Winchester from 1070 to 1098,

[1] G. Zarnecki, '1066 and architectural sculpture', *Proc. Brit. Acad.*, LII (1966), pp. 87–104.
[2] *Ibid.*, p. 87.   [3] *Ibid.*, p. 88.
[4] Knowles, *Historian and Character* (1963), p. 184.

began reconstituting the great cathedral which today bears such emphatic witness to antiquity. At the same time, Abbot Serlo from Le Mont-St-Michel started to give new form to the abbey at Gloucester where the great romanesque nave can still be admired; and during the same years at Ely, there began to arise in its present form what was to be the dominating cathedral of the Fens. Modern Londoners can contemplate the results of this activity at St Bartholomew's at Smithfield and at St John's chapel in the Tower, and the same energy which stretched across England from Exeter to St Albans, and northwards to its climax at Durham, was exemplified also in very many of the parishes and villages of England.[1]

The character of this Norman romanesque building is familiar to all Englishmen since it was by the Normans that the massive round arch which had once glorified the triumphs of Titus and Severus came to find a permanent place in the English shires. The greater Norman churches were, generally speaking, much larger in concept and size than those which they replaced. They were marked in particular by long naves and by more ceremonial space in front of the high altars. At the same time many elaborate chapels were added in honour of Our Lady in response to the developing cult.[2] In all these ways, the Normans must here be regarded as innovators, but it should be added that the earlier Norman churches in England were normally erected on the sites of existing buildings. This frequently entailed the destruction of earlier structures but there seems to have been no desire to discourage the work of native craftsmen. Indeed, some smaller churches designed on the older pattern were actually erected in England after the Norman Conquest. The little church of Sompting in Sussex, for example, is wholly 'Anglo-Saxon' in spirit, but it was constructed out of Caen stone, and built after the Norman Conquest.[3]

Both in England and in the south, the development of architecture at this time owed more to Norman rulers than to Norman artists. But their achievement is not for that reason to be belittled. In England what the Normans accomplished gave high distinction to a great age of ecclesiastical building, which stood in special relation to what came after. The men who were responsible for the cathedral at Durham need no apology as sponsors of architecture, and in the older parts of the cathedrals of Peterborough and Ely, as in the choirs of York and Ripon

[1] Plates V and X.   [2] *Op. cit.*, pp. 184, 185.
[3] Zarnecki, *op. cit.*, p. 91.

may be seen the stages by which Gothic architecture in England was evolved out of the Norman romanesque. In the south too, the same driving energy produced results of similar magnitude. In Italy, Lombard and Greek artists were made to work side by side, and together with Saracens in Sicily, they combined to produce, both on the mainland and in the island, an architectural style of strong individuality and great beauty.

Such memorials endure, and when all has been rightly said of the artistic debt of the Normans to the peoples they ruled, their own contribution to ecclesiastical architecture is not to be minimized. In England many of our most venerated cathedrals and abbey churches – Winchester for instance, or Gloucester, or St Albans, or Tewkesbury, or Exeter – would have been very different and vastly inferior apart from the Normans. And without the Normans there would have been no Monreale, no Cefalù, no St Nicholas at Bari, and there would have been a very different church at Salerno. These, with the oriental domes of the Eremiti, or the mosaics of the Martorana, were moreover but outstanding examples of the success with which the Normans co-ordinated so many of the artistic energies of their subjects. Little remains of Lanfranc's cathedral at Canterbury, and what Holy Trinity, Mileto and St Eufemia looked like when they were first built is not now to be discovered. But a man who wishes to realize at once the concerted effort, and the diverse results, of this far-flung Norman endeavour need do no more than contemplate the small parish churches of Kilpeck on the Welsh border, and of Melbourne in Derbyshire, and then pass overseas to visit the little church of St Nicholas of Norman origin, which stands besides the Roman amphitheatre at Syracuse.[1] And he may with equal profit linger within the astonishing cathedral in the same city. For Roger, the 'Great Count', re-established the bishopric of Syracuse after long Moslem domination. It was fitting therefore that he should have given a new roof to the great temple of Minerva (one commemorated by Cicero), and should have restored it once more as the Christian cathedral which it still remains.[2]

[1] The tradition that Jordan, bastard son of Roger I was buried there perhaps derives from a misreading of Malaterra (IV, c. 17). The body was certainly carried to Syracuse, but it was buried at St. Nicholas at Troina.

[2] Ecclesia Syracusana prima filia Divi Petri et prima post Antiocham Christo dicata.

EPILOGUE

The great movements of intellectual and artistic fusion that occurred in the Norman lands might be taken as symbolic of the Norman achievement which has been commemorated in this book. Thus, what was then accomplished in secular dominion derived not only from the quality of Norman rule, but also from the Norman ability to respect the traditions, and to utilize the aptitudes of those they governed. And a similar duality has been found pervading the vast extension of Norman power which took place between 1050 and 1100. This was due in the first instance, and primarily, to the overmastering energy of a dominant people, to the particular enthusiasms which inspired them, and to the special military techniques which, under skilled leadership, they everywhere successfully applied. Thus was created the self-conscious Norman world of the eleventh century which was pervaded by sentiments shared in common, and knit together by its subjection to inter-related groups of great families. None the less, within this integrated Norman world, there was always left full scope for a proper diversity among its several parts. If in the future the Normans were, so to speak, to be absorbed into the countries they conquered, they were merged into communities whose individuality they had fostered, and whose future development they had done much to determine.

This, as has been seen, occurred in England, in Italy, in Sicily, and even in Norman Antioch. It would be idle to speculate on what might have been the political, social and ecclesiastical future of these countries had they not been made subject to the Normans – if England for instance, had continued on the course on which she was set in 1053, or if the competing Greek, Lombard and Moslem states in the south had not been brought under Norman rule. But it may be legitimately surmised that apart from the Normans, the later development of these peoples would not have been either more distinguished or more distinct. And as was the case with those countries which the Normans conquered, so also was it with Europe as a whole. Of course, neither the achievements of the Hildebrandine papacy nor the cultural revival in the West, nor the Crusades were the creation of the Normans. But they would not have taken place as, and when, they did, apart from the Normans. Again (to offer a pejorative example) the lamentable schism of Christendom which in 1204 was to culminate in the sack of Constantinople would probably in any case have occurred, but it was precipitated and made inevitable by Norman policy. Finally, it may be recalled that both the 'Angevin empire', dominating the Atlantic coast, and the kingdom of Roger II, controlling both shores of the central Mediterranean, were in their turn the direct outcome of earlier Norman endeavour. It might be said that the full consequences of the Norman impact upon Europe were not revealed until the twelfth century was well advanced – perhaps indeed not until the age of Innocent III. But the character of the enduring influence of the Normans upon history had already been disclosed, and its extent had already been determined, by Norman action between 1050 and 1100.

It may be fitting, therefore, to end this study beside the tombs of some of those who were primarily responsible for that swift advance, since these monuments are themselves in some sense a reflexion of what the Normans had achieved during these five momentous decades. It was in his own duchy, in the church of St Stephen at Caen which he had built, that in 1087 William the Conqueror was laid to rest. His tomb was soon to be adorned by a foreign craftsman living in England,[1] but the grave was subsequently ravaged, and the original erection has now totally disappeared. The setting was none the less wholly appropriate,[2] and it was equally fitting that in 1085 Robert Guiscard should have been brought from Cephallonia to Venosa, the birth-place of Horace, there to be buried in the abbey he had so lavishly enriched alongside the Norman wife he had so cruelly repudiated. His tomb also has perished, but its contemporary fame spread to far-off Wiltshire where a monk proudly set down the epitaph which surmounted it. Evidently the exploits of the Norman duke of Apulia, 'the terror of the world', and particularly his victories over the emperors of the West and the East, were a matter of pride in Norman England.[3] As for Roger I it need only be added that he was buried not in Syracuse or Palermo or even at

[1] This was 'Otto the Goldsmith'. His family prospered and held estates in England, and were benefactors of the abbey of Bury St Edmunds (Douglas, *Feudal Documents*, p. cxxxix, and no. 20).

[2] Appropriate also was the resting place of the Conqueror's diminutive wife Matilda in the Abbaye aux Dames which she built at the other end of the town. The original stone slab is still in the church, and the curious may read the beautiful inscription in the plate given by J. S. Cotman, *Architectural Antiquities of Normandy* (1822), I, plate XXXIII.

[3] Will. Malms., *Gesta Regum*, II, p. 322.

Messina (as might perhaps have been expected) but in his own abbey of Holy Trinity outside Mileto, the city which he had raised to cosmopolitan fame, which had watched his rise to power, and which speedily declined after his death.[1]

Even more remarkable in this respect are the existing monuments to the eleventh-century Norman leaders of the next generation. There is for example the gaunt black stone which appropriately covers the body of William Rufus who was brought in 1100 from his mysterious death in the New Forest accompanied by a lamenting English crowd to his burial in Winchester Cathedral.[2] There is also the sepulchre of Robert, that other son of the Conqueror, who won fame in Syria, and then suffered misfortune in the West until after long imprisonment he was interred at last in the abbey church of St Peter at Gloucester.[3] The wooden effigy which commemorates him is of later medieval date, and much restored, but his tomb may none the less be suitably compared with the monument to Bohemund, Robert's companion on the First Crusade. This (which is perhaps the strangest and most revealing of all the Norman tombs) is to be found outside the cathedral at Canosa (between Bari and Foggia) and it is oriental in structure and Moslem in spirit. It is not like a sarcophagus placed in the *atrium* or nave of a Christian Church. Rather, with its cupola resting on a square base it resembles a Moslem tomb, or *turbeh*, such as might be found outside a mosque. The grandiose inscription certainly exalts the victories of this 'faithful athlete of Christ', and claims that he had not only subdued Syria but three times ravaged Greece, and brought terror to Parthia. But the monument which covers the body of Bohemund of Taranto, prince of Antioch, derives its inspiration as much from the Moslem east as from the Christian west.[4]

It is a far cry from Gloucester to Canosa, and the contrasting tombs of Robert and his friend Bohemund may serve to call attention to the many fields of Norman action in their time. Perhaps however, a final synthesis might be sought at Palermo in the great cathedral, once a mosque which the Normans restored to Christendom in 1072. There, in 1097, was brought for burial William the Conqueror's half-brother, Odo, bishop of Bayeux and earl of Kent, and his funeral service was conducted by the same bishop of Évreux in Normandy who ten years

---

[1] Edrisi in Amari, *Bibliotheca*, I, p. 37; Chalandon, *Domination normande*, I, p. 354. The sarcophagus is now at Naples.

[2] E. A. Freeman, *William Rufus*, Appendix 'TT'. [3] Plate XII.

[4] Bertaux, *op. cit.*, pp. 312–16; Plate XIII.

before had preached the sermon at the obsequies of the Conqueror himself.[1] There, too, is the evocative chapel which contains the tomb of King Roger II of Sicily. His father had started his Italian career as a cattle-thief, continued it as a notable soldier, and ended it as a constructive statesman. And now the son lies in state beside his own daughter Constance, and beside the two emperors, Henry VI and Frederick II, who were his close kinsfolk. If St Stephen's, Caen, stark and dignified, was the appropriate resting place for William the Conqueror, and if Norman romanesque building reasonably reached its climax not in the duchy but in the north of England, so also might a fitting symbol of Norman endeavour be found in the lovely porphyry monument which now enshrines the royal son of Roger the 'Great Count'. The results of the Norman achievement between 1050 and 1100 were in truth to be various and widely stretched. But there was an inherent unity in all the Normans wrought.

[1] Ord. Vit., IV, pp. 17, 18.

MAPS

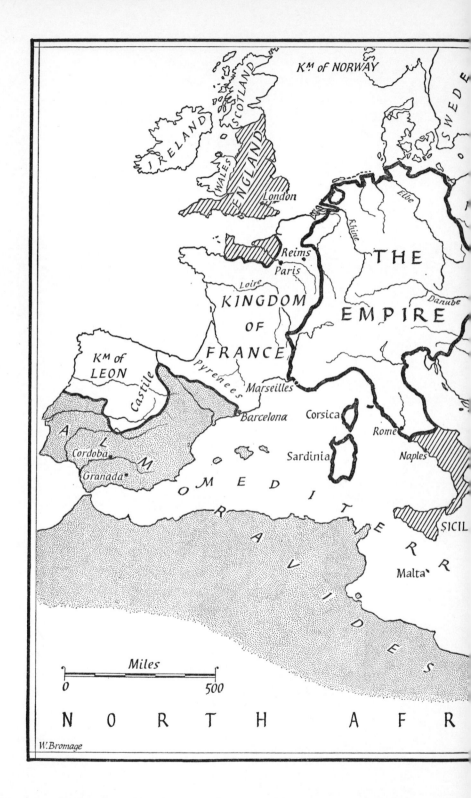

Kᴹ of NORWAY

SWEDE

IRELAND

SCOTLAND

WALES

ENGLAND

London

Elbe

Rhine

THE

Reims

Paris

EMPIRE

Loire

Danube

KINGDOM

OF

FRANCE

Pyrenees

Kᴹ of
LEON

Castile

Marseilles

Barcelona

Corsica

Rome

A

L

Cordoba

M

Sardinia

Naples

Granada

M

O

R

A

V

I

D

E

S

E

D

I

T

E

R

R

SICIL

Malta

Miles

0   500

N   O   R   T   H   A   F   R

W. Bromage

EUROPE
c. 1100

Lands under
Norman rule

Lands under
Moslem rule

ND

Buda

Danube

EASTERN

Durazzo

Constantinople

Smyrna

Athens

Crete

EAN *SEA*

Cyprus

BLACK SEA

Caucasus

EMPIRE

Antioch

Latakia

Aleppo

SELJUK

EMPIRE

Damascus

Acre

Jerusalem

Alexandria

Cairo

FATIMITE CALIPHATE

C A

RED SEA

ARABIA

ENGLAND &
NORMANDY
at the time of
WILLIAM the
CONQUEROR

Newcastle
Durham
Richmond
Ripon
Tadcaster · York
Pontefract
Lincoln
Chester Nottingham Belvoir
Shrewsbury
Lichfield Stamford · Peterborough · Norwich
Coventry Ely
Worcester Warwick Bury
Hereford Cambridge Colchester
Gloucester Oxford Berkhamstead
Bristol LONDON
Wells · Bath Rochester · Canterbury
Glastonbury Winchester Tonbridge Dover
Salisbury Hastings
Exeter Dorchester Pevensey
Totnes FLANDERS

St-Valéry-sur-Somme PONTHIEU
Amiens

Fécamp
Channel ROUEN
Islands Jumièges Beauvais
Bayeux Lisieux PARIS
Caen Évreux
Coutances ISLE DE
Mont-St-Michel Avranches NORMANDY
Dol Mortain FRANCE
BRITTANY MAINE BLOIS Orleans
Rennes LeMans
Angers Tours
ANJOU TOURAINE

Miles
0 50 100 150
POITOU

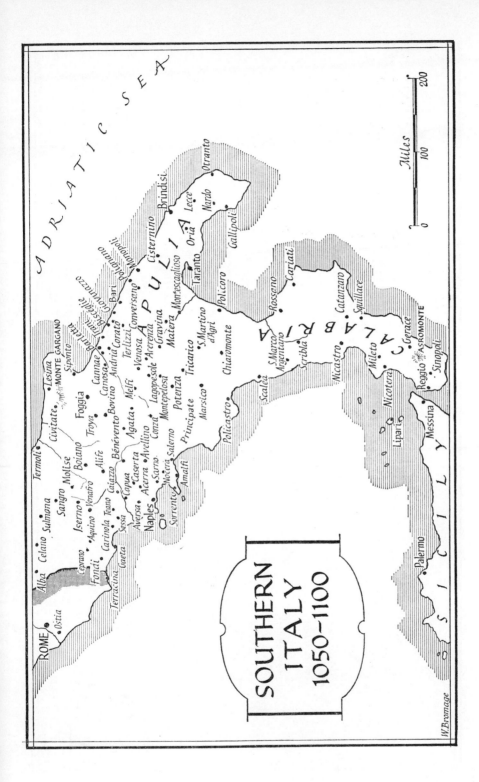

ADRIATIC SEA

SICILY

SOUTHERN ITALY 1050–1100

Miles

0   100   200

ROME
Ostia
Alba
Celano
Sulmona
Sangro
Molise
Iserno
Boiano
Aquino
Venafro
Alife
Carinola
Teano
Caiazzo
Capua
Caserta
Acerra
Aversa
Naples
Sorrento
Amalfi
Nocera
Salerno
Sarno
Avellino
Conza
Montepelosi
Potenza
Principate
Marsico
Policastro
Scalea
S.Marco Argentano
Scribla
Nicastro
Mileto
Nicotera
Lipari
Messina
Reggio
ASROMONTE
Sinopoli
Gerace
Squillace
Catanzaro
Cariati
Rossano
Policoro
Taranto
Chiaromonte
Tricarico
S.Martino d'Agri
Matera
Montescaglioso
Gravina
Acerenza
Venosa
Terlizzi
Lagopesole
Andria
Coratò
Canosa
Cannae
Bovino
Troya
Foggia
Melfi
Agata
Civitate
Lesina
MONTE GARGANO
Siponto
Bari
Bisceglie
Trani
Barletta
Giovinazzo
Polignano
Monopoli
Cisternino
Oria
Lecce
Nardo
Gallipoli
Otranto
Brindisi
Termoli
Gaeta
Fondi
Copano
Terracina

APULIA

CALABRIA

Palermo

W.Bromage

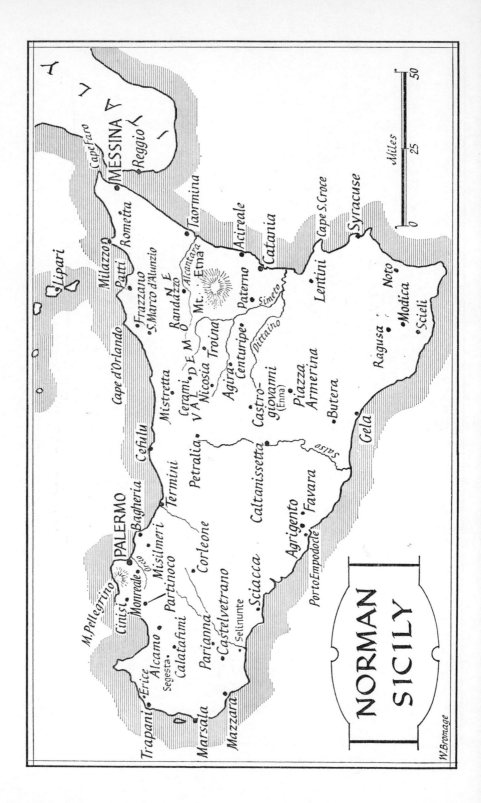

NORMAN SICILY

W.Bromage

Miles
0 25 50

MESSINA
Cape Faro
Reggio
Milazzo
Patti
Rometta
Frazzano
S.Marco d'Alunzio
N.E
Randazzo
Taormina
Alcantara
Mt. Etna
Acireale
Catania
Paterno
Simeto
Cape S.Croce
Syracuse
Lipari
Cape d'Orlando
Mistretta
Cerami
D E M O N E
Nicosia
Troina
Agira
Centuripe
Dittaino
Lentini
Noto
Modica
Scieli
Castro-
giovanni
(Enna)
Piazza
Armerina
Ragusa
V A L
Butera
Gela
Petralia
Cefalu
Termini
Caltanissetta
Salso
Salso
Bagheria
PALERMO
Misilmeri
Corleone
Sciacca
Agrigento
Favara
M.Pellegrino
Cinisi
Monreale
Partinoco
Oreto
Alcamo
Parianna
Castelvetrano
Selinunte
PortoEmpodocle
Erice
Segesta
Calatafimi
Trapani
Marsala
Mazzara
Castelvetrano
Centuripe

SELECT GENEALOGIES

NOTE

It must be emphasized that the sketch-pedigrees which follow are in no way intended to give a complete representation of the families concerned. They are designed simply to indicate the relationship between some of the chief personages mentioned in this book, and in particular to illustrate the significance of those connexions which are discussed in chapters 6 and 9.

Robert I, Duke of Normandy = Herleve
1027–1035   d. of Fulbert, a tanner
   of Falaise

= Herluin
vicomte of Conteville

William the Conqueror = Matilda
duke of Normandy 1035–87   d. of
king of England 1066–87   Baldwin V, count
   of Flanders

Odo
bishop of Bayeux
1049–90
Made earl of Kent
1067

Robert
count of Mortain
Large land-owner
in England 1086
d. 1091

Robert II = Sibyl
duke of   d. of Geoffrey
Normandy   of Brindisi, Count of
1087–1106   Conversano, and great
d. 1134   niece of Robert Guiscard

Richard
d. s.p.l.
c. 1075

William II
king of England
1087–1100

Henry I = Matilda
king of   d. of Malcolm III
England   king of Scotland
1100–35   and niece of
duke of   Edgar Atheling
Normandy
1106–35

daughters

Table 1. The Norman ducal dynasty

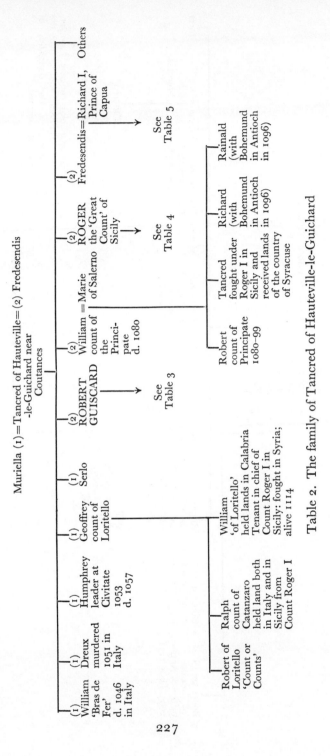

Table 2. The family of Tancred of Hauteville-le-Guichard

227

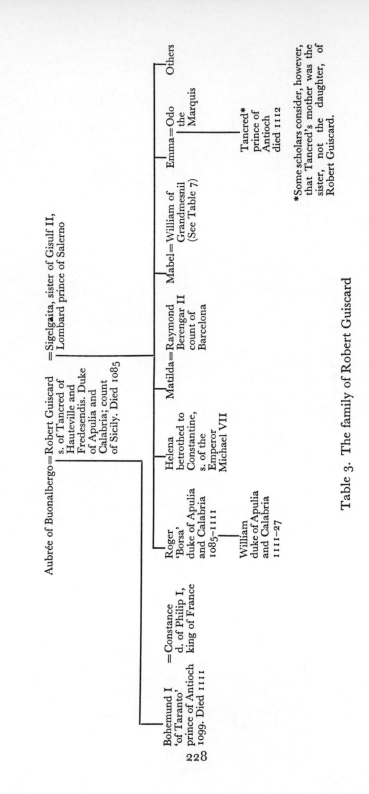

Aubrée of Buonalbergo = Robert Guiscard, s. of Tancred of Hauteville and Fredesendis. Duke of Apulia and Calabria; count of Sicily. Died 1085 = Sigelgaita, sister of Gisulf II, Lombard prince of Salerno

Bohemund I 'of Taranto', prince of Antioch 1099. Died 1111 = Constance d. of Philip I, king of France

Roger 'Borsa', duke of Apulia and Calabria 1085–1111

William duke of Apulia and Calabria 1111–27

Helena betrothed to Constantine, s. of the Emperor Michael VII

Matilda = Raymond Berengar II count of Barcelona

Mabel = William of Grandmesnil (See Table 7)

Emma = Odo the Marquis

Tancred* prince of Antioch died 1112

Others

*Some scholars consider, however, that Tancred's mother was the sister, not the daughter, of Robert Guiscard.

228

Table 3. The family of Robert Guiscard

Roger I
youngest s. of Tancred of
Hauteville; 'the great count'
of Sicily; in occupation of
Palermo 1072. Died 1101
= (1) Judith
d. of William, count of Évreux
and grand-d. of Archbishop Robert I
of Rouen; half-sister of Hugh and
Robert II of Grandmesnil (see Table 7)
(2) Eremberga, d. of William, count
of Mortain
(3) Adelaide, d. of Manfred,
the 'Marquis'

Matilda = Raymond of Provence

Constance = Conrad, rebel s. of the Emperor Henry IV

Busila = Carloman king of Hungary

daughter = Rannulf count of Alife

daughter = Ralph Maccabees count of Montescaglioso

(3)
Simon count of Sicily 1101–05

(3)
Elvira of Castile = Roger II count of Sicily 1105–54 duke of Apulia 1122–54 king 1130–54 = Beatrice of Rethel

William I king of Sicily 1154–60

William II king of Sicily 1166–88

Constance = Henry VI king of Sicily; Emperor 1190–97

Frederick II king of Sicily 1198; Emperor 1212–50

Others

Roger I had illegitimate sons:
1. Jordan, died campaigning in Sicily 1092
2. Geoffrey, became a monk
3. Mauger, who was still living in 1098

229

Table 4. The family of Roger I, count of Sicily

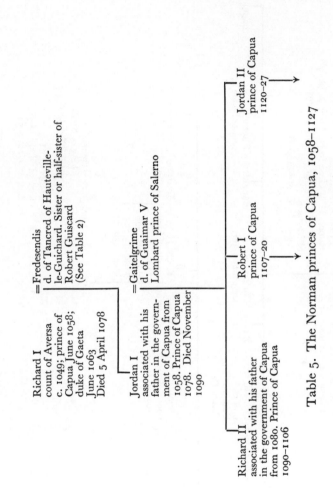

Richard I
count of Aversa
c. 1049; prince of
Capua June 1058;
duke of Gaeta
June 1063
Died 5 April 1078

= Fredesendis
d. of Tancred of Hauteville-
le-Guichard. Sister or half-sister of
Robert Guiscard
(See Table 2)

Jordan I
associated with his
father in the govern-
ment of Capua from
1058. Prince of Capua
1078. Died November
1090

= Gaitelgrime
d. of Guaimar V
Lombard prince of Salerno

Richard II
associated with his father
in the government of Capua
from 1080. Prince of Capua
1090–1106

Robert I
prince of Capua
1107–20
→

Jordan II
prince of Capua
1120–27
→

Table 5. The Norman princes of Capua, 1058–1127

230

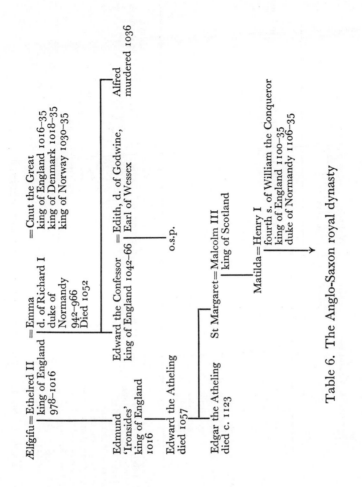

Table 6. The Anglo-Saxon royal dynasty

Robert I of Grandmesnil = Hawisa, d. = William, count of Évreux
of Géré of s. of Archbishop Robert I
Échauffour of Rouen

Hugh
born c. 1032;
1060 custodian of Neufmarché;
1066 fought at Hastings;
1067–69 custodian of Winchester,
later established at Leicester;
1086 very large landowner in England
died 1088 = Adeliza of Beaumont

Robert II
abbot of St Évroul c. 1059;
deposed and went to Italy
followed by many of his monks.
Became abbot of S. Eufemia in
Calabria. Held Vicalvi for
Robert Guiscard. Established
monastic colonies at Venosa
and Mileto; visited Normandy
in 1077; died 1082

Arnulf
went as a
youth to
Italy

Adeliza = Humphrey
of Tilleul

(See Table 9)

**Judith = Roger I, coun
of Sicily**

(See Table 4)

Robert
received the
Norman lands

William
born c. 1060; left for Italy
as a young man; some time
in favour at the imperial
court at Constantinople;
acquired large estates in
Italy; established at Rossano;
1081 accompanied Robert
Guiscard to the siege of
Durazzo; 1098 at Antioch;
died before 1114 in Italy

= Mabel
daughter of
Robert Guiscard

Hugh
died young in
1087

Yves
received English lands
which he pawned to
go on Crusade in 1096;
1098 at Antioch;
returns to Normandy;
1102 leaves for Syria
with his wife.
Dead 1102

Aubrey
at Antioch
1098

Others

Table 7. Some members of the family of Grandmesnil, 1050–1100

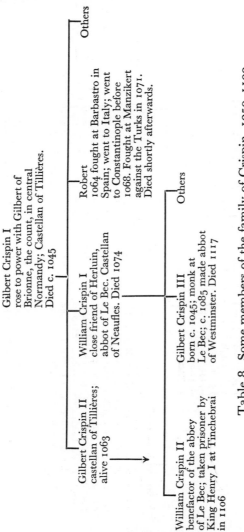

Gilbert Crispin I
rose to power with Gilbert of Brionne, the count, in central Normandy; Castellan of Tillières. Died c. 1045

Gilbert Crispin II
castellan of Tillières; alive 1063

William Crispin II
benefactor of the abbey of Le Bec; taken prisoner by King Henry I at Tinchebrai in 1106

William Crispin I
close friend of Herluin, abbot of Le Bec. Castellan of Neaufles. Died 1074

Gilbert Crispin III
born c. 1045; monk at Le Bec; c. 1085 made abbot of Westminster. Died 1117

Others

Robert
1064 fought at Barbastro in Spain; went to Italy; went to Constantinople before 1068. Fought at Manzikert against the Turks in 1071. Died shortly afterwards.

Others

Table 8. Some members of the family of Crispin, 1050–1100

233

Humphrey of Tilleul-en-Auge established in Normandy about 1050; visits English court of Edward the Confessor; joins William's expedition against England in 1066 and becomes castellan of Hastings Castle. 1069 returns to Normandy

= Adeliza daughter of Robert I of Grandmesnil (see Table 7)

Robert 'of Rhuddlan' comes with his father to England and wins favour of Edward the Confessor; joins William's expedition in 1066; becomes baron of Hugh of Avranches, earl of Chester; takes prominent part in Norman advance into South Wales. Present at the Conqueror's court at Laycock, 1086; is large landowner in England in 1086; killed by the Welsh 3 July 1088

William monk of St Évroul migrates to S. Eufemia in Calabria; becomes second abbot of S. Eufemia c. 1082, witnesses charter for Mileto, and Count Roger's foundation charter for the bishopric of Catania. Died c. 1103

Arnold monk of St Évroul. In 1088 brings back the body of his brother Robert of Rhuddlan to St Évroul for burial; and collects money from his relatives in Italy for the erection of a family tomb

Table 9. Some members of the family of Tilleul-en-Auge, 1050–1100

SCHEDULE OF SELECTED DATES

The schedule which follows sets out some of the dates of events which have been recorded in this book. No finality however is claimed for this list since the chronology of the age is beset with difficulties, and even in respect of some of the most important events the evidence is less conclusive than might be desired.

1035   (July) Accession of William the Conqueror (then a child) as duke of Normandy.
(12 November) Death of Cnut the Great, king of England, Denmark and Norway.

1042   Accession of Edward 'the Confessor' as king of the English.

1047   (January) Defeat of the Norman rebels at Val-ès-Dunes. Beginning of the effective reign of Duke William of Normandy.
Arrival of Robert Guiscard in Italy.

1048   Leo IX becomes pope.

1049   (October) Opening of the Council of Rheims.

1050   (early) Duke William of Normandy regains possession of Rouen.

1050? Marriage of Robert Guiscard with Aubrée of Buonalbergo.

1051   Robert, formerly Abbot of Jumièges, becomes archbishop of Canterbury.
Unsuccessful rebellion of Earl Godwine and his sons against Edward the Confessor. They are sent into exile.
(10 August) Dreux, son of Tancred of Hauteville, murdered in Italy.

1051? Marriage of Duke William of Normandy to Matilda of Flanders.

1052   (6 March) Death of Emma, mother of Edward the Confessor and widow of Cnut the Great.
(Before September) Earl Godwine and his sons effect their return to England by force. Expulsion of many Normans from England. Stigand is given the archbishopric of Canterbury.

1053   (February) Defeat of Argyrus by the Normans in south Italy.
John, abbot of Fécamp, visits Leo IX in Rome.
(13 April) Death of Earl Godwine. He is succeeded as Earl of Wessex by his son Harold.
(18 June) Battle of Civitate. Defeat of Leo IX and his German allies by the Normans.
(25 June) Leo IX brought by the Normans to Benevento.

1054   (January) Invasion of Normandy by King Henry I of France.
(February) Battle of Mortemer.
(February) Letter of Leo IX to the Emperor Constantine IX.
(February) Mission headed by Humbert of Silva Candida sent by Leo IX to Constantinople.

(18 March) Leo IX returns to Rome.

(19 April) Death of Leo IX.

(16 July) Bull excommunicating Michael Caerularius patriarch of Constantinople, laid on the altar of Santa Sophia. 'Schism of Caerularius.'

1056   Roger, youngest son of Tancred of Hauteville, arrives in Italy.

Bisignano and Nicastro submit to Robert Guiscard.

(October) Death of the Emperor Henry III. He is succeeded by his son Henry IV then a minor.

1057   (August) Death of Humphrey, son of Tancred of Hauteville.

Visit to England of Edward the Atheling, heir to Edward the Confessor. He dies suddenly in strange circumstances.

1058   (June) Richard, count of Aversa, having ousted the Lombard dynasty, takes title of prince of Capua.

(June) Nicholas II becomes pope.

Robert Guiscard repudiates his wife Aubrèe and marries Sigelgaita sister of Gisolf, the Lombard prince of Salerno.

Desiderius becomes abbot of Monte Cassino.

Alfanus I becomes archbishop of Salerno.

1059   (March–April) Easter Council at Rome: promulgation of decrees concerning the freedom of papal elections, and other reforms.

(August) Synod of Melfi. Richard of Aversa and Robert Guiscard receive papal recognition as, respectively, prince of Capua and duke of Apulia and Calabria. In return they promise to defend the freedom of papal elections.

Rossano, Cosenza, and Gerace submit to the Normans.

Count Roger established at Mileto.

Norman assaults on Reggio and Squillace.

1060   (April) Reforming Council at Rome.

(May) Robert Guiscard seizes Taranto.

(4 August) Death of Henry I, king of France: he is succeeded by Philip I then a minor.

(September) First raid of Count Roger on Sicily.

Norman occupation of Reggio and Scilla.

1061   (February) Second raid on Sicily by Count Roger I, with the aid of Ibn at Timnah.

(May) Robert Guiscard and Count Roger I take expedition to Sicily and capture Messina.

(27 July) Death of Nicholas II. He is succeeded as pope by Alexander II.

1062   (February) Capture of Petralia in northern Sicily by Count Roger I.

(March) Murder of Ibn at Timnah.

(May) Cadalus the anti-pope expels Alexander from Rome.

1063   (Summer) Count Roger I defeats the Saracens at the battle of Cerami.

The Normans give armed support to Pope Alexander II against the anti-pope.

Conquest of Maine by Duke William of Normandy.

1064   Christians capture Barbastro in Spain from the Moors with Normans participating.

1064? Harold Godwineson takes oath of fealty to Duke William of Normandy.

1065   Revolt of Northumbria against Edward the Confessor. Earl Tosti, son of Godwine, is exiled.

1066   (5 January) Death of Edward the Confessor.

(6 January) Coronation of Harold Godwineson, earl of Wessex, as king of the English.

(Spring) Norman mission to Rome to obtain papal support for the expedition against England.

(August–September) William's fleet, recently built, assembles in the Dives.

(8 September) Harold Godwineson in southern England disbands his army, and disperses his fleet.

(September) William's fleet at St Valéry-sur-Somme.

(September) Invasion of England by Harold Herdraada, king of Norway, and Tosti Godwineson.

(20 September) Battle of Stamford Bridge.

(14 October) Battle of Hastings.

(Autumn) Submission of Winchester and Canterbury.

(December) Assembly at Berkhampstead.

(25 December) Coronation of Duke William as king of the English.

Count Roger I builds castle at Petralia in Sicily.

1067   Odo, bishop of Bayeux, becomes earl of Kent.

Norman assaults on Brindisi and Otranto.

1068   (early) Subjection of Exeter. Submission of Bristol.

William's first entrance into York.

Victory of Count Roger over the Saracens, at Miselmeri near Palermo.

Castles built at York, Warwick, Lincoln, Huntingdon and Cambridge.

Robert Guiscard begins siege of Bari.

1069   Revolt of Maine against the Normans.

Invasion of Yorkshire by the Danes. General rebellion in the north of England supported by Malcolm, king of Scotland.

Siege of Bari continues.

William recaptures York.

1070   Sweyn Estrithson enter Humber with a fleet.

(January–March) Harrying of the North.

(15 August) Stigand having been deposed, Lanfranc becomes Archbishop of Canterbury.

(Summer) King Malcolm of Scotland ravages the north of England.

A Greek fleet fails in its attempt to relieve Bari.

1071   (16 April) Capture of Bari by the Normans from the Greeks.

(19 August) Battle of Manzikert. Alp Arslan defeats the Emperor

Romanus IV. The Seljuk Turks occupy many of the eastern provinces of the empire.

Robert Guiscard and Count Roger I invade Sicily and take Catania.

The Normans advance by sea and land against Palermo.

The siege of Palermo begins.

(October) Dedication of the new church at Monte Cassino by Pope Alexander II.

Suppression of the rebellion of Hereward in the Fens.

Capture of Jerusalem by the Turks.

1072 (January) The Normans capture Palermo from the Saracens.

(Autumn) King William I invades Scotland by sea and land. King Malcolm of Scotland submits to the Pact of Abernethy.

(November) King William I at Durham.

Castles built by the Normans at Rossano, and (in Sicily) at Mazzara and Palermo.

1073 (early) King William I invades and reconquers Maine. He re-enters Le Mans.

(21 April) Death of Alexander II. He is succeeded as pope by Gregory VII (Hildebrand).

(Before May) archbishopric of Palermo restored.

Normans take Trani.

1074 Castle built by Count Roger I at Calascibetta.

First excommunication of Robert Guiscard by Gregory VII.

1075 Revolt in England of the Earls of Hereford and Norfolk. Ralph, earl of Norfolk, escapes to his Breton lordship.

Treaty between Count Roger I and Tamin, sultan of Mehdia.

Ecclesiastical Council in London. Reconstitution of the English bishoprics begins.

1076 Siege of Salerno by the Normans begins.

Richard of Capua and Robert Guiscard reconciled by Abbot Desiderius.

(March) 'Dictatus Papae'.

(November) King William I defeated at Dol.

1077 (May) Capture of Salerno by Robert Guiscard.

Capture of Trapani by Count Roger I.

1078 (5 April) Death of Richard I, prince of Capua. He is succeeded by Jordan I.

Tutush brother of Malik Shah, sultan of Baghdad, becomes Seljuk ruler of Syria and Palestine.

1079 (January) King William I defeated at Gerberoi.

(15 August–8 September) Devastation of the north of England by Malcolm, king of Scotland.

(October) Artuk occupies Jerusalem on behalf of Tutush.

Establishment of the bishopric of Troina in Sicily.

1080 Robert 'Curthose' (eldest son of King William I) invades Scotland. Foundation of Newcastle.

(June) Robert Guiscard regains support of Gregory VII at synod at Ceprano.

1080? Gregory VII makes (or renews) to King William a demand for fealty in respect of the English kingdom. This is refused.

1081 Gregory VII issues letter to the bishops of Apulia and Calabria supporting the project of Robert Guiscard to invade the eastern empire.
(March) Robert Guiscard assembles fleet at Otranto.
(May) Robert Guiscard and his son Bohemund take Corfu.
(June) Siege of Durazzo begins.
(July) Naval defeat of the Normans by the Venetians.
(October) First engagement between Alexis and the Normans. The Normans repulsed.
Siege of Durazzo continues.
Alexis I becomes emperor.

1082 (21 February) Capture of Durazzo by the Normans.
Prelates of the Roman allegiance installed at Mileto and Reggio.
(Late) Robert Guiscard returns to Italy to deal with his rebellious vassals, and to support the pope against the Emperor Henry IV.

1083 Bohemund after a successful campaign in Greece, advances towards Constantinople but is repelled by Alexis I at Larissa.

1084 Robert Guiscard in answer to appeals from Gregory VII advances towards Rome to help the pope.
(May) Capture and sack of Rome by the Normans.
Bohemund returns to Italy.

1085 (25 May) Death of Pope Gregory VII.
(17 July) Death of Robert Guiscard. Roger Borsa, his son by Sigelgaita, is nominated as his successor.
(   ) Death of Alfanus I, archbishop of Salerno.
Threatened invasion of England from Scandinavia.
(25 December) Domesday Survey planned at Gloucester.

1086 Domesday Survey takes place.
(May) Count Roger I begins siege of Syracuse.
(August) Feudal Assembly of King William's greater tenants at Salisbury.
(23 October) Battle of Sagrajas. Christians heavily defeated by the Almorovids.
(October) Syracuse captured by the Normans.

1087 (Summer) William invades the Vexin and sacks Mantes.
(9 September) William I dies in the suburbs of Rouen. He is succeeded as duke of Normandy by his son Robert (Curthose) and as king of the English by his son William II ('Rufus').
(July) Capture of Agrigento by the Normans.
(August) Expedition from Pisa and other Italian cities against the Saracen Sultanate of Mehdia.
Capture of Castrogiovanni by Count Roger I from the Emir Hamud, who becomes a Christian.

239

1087–1088   Establishment of the bishoprics of Agrigento, Mazzara, Catania, Messina, and Syracuse.

1088   Civil war in England between King William II and Duke Robert (Curthose).
Urban II becomes pope.
(November) Trial of William of St Calais, bishop of Durham.

1089   (24 May) Death of Archbishop Lanfranc.

1090   (July) Count Roger I takes possession of Malta and Gozo.
War between Bohemund and Duke Roger (Borsa) of Apulia.
Bohemund occupies Bari.
(20 November) Death of Jordan I, prince of Capua. He is succeeded by his son, Richard II.
Suppression of rebellion in the north of England.

1090–1095   Civil war in Normandy between Duke Robert, King William II and their brother Henry.

1091   Norman conquest of Sicily completed.
Count Roger I suppresses revolt at Cosenza.

1090–1093   Feudal assembly at Mazzara of the greater tenants of Count Roger I. Distribution of the Sicilian fiefs.

1092   (May) Normans capture and colonize Carlisle.
(November) Death of Malik Shah, son of Alp Arslan and sultan of Baghdad. Civil war ensues.

1093   (March) Anselm installed as archbishop of Canterbury.

1094   Death of Hugh of Grandmesnil.

1095   (February) Death of Tutush, brother of Malik Shah. He is succeeded in Aleppo by his son, Ridwan; and in Damascus by his son, Duqaq.
(March) Council of Piacenza. Alexis I asks for help from the West against the Turks.
(March) Council of Rockingham. Bishops in England support King William II against Anselm.
Unification of the sees of Troina and Messina.

1096   Normandy placed in pledge to King William II by Duke Robert (Curthose).
Normans besiege Amalfi.
Duke Robert (Curthose) and others start on Crusade. They meet the Normans outside Amalfi. Bohemund takes the Crusaders' oath.

1097   (February) Death of Odo, bishop of Bayeux at Palermo.
(April–May) Bohemund at Constantinople.
(1 July) Battle of Dorylaeum. Bohemund present. Crusaders are victorious.
(October) Anselm, archbishop of Canterbury is exiled from England. He reaches Italy.
(October) Crusaders begin the siege of Antioch.

1098   (March) Attempt made by Ridwan of Aleppo to relieve Antioch, is beaten off by Bohemund.

(3 June) The Crusaders capture Antioch. Bohemund claims the city for himself and takes the title of prince.

Kerbogha of Mosul prepares to relieve Antioch.

(28 June) 'Great Battle of Antioch'. Defeat of Kerbogha.

(26 August) The Fatimids take Jerusalem from the Seljuk Turks.

(September) 'Letter of the Princes' sent to Urban II.

(October) Council of Bari under presidency of Urban II (Anselm, archbishop of Canterbury, present).

Siege of Capua by Count Roger I.

Bull of Urban II granting legatine privileges to Count Roger I.

Primatial rights granted by Urban II to the archbishopric of Salerno at the request of Duke Roger (Borsa).

1099   (15 July) The Crusaders capture and sack Jerusalem.

(19 July) Death of Urban II: he is succeeded as pope by Paschal II.

Prelates of the Roman allegiance installed at Tarsus, Artah, Mamistra and Edessa.

1100   Bernard of Valence becomes Latin patriarch of Antioch.

(2 August) Death of King William II.

(5 August) Coronation of Henry I as king of the English.

1100–1103   Bohemund is a prisoner of the Turks. Antioch is ruled by his nephew, Tancred.

1101   (22 June) Death of Roger I ('The Great Count').

1104–1106   Bohemund, having been released by the Turks, is in Western Europe. Paschal II supports his call for a Crusade against the eastern empire.

1106   (28 September) Battle of Tinchebrai. Normandy and England re-united under King Henry I.

1107   Bohemund invades the eastern empire, and is decisively defeated by Alexis I. He retires to Italy where he dies in 1111. Tancred (died 1112) rules in Antioch.

CONTEMPORARY RULERS

DUKES OF NORMANDY

Robert I, 1027–35
William II (the Conqueror), 1035–87
Robert II ('Curthose'), 1087–1106
Henry I (k. of England), 1106–35

KINGS OF ENGLAND

Ethelred II (the 'Unready'), 979–1016
Cnut the Great, 1016–35
Harold I, 1035–40
Harthacnut, 1040–2
Edward the Confessor, 1042–66
Harold II, 1066
William I (the Conqueror), 1066–87
William II ('Rufus'), 1087–1100
Henry I, 1100–35

NORMAN DUKES OF APULIA AND CALABRIA

Robert Guiscard, recognized as duke 1059, d. 1085
Roger 'Borsa', 1085–1111
William, 1111–27

NORMAN RULERS OF SICILY

Robert Guiscard, claimant as 'count', 1059–85
Roger I, 'the Great Count', effective ruler as count, 1072–1101.
Simon, count, 1101–1105
Roger II, count of Sicily, 1105–54
  duke of Apulia,   1127–54
  king,   1130–54

KINGS OF FRANCE

Henry I, 1031–60
Philip I, 1060–1108

POPES

Leo IX, 1048–54
Victor II, 1055–7
Stephen X, 1057–8
Nicholas II, 1059–61
Alexander II, 1061–73
Gregory VII (Hildebrand), 1073–85
Victor III, 1087
Urban II, 1088–99
Paschal II, 1099–1118

EMPERORS IN THE WEST

Henry III, 1039–56
Henry IV, 1056–1106
Henry V, 1110–25

EMPERORS IN THE EAST

Constantine IX, 1042–54
Theodora, 1054–6
Michael VI, 1056–7
Isaac I, 1057–9
Constantine X, 1059–67
Romanus IV, 1067–71
Michael VII, 1071–8
Nicephorus III, 1078–81
Alexis I (Comnenus), 1081–1118
John II, 1118–43

SELECT BIBLIOGRAPHY

The list which follows is in no sense to be regarded as representing the vast literature which has been devoted to the history of the Normans between 1050 and 1100. Some idea of the enormous extent of that literature, and of the original sources upon which it is based may be obtained by reference to the bibliographies given in, F. Chalandon, *Domination normande en Italie et en Sicile*, vol. I, pp. v–xcii; in David C. Douglas, *William the Conqueror*, pp. 427–47; and in Sir Steven Runciman, *History of the Crusades*, vol. I, pp. 327–35, and pp. 342–60. The purpose of the very restricted bibliography here given is limited to indicating some of the principal authorities on which the author has relied for his comparative study, and to suggesting some possible instruments for further research in this field. The conventional distinction between primary and secondary authorities has been retained, but it must be emphasized that many of the works cited in the later category contain texts of original documents, and are often here included for that reason.

A

ORIGINAL AUTHORITIES AND COLLECTIONS OF SOURCES

Acta Lanfranci (Earle and Plummer, *Two of the Saxon Chronicles Parallel*, vol. I, pp. 283–92).

Aguileis, Raymond of, *Historia Francorum qui ceperunt Jerusalem* (*Rec. Hist. Crois. Occ.*, III, pp. 235–309).

Alfanus I, archbishop of Salerno, *Opera* (*Pat. Lat.*, CXLVII).

Amari, M., *Bibliotheca Arabo-Sicula*, 2 vols. (Turin and Rome, 1880, 1881).

Amatus. *See* Monte Cassino.

Anglo-Saxon Chronicle. A revised translation edited by D. Whitelock, with D. C. Douglas and S. I. Tucker (London, 1961).

Anna Comnena, *Alexiad*, ed. B. Leib, 3 vols. (Paris, 1937–45).

—— —— trans. E. A. Dawes (London, 1967).

Annales Barenses (Bari) (*Mon. Germ. Hist. SS.*, V, pp. 51 et seq.).

Annales Beneventani (Benevento) (*Mon. Germ. Hist. SS.*, III, pp. 173 et seq.).

Annales Casinenses (Monte Cassino) (*Mon. Germ. Hist. SS.*, XIX, pp. 305 et seq. – several recensions).

Annales Cavenses (La Cava) (*Mon. Germ. Hist. SS.*, III, pp. 233 et seq.).

Annales Rothomagenses (Rouen) (*Mon. Germ. Hist. SS.*, XXVI, pp. 498 et seq.).

Annales Siculi (Sicily) – (printed in the edition of the chronicle of Geoffrey Malaterra by E. Pontieri (q.v.) at pp. 114–20).

Apulia, William of, *Gesta Roberti Wiscardi*, edited with a translation into French by M. Mathieu ('Guillaume de Pouille' – Palermo, 1961). (Also in *Mon. Germ. Hist. SS.*, IX and *Pat. Lat.* CLXIX).

Bayeux Tapestry, ed. F. M. Stenton (London, 1957); also ed. F. R. Fowke (London, 1875).

Bessin, G., *Concilia Rothomagensis Provinciae* (Rouen, 1717).

Bonizo, *Liber ad Amicum* (Jaffé, *Monumenta Gregoriana*, pp. 577–689).

Caen, Ralph of, *Gesta Tancredi* (*Rec. Hist. Crois. Occ.*, III).

Carmen de Hastingae Proelio, ed. H. Petrie *Monumenta* (1848).

Cartulaire de S. Père de Chartres, ed. B. E. C. Guérard, 2 vols. (Paris, 1840).

Catalogus Baronom Neapolitano in regno versantium. Printed in Del Re, *Cronisti e Scrittori*, II, pp. 571–615 (Naples, 1868). A new edition is now in preparation.

Chabannes, Adémar of, *Chronicon*, ed. J. Chavanon (Paris, 1897).

Chanson de Roland, ed. J. A. Jenkins (Oxford, 1929).

——, '*The Song of Roland done into English*' by C. Scott Moncrieff (London, 1920).

Chartres, Fulcher of, *Gesta Francorum Iherusalem Peregrinantium* ed. H. Hagenmeyer (Heidelberg, 1015).

Chronicon Casinense. See: Ostia, Leo of.

Chronicon Monasterii de Abingdon, 2 vols. (London, 1858).

Clare, Osbert of, *Letters*, ed. E. W. Williamson (Oxford, 1929).

Codice Diplomatico Barese, 18 vols. (Bari, 1897–1950).

Codice Diplomatico Brindisiano, vol. I (Trani, 1940).

Codice Diplomatico normannico d'Aversa, ed. A. Gallo (Naples, 1926).

Cusa, S., *I Diplomi Greci e Arabi di Sicilia* (Palermo, 1896–8).

Davis, H. W. C. *See: Regesta Regum Anglo-Normannorum.*

Damascus Chronicle of the Crusade, edited and translated by H. A. R. Gibb (London, 1932).

Domesday Book, ed. Record Commission, 2 vols. (1783).

Durham, Simeon of, *Opera Omnia*, ed. T. Arnold, 2 vols. (London, 1882, 1883).

Eadmer, *Historia Novorum*, ed. M. Rule (London, 1884).

——, *Vita Anselmi*, ed. R. W. Southern (Edinburgh, 1962).

Edward the Confessor, *Vita Edwardi Confessoris*, ed. F. W. Barlow (Edinburgh, 1962).

Facsimiles of English Royal Writs to 1100 A.D., ed. T. A. Bishop and P. Chaplais (Oxford, 1957).

Feudal Documents from the Abbey of Bury St Edmunds, ed. David C. Douglas (London, 1931).

Fulcher. *See:* Chartres.

Gallia Christiana, vol. XI (Paris, 1759).

Garufi, C. A., *I Documenti inediti dell epoca Normannia: Documenti per servire alla storia di Sicilia*, Soc. Siciliana di Storia Patria: Ser. Diplomatica, XVIII (Palermo, 1899).

Gattola, E. , *Historis Abbatiae Cassinensis – Accessiones*, 2 vols. (Venice, 1724).

Gesta Francorum et aliorum Hierosolimitanorum, ed. R. Hill (Edinburgh, 1962). Another edition is by H. Hagenmeyer (Heidelberg, 1890).

Glaber, Rodulf, *Francorum Historia*, ed. M. Prou (Paris, 1886).

Gregory VII, Pope, *Monumenta Gregoriana*, ed. Ph. Jaffé (Berlin, 1865).

——, *Registrum Papae Gregoriii VII*, ed. E. Caspar (*Mon. Germ. Hist.*, 2 vols., Berlin, 1893).

Guillaume, P., *Essai historique sur l'abbaye de Cava* (Cava, 1877). [Important appendix of charters.]

Hagenmeyer, H., *Die Kreuzzugsbriefe aus den Jahren 1088–1100* (Innsbruck, 1902).

Ibn el Athir, *Chronicle. See:* Amari, *Bibliotheca*, vol. I.

Ibn Jubair, *Chronicle. See:* Amari, *Bibliotheca*, vol. I.

Jaffé, Philip, *Regesta Pontificum Romanorum*, 2nd. edition, ed. by E. Wattenbach, S. Loewenfeld and others. 2 vols. (Leipzig, 1885–8). [Cited as 'Jaffé-Loewenfeld'.]

Jumièges. *Chartes de l'abbaye de Jumièges*, ed. J. J. Vernier, 2 vols. (Rouen, 1916).

Jumièges, William of, *Gesta Normannorum Ducum*, ed. J. Marx (Rouen, 1914).

Kehr, P. F., *Regesta Pontificum Romanorum – Italia Pontificia*, vol. VII, *Regnum Normannorum – Campania* (Berlin, 1936).

Lair, J., *Guillaume Longue Epée* (Paris, 1893). [Contains in the facsimile the text of the 'Lament'.]

Leo IX, Pope, *Epistolae, etc.* (*Pat. Lat.*, CXLIII).

'Letter of the Princes' (1098), *see:* H. Hagenmeyer, *Kreuzzugsbriefe*, pp. 161–5.

Liber Pontificalis, ed. L. Duchesne, 2 vols. (Paris, 1886–92).

Liebermann, F., *Ungedruckte Anglo-Normannische Geschichtsquellen* (Strassburg, 1879).

Lupus Protospatarius, *see: Annales Barenses*.

Malaterra, Geoffrey, *De Rebus Gestis Rogerii Calabriae et Siciliae Comitis* ('*Historia Sicula*'), ed. E. Pontieri (Muratori *Scriptores* – new edition – vol. I, part I (Bologna, 1924). Also *Pat. Lat.*, CLXIX.

Malmesbury, William of, *Gesta Regum Anglorum*, ed. W. Stubbs (London, 1870).

Mas Latrie, *Traités de Paix et de Commerce* (Paris, 1866).

Mazzoleni, J., *Le Pergamene di Capua*, I (Naples, 1957).

Ménager, L. R., 'Documents . . . sur quelques monastères grecs de Calabrie a l'époque normand' (*Byzantinische Zeitschrift*, vol. L).

——, *Les Actes latines de S. Maria di Messina* (Palermo, 1961).

——, And see below p. 250.

Monasticon Anglicanum, ed. W. Dugdale, new edition, 8 vols. (London, 1817–30).

Monte Cassino, Amatus of, *Ystoire de li Normant*, ed. V. de Bartholomeis. (Amato di Montecassino, *Storia di Normanni*, Rome, 1935.) Also, ed. O. Delarc (Rouen, 1892). [Cited by book and chapter as 'Amatus'.]

Musset, L., *Actes inédites du XIe. siècle* in *Bull. Soc. Antiquaries de Normandie*, vol. LII, pp. 117–55, vol. LIV, pp. 115–54.

Neustria Pia, ed. A. de Monstier (Rouen, 1163).

Nogent, Guibert of, *Historia Hierosolymitarii* (*Rec. Hist. Crois. Occ.*, IV, pp. 115–263).

Ordericus Vitalis, *Historia Ecclesiastica*, ed. A. Le Prévost and L. Delisle, 5 vols. (Paris, 1838–55).

Ostia, Leo of, *Chronicon Casinense* (*Mon. Germ. Hist. SS.*, VII, pp. 574 et seq. Also *Pat. Lat.*, CLXXIII).

Paschal, II, Pope, *Epistolae, etc.* (*Pat. Lat.*, CLXIII).

Peter the Deacon, *Chronicon Casinense*. This is an (inferior) continuation of the chronicle of Leo of Ostia (q.v.).

Pirro, R., *Sicilia Sacra*, 3rd. ed. (Palermo, 1733).

Placita Anglo-Normannica, ed. M. M. Bigelow (Boston, 1879).

Poitiers, William of, *Gesta Guillemi Ducus Normannorum et Regis Anglorum*, ed. R. Foreville (Paris, 1952).

Recueil des Actes des Ducs de Normandie de 911 a 1066, ed. M. Fauroux (Paris, 1961).

Recueil des Historiens des Croisades: Historiens Occidentaux, 5 vols. (Paris, 1844–1895).

Recueil des Historiens des Gaules et de la France ('Dom Bouquet') 24 vols. (Paris, 1738–1924).

Regesta Regum Anglo-Normanorrum, ed. H. W. C. Davis, vol. I (Oxford, 1913).

Regesta Regni Hierosolymiti, ed. R. Röhricht (Innsbruck, 1893).

Robert the Monk, *Historia Hierosolymitana* (*Rec. Hist. Crois. Occ.*, III, pp. 717–82.

Round, J. H., *Calendar of Documents preserved in France illustrative of the history of Great Britain and Ireland* (London, 1899).

Scotland. *Early Scottish Charters*, ed. A. C. Lawrie (Glasgow, 1905).

Starrabba, R. *Contributo allo Studio della diplomatica Siciliana dei tempi normanni: Diplomi di fundazione delle chiese episcopali di Sicilia* (*Archivio Storico Siciliano*, Nuova Serie, XVIII, Palermo, 1893).

Taccone Galluci, *Regesti dei Pontifici Romani per le Chiese della Calabria* (Rome, 1902).

'Tractatus Eboracenses' (*Mon. Germ. Hist.: Libelli de Lite*, vol. III). By the 'Norman Anonymous' of Rouen or of York.

Ughelli, F., *Italia Sacra*, 2nd. ed. 10 vols. (Venice, 1717–22).

Urban II, Pope, *Epistolae* etc. (*Pat. Lat.*, CLI).

Watterich, J. M., *Pontificum Romanorum qui fuerunt inde ab exeunte saeculo IX usque ad finem saeculi XIII*, . . . *Vitae*, 2 vols. (Leipzig, 1862).

Wharton, H., *Anglia Sacra*, 2 vols. (London, 1691).

Wilkins, D., *Concilia Magnae Britanniae et Hiberniae*, 4 vols. (London, 1837).

Worcester, Florence of, *Chronicon*, ed. B. Thorpe, 2 vols. (London, 1748, 1849).

B

SECONDARY AUTHORITIES AND WORKS OF REFERENCE

Alphandéry, P., *La Chrétienté et l'idée de Croisade* (Paris, 1954).

Amann, E., 'Michel Cerulaire', article in *Dictionnaire de Théologie catholique*, ed. Vacant, A., and Mangenot, E.

Amann, E. and Dumas, A., *L'Église au Pouvoir des laïques* (Paris, 1942).

Amari, M., *Storia dei Musulmani di Sicilia*, 3 vols. (Catania, 1933–7).

Andrieu-Guitrancourt, P., *Histoire de l'Empire normand* (Paris, 1932).

Armitage, E., *The Early Norman Castles of the British Isles* (London, 1912).

Avery, M., *The 'Exultet Rolls' of South Italy* (Princeton, 1936).

Barlow, Frank, *The English Church 1000–1066* (London, 1963).

——, *William I and the Norman Conquest* (London, 1965).

Barlow, J. W., *A Short History of the Normans in South Europe* (London, 1886).

Barrow, G. W. S., *The Border* (Durham, 1962).

——, 'Les Familles normandes d'Ecosse' (*Annales de Normandie*, XV, 1965).

Battifol, P., *L'abbaye de Rossano* (Paris, 1891).

Baynes, N. H., *The Byzantine Empire* (London, 1925).

Baynes, N. H. and Moss, H. St. L. B. (eds.) *Byzantium* (Oxford, 1948).

Bédier, J., *Les Légendes épiques*, 4 vols. (Paris, 1908–13).

Beeler, J., *Warfare in England* (Cornell U.P., 1966).

Bentham, J., *History and Antiquities of the . . . Cathedral Church of Ely*, 2 vols. (Cambridge–Norwich, 1771–1817).

Bertaux, E., *L'Art dans l'Italie méridionale* (Paris, 1903).

Bishop, E., *Liturgica Historica* (Oxford, 1918).

Bloch, H. M., 'Monte Cassino, Byzantium and the West' (*Dumbarton Oaks Papers*, III, 1945).

Bloch, Marc., *Feudal Society*, trans. L. A. Manyon (London, 1961).

——, *Mélanges historiques*, 2 vols. (Paris, 1963).

——, *Les Rois thaumaturges* (Strassburg, 1924).

Boase, T. S. R., 'Recent developments in Crusading historiography' (*History*, XXII (1937, pp. 110–25).

Boissonade, P., *Du nouveau sur la Chanson de Roland* (Paris, 1923).

Borino, G. B. (ed.), *Studi Gregoriani*, 7 vols. (Rome, 1967 etc.).

Bouard, M. de, 'De la Neustrie carolingien à la Normandie feodale' (*Bull. Institute of Historical Research*, XXVII (1955, pp. 1–17).

——, *Guillaume le Conquérant* (Paris, 1958).

Brackmann, A., 'The Beginning of the National State in medieval Germany, and the Norman monarchies', trans. in Barraclough, *Medieval Germany*, II, pp. 281–99.

Bréhier, L., *L'Église et l'Orient* (Paris, 1928).

——, *La Monde Byzantine*, II, *Les Institutions* (Paris, 1949).

——, *Le Schisme oriental du XIe siècle* (Paris, 1899).

Bréhier, L., review of Erdmann, *Kreuzzugsgedankens* (q.v.) in *Rev. Histoire Ecclésiastique*, XXXII, pp. 671–6.

Brooke, Z. N., *The English Church and the Papacy from the Conquest to the reign of John* (Cambridge, 1931).

Brown, R. A., *English Castles* (London, 1962).

——, *The Normans and the Norman Conquest* (London, 1969).

Buckler, G., *Anna Comnena* (Oxford, 1928).

Cahen, C., *Le Régime féodale de l'Italie normande* (Paris, 1940).

——, *La Syrie du Nord à l'époque des Croisades et la principalité franque d'Antioche* (Paris, 1940).

Casinensia. [Two commemorative volumes published at Monte Cassino in 1929].

Capparoni, P., 'Il Trattato "De quattuor Humoribus" di Alfano I' (*Casinensia* I, pp. 152–7).

Caspar, E., *Die Gründungsurkunden der Sicilischen Bistümer und die Kirchenpolitik Graf Rogers I* (Innsbruck, 1902). [This was reprinted as an Appendix to the author's work on Roger II.]

——, *Roger II und die Gründung der normannisch-sicilischen Monarchie* (Innsbruck, 1904).

Castro, A., *The Structure of Spanish History* (Princeton, 1948).

Chadwick, H. M., *The Study of Anglo-Saxon* (Cambridge, 1941).

Chalandon, F., *Histoire de la Domination normande en Italie et en Sicile*, 2 vols. (Paris, 1907).

——, *Essai sur le regne d'Alexis I* (Paris, 1900).

——, *Histoire de la première Croisade* (Paris, 1925).

Charanis, P., 'Byzantium, the West, and the origin of the First Crusade' (*Byzantion*, XIX, 1949).

Clapham, A. W., *English Romanesque Architecture after the Conquest* (London, 1934).

Complete Peerage of England, Scotland, Ireland, Great Britain and the United Kingdom, by G. E. C., new edition, 13 vols. in 14 (London, 1910–59).

Cotman, John Sell, *Architectural Antiquities of Normandy; accompanied by Historical and Descriptive Notices by Dawson Turner*, 2 vols. (London, 1822).

Cottineau, L. H., *Répertoire Topo-bibliographique des abbayes et prieurés*, 2 vols. (Macon, 1935, 1937).

Crawford, F. Marion, *The Rulers of the South: Calabria, Sicily, Malta*, 2 vols. (London, 1900).

Cronne, H. A., 'The Origins of Feudalism' (*History*, XXIV (1939), pp. 251–9).

Curtis, E., *Roger of Sicily* (New York, 1912).

Darlington, R. R., *Anglo-Norman Historians* (London, 1947).

——, *The Norman Conquest* (London, 1963).

David, C. W., *Robert Curthose* (Harvard U.P., 1920).

Dawson, C., *Medieval Essays* (London, 1953).

Delarc, O., *Les Normands en Italie* (Paris, 1883).

Demus, O., *The Mosaics of Norman Sicily* (London, 1950).

Diehl, C., *History of the Byzantine Empire*, trans. G. B. Ivan (Princeton, U.P. 1925).

——, *Palerme et Syracuse* (Paris, 1907).

Douglas, David C., *The Norman Conquest and British Historians* (Glasgow, 1946).

——, *The Rise of Normandy* (*Proc. Brit. Acad.*, XXXIII (1947) – and separately).

——, 'The "Song of Roland" and the Norman Conquest' (*French Studies*, XIV (1960), pp. 99–116).

——, 'Les Réussites normandes' (*Revue historique* (1967)).

——, *William the Conqueror* (London, 1964).

Douglas, Norman, *Old Calabria*, 4th ed. (London, 1955).

Duchesne, L., *Les Premiers temps de l'état pontificale* (Paris, 1904).

——, 'Les évêchés de Calabrie', in *Mélanges . . . Paul Fabre*, pp. 1–16 (Paris, 1902).

——, *The Origins of Christian Worship*, trans. McClure (London, 1912).

Edwards, J. G., 'The Normans and the Welsh March' (*Proc. Brit. Acad.*, XLII (1956), pp. 155–78).

Erdmann, C., *Die Enstehung des Kreuzzugsgedankens* (Stuttgart, 1935).

Every, G., *The Byzantine Patriarchate* (London, 1947).

Fliche, A., *La Reforme gregorienne*, 2 vols. (Paris, 1924, 1925).

Freeman, E. A., *The Norman Conquest of England*, 6 vols. (London, v.d.).

——, 'The Normans at Palermo in *Historical Essays* III, pp. 437–76 (London, 1879).

——, *Sketches of Travel in Normandy and Maine* (London, 1897).

——, *The Reign of William Rufus*, 2 vols. (London, 1882).

Frère, E., *Manuel du bibliographe normand*, 2 vols. (Rouen, 1858, 1860).

Fuller, J. F. C., *Decisive Battles of the Western World*, I (London, 1954).

Gallo, A., *Aversa normanna* (Naples, 1938). See also above, p. 243, sub. 'Codice diplomatico'.

Gams, B., *Series Episcoporum Ecclesiae Catholicae* (Regensburg, 1873).

Gattola, E., *Historia Abbatis Cassinensis*, 2 vols. (Venicc, 1723).

Garufi, C. A., *Censimento e Catasto della populazione servile – Nuovi Studi . . . sull' ordinamento administrativo dei Normanni in Sicilia* (*Archivio Storico Siciliano*, n.s. XLIX (1928)).

Gay, Jules, *L'Italie meridionale et l'empire byzantine* (Paris, 1904).

——, *Les Papes de XIe siècle et la chrétienté* (Paris, 1926).

Gibbon, E., *Decline and Fall of the Roman Empire*, ch. I.VI.

Gieyzstor, A., 'The Genesis of thc Crusades' (*Medievalia et Humanistica*, V and VI).

Grégoire, Henri, 'La Chanson de Roland de l'an 1085' (*Bull. Acad. Royale de Belgique*. Classes des Lettres. Serie XXV (1939)).

——, 'La Chanson de Roland et Byzance' (*Byzantion*, XIV, 1939)).

Gregorovius, F., *History of Rome in the Middle Ages*, vol. IV, trans. Hamilton (London, 1905).

Grousset, R., *Histoire des Croisades*, vol. I (Paris, 1934).

Haskins, Charles H., 'England and Sicily in the Twelfth century (*Eng. Hist. Rev.*, XXVI (1916), pp. 435–47; 641–65).

——, 'Albericus Casinsensis' *Casinensia*, I, pp. 115–25 (1929).

——, *The Normans in European History* (New York, 1915).

——, *Norman Institutions* (Harvard U.P., 1918).

——, *The Renaissance of the Twelfth Century* (Harvard U.P., 1927).

——, *Studies in the History of Medieval Science* (Harvard U.P., 1927).

Heer, Friedrich, *The Medieval World*, trans. J. Sondheimer (London, 1961).

Hefele, *Histoire des Conciles*, ed. H. Leclerc, 11 vols. (Paris, 1907–52). [Cited as 'Hefele-Leclerc'.]

Heinemann, L., *Geschichte der Normannen in Unteritalien und Sicilien* (Leipzig, 1894).

Hollister, C. W., *The Military Organization of Norman England* (Oxford, 1965).

——, 'The Norman Conquest and the Genesis of English feudalism' (*Amer. Hist. Rev.*, LXVI, pp. 641–66 (1961).

Hussey, J. M., 'The Byzantine Empire in the eleventh century' (R. Hist. Soc., *Trans.* Ser. 4, XXXII (1905)).

Jamison, Evelyn C., *The Admiral Eugenius of Sicily* (London, 1957).

——, 'The Norman administration of Apulia and Capua' (*Papers of the British School at Rome*, VI (1913), pp. 221–481).

——, 'Some Notes on the *Anonymi Gesta Francorum* with special reference to the Norman contingents from South Italy and Sicily in the First Crusade' (*Studies Presented to . . . M. K. Pope*) (Manchester U.P., 1939).

——, 'The Sicilian Norman Kingdom in the mind of Anglo-Norman contemporaries' (*Proc. Brit. Acad.*, XXIV (1938).

Joranson, E., 'The Inception of the career of the Normans in Italy: Legend and History' (*Speculum*, XXIII (1948), pp. 353–96).

Jordan, E., 'La politique ecclésiastique de Roger I' (*Moyen Age*, XXIII (1922), XXIV (1923)).

Jugie, M., *Le Schisme byzantin* (Paris, 1941).

Kantorowicz, E. H., *The King's Two Bodies: a study of medieval political theory* (Princeton U.P., 1957).

——, *Laudes Regiae* (California U.P., 1946).

Keeton, G. W., *The Norman Conquest and the Common Law* (London, 1966).

Kern, F., *Kingship and Law in the Middle Ages*, trans. S. B. Chrimes (London, 1939).

Knowles, M. D., *The Historian and Character* (Cambridge, 1963).

——, *The Monastic Order* (Cambridge, 1940).

Knight Gally, *Saracenic and Norman remains to illustrate the Normans in Sicily* (London, 1840).

Krey, A. C., 'Urban's Crusade: success or failure' (*Amer. Hist. Rev.*, XI (1948)).

——, 'A neglected passage in the *Gesta*' (*Essays for . . . D. C. Munro* (1928) pp. 55–79).

——, *The First Crusade: Accounts of Eye-Witnesses* (Princeton U.P., 1921).

La Monte, J. L., *Feudal Monarchy in the Latin kingdom of Jerusalem* (Harvard U.P., 1932).

——, 'Some Problems of Crusading historiography (*Speculum*, XV (1940)).

Laporte, J., 'Les Operations navales en Manche et Mer du Nord pendant l'année 1066' (*Annales de Normandie*, XVII (1967)).

Leib, O., *Rome Kiev et Byzance à la fin de XIe siècle* (Paris, 1924).

Lenormant, F., *La Grande Grèce*, 3 vols. (Paris, 1881–4).

Lewis, C. S., *The Discarded Image* (Cambridge, 1964).

Longnon, Jean, *Les Français d'Outre-Mer au Moyen Age* (Paris, 1929).

Lopez, R., 'The Norman Conquest of Sicily' (Setton and Baldwin, *The Crusades* (q.v.), vol. I, ch. ii c.).

Lot, F., 'Etudes sur les légendes épiques française: 'La Chanson de Roland' (*Romania*, LIV (1928), pp. 357–80).

Lowe, E. A., *The Beneventan Script* (Oxford, 1914).

——, 'The unique manuscript of Tacitus' *Histories*' (*Casinensia*, I).

Loyd, L. C., *The Origins of some Anglo-Norman Families* (Harleian Soc., CIII, 1951).

Macdonald, A. J., *Lanfranc* (Oxford, 1926).

Ménager, L. R., 'Les Fondations monastiques de Robert Guiscard' (*Quellen und Forschungen aus Italienischen Archiven und Bibliotheken*, XXXIX (1959), pp. 1–116).

——, La Politique monastique des Normands d'Italie (*Rev. Histoire Ecclesiastique*, LIII (1958), pp. 747–74; LIV (1959), pp. 5–40).

Menendez Pidal, *La Chanson de Roland* (Paris, 1960).

——, *The Cid and his Spain* (London, 1934).

Munro, D. C., 'The Speech of Urban II at Clermont' (*Amer. Hist. Rev.*, XI (1906), pp. 231 et seq.).

——, *Essays . . . presented to* (New York, 1928).

Norwich, John Julius, Lord, *The Normans in the South*, 2 vols. (London, 1966).

Palmarocchi, R., *L'abbazia di Montecassino e la conquista normanna* (Rome, 1923).

Paris, G., 'La Sicile dans la litterature française' (*Romania*, V (1876).

Pontieri, E., *Tra i Normanni nel Italia meridionali* (Naples, 1848).

Pollock, F. and Maitland, F. W., *History of English Law before the Time of Edward I*, 2nd ed., 2 vols. (Cambridge, 1898).

Poole, A. L., *From Domesday Book to Magna Carta* (Oxford, 1949).

Poole, R. L., *Lectures on the History of the Papal Chancery* (Cambridge, 1915).

——, *Studies in Chronology and History* (Oxford, 1934).

Prestwich, J. O., 'War and Finance in the Anglo-Norman state' (R. Hist. Soc., *Trans.*, Ser. 5, IV (1954)).

—— ——, 'Anglo-Norman Feudalism' (*Past and Present*, 1963).

Rey, E. G., 'Les Dignitaires de la Principauté d'Antioche' (*Rev. de l'Orient Latin*, VIII, 1900).

Ritchie, R. L. G., *The Normans in England before Edward the Confessor* (Exeter, 1948).

Ritchie, R. L. G., *The Normans in Scotland* (Edinburgh, 1954).

Robinson, J. A., *Gilbert Crispin, Abbot of Westminster* (Cambridge, 1911).

Round, J. H., *Feudal England* (London, 1895).

Rousset, P., *Les Origines et les caractères de la première croisade* (Neufchatel, 1945).

Runciman, Steven, *A History of the Crusades*, 3 vols. (Cambridge, 1951–4).

——, *The Eastern Schism* (Cambridge, 1955).

——, 'The Holy Lance found at Antioch' (*Analecta Bollandiana*, LXVIII (1950)).

Sackur, E., *Die Cluniacenser*, 2 vols. (Halle, 1892–4).

Saunders, J. J., *Aspects of the Crusades* (Christchurch, N.Z., 1962).

Schipa, M., 'Una Triade illustré di Montecassino' (*Casinensia*, I (1929)).

Schlumberger, G., 'Deux chefs normands des armées byzantines' (*Revue historique*, XVI (1881)).

Setton, K. M. and Baldwin, M. W. (eds.), *A history of the Crusades*; vol. I, *The First Hundred Years* (Philadelphia, 1955).

Smail, R. C., *Crusading Warfare* (Cambridge, 1956).

Southern, R. W., *St Anselm and his Biographer* (Cambridge, 1963).

——, 'The Place of England in the Twelfth Century Renaissance' (*History*, XLV (1960)).

——, *The Making of the Middle Ages* (London, 1953).

——, 'The English Origins of the "Miracles of the Virgin" ' (*Medieval and Renaissance Studies*, IV (1958), pp. 183–200).

Spatz, W., *Die Schlacht von Hastings* (Berlin, 1896).

Stenton, F. M., *Anglo-Saxon England* (Oxford, 1943).

——, *The First Century of English Feudalism* (Oxford, 1952).

Stephano, A. de, *La cultura in Sicilia nel periodo normanno* (Palermo, 1938).

Stephenson, C., 'Feudalism and its antecedents in England' (*Amer. Hist. Rev.*, XLVIII (1943)).

Stevenson, W. B., *The Crusaders in the East* (Cambridge, 1907).

Tellenbach, G., *Church State and Christian Society at the time of the Investitures Contest* (Oxford, 1940).

Thorndike, L., *History of Magic and Experimental Science*, vol. I (New York, 1923).

Torraca, F., 'Amato di Montecassino et il suo traduttore' (*Casinensia*, I (1929), pp. 155–61).

Tritz, H., 'Die Hagiographischen Quellen zur Geschichte Papst Leo IX' (*Studi Gregoriani*, ed. G. B. Borino, IV, pp. 191–364).

Ullmann, W., *Medieval Papalism: the political theories of medieval canonists* (London, 1949).

Verbuggen, J. F., *De Krijskunst in West-Europa in den middeleeuwen* (Brussels, 1954).

Villars, J. B., *Les Normands en Méditerranée* (Paris, 1951).

Waley, D. P., 'Combined Operations in Sicily A.D. 1060–78' (*Papers of the British School at Rome*, XXII (1954)).

Waern, C., *Mediaeval Sicily* (London, 1910).

Weiss, R. 'The Greek culture of Southern Italy in the later Middle Ages' (*Proc. Brit. Acad.*, XXXVI, 1951, pp. 23–50).

White, L. T., *Latin Monasticism in Norman Sicily* (Harvard U.P., 1938).

Williams, G. H., *The Norman Anonymous of 1100 A.D.* (Harvard U.P., 1938).

Yewdale, R. B., *Bohemund the First* (New York, 1917).

Yver, Jean, 'Le Bref anglo-normand' (*Revue Histoire de Droit*, XXIX, 1962).

——, 'Les Châteaux forts en Normandie jusqu'au mileu du XIIe siècle' (*Bull. Soc. Antiquaires de Normandie*, LIII (1956), pp. 26–121).

Zarnecki, George, '1066 and Architectural Sculpture' (*Proc. Brit. Acad.*, LII (1966)).

INDEX

Abbo, abbot of Fleury, 13
Abernethy, 50, 129
Abingdon, abbey of, 176
—, knights of, 176, 177
Abruzzi, 64
Acerenza, archbishopric of, 156, 205
Acerra (near Caserta), comté of, 175
Adela, d. of William the Conqueror, 162
Adelard of Bath, scholar, 209
Adhémar, bishop of Le Puy, papal legate, 165
Adriatic sea, 61, 83
Ælfgar, earl of Mercia, 31
Agrigento (Sicily), 57
—, bishopric of, 121, 139
Al Aziz, khalif of Cairo, 8, 150
Al Mansour, khalif of Cordova, 8, 150
Albania, 61
Alberic of Monte Cassino, scholar, 197
Alcher, archbishop of Palermo, 145
Aldred, archbishop of York, 47, 48
Alençon, 79
Aleppo, 91, 160, 164; see also Ridwan
Alexander II, pope, 56, 101, 102, 132, 133, 155, 196
Alexandria, patriarchate of, 151
Alexiad. See Anna Comnena
Alexis I, Emperor, 61, 108, 158, 160
—, policy towards papacy, 159–61
—, policy towards Normans, 61, 163–8
—, relations with Robert Guiscard, 61, 163
—, relations with Bohemund, 60–3, 164–168
—, see also Antioch; Durazzo; Urban II
Alfanus I, archbishop of Salerno, 193
—, monk at Monte Cassino, 196, 198
—, travels in the east, 198
—, friendship with Normans, 193, 198, 199
—, poet, 198
—, medical student, 199
—, patron of arts and sciences, 198–200
Alfred the Atheling, 14, 30

Alife (Calabria), comté of, 175
Ali ben Abas, medical student, 200
Almorovids, 158, 159, 161
Alphonzo VI, king of Leon, 161
Amalfi, 34–6, 59, 60, 64, 71, 196
Amatus of Monte Cassino, historian, 17, 69, 103, 104, 109, 110
—, also wrote poetry, 197
—, familiar with Latin classics, 197
—, value of his work as evidence, 17
Ambrose, abbot of Lipari, 120
'Angels of Mons', 15
'Angevin Empire', 190, 216
Anglo-Norman aristocracy, 27
—, establishment of, 12, 113, 173, 174
—, character of, 88, 181
Anglo-Norman Kingdom, 67, 173–80
—, political cohesion of, 49, 173
—, defence of, 49–53
Anglo-Saxon Chronicle, 18
Anglo-Saxon England, 35
—, architecture in, 212
—, culture in, 207–12
—, monarchy in, 30–4
—, earldoms in, 31–3
—, hundreds in, 186
—, shires in, 186
—, military organization of, 79
—, vernacular literature in, 207, 208
—, —, effect of Norman conquest on, 210, 211
Anjou, 10, 28, 49; see also Fulk Nerra; Geoffrey Martel
Anna Comnena, 20, 41, 69, 74, 75, 108, 160
Annals:
—, Anglo-Saxon, 18, 33, 48, 49
—, Norman, 18
—, of Bari, 18, 56
—, of Benevento, 18, 38
—, of Monte Cassino, 18, 37, 38
Anscher, bishop of Catania, 119, 121
Anselm, St, archbishop of Canterbury, 14, 28, 107, 122, 141–3, 189, 208

255

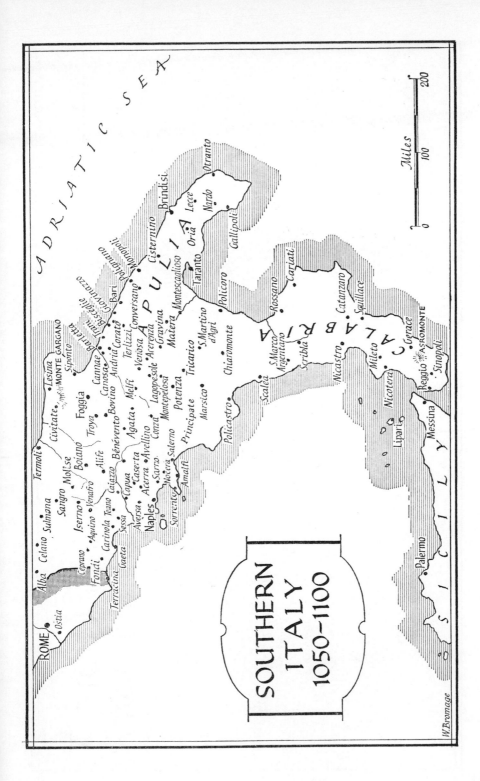

SOUTHERN
ITALY
1050-1100

ADRIATIC SEA

Miles
0   100   200

ROME
Ostia
Alba
Celano
Sulmona
Sangro
Termoli
Iserno
Boiano
Molise
Aquino
Venafro
Alife
Carinola
Teano
Sessa
Gaeta
Fondi
Copano
Terracina
Civitate
MONTE GARGANO
Siponto
Foggia
Troya
Cannae
Canosa
Bovino
Andria
Corato
Bari
Bisceglie
Trani
Barletta
Giovinazzo
Polignano
Monopoli
Cisternino
Brindisi
Oria
Lecce
Nardò
Otranto
Gallipoli
Taranto
APULIA
Conversano
Terlizzi
Agata
Melfi
Venosa
Acerenza
Gravina
Matera
Montescaglioso
Policoro
S.Martino
d'Agri
Tricarico
Chiaromonte
Lagopesole
Montepeloso
Potenza
Principate
Marsico
Conza
Salerno
Nocera
Amalfi
Sorrento
Naples
Aversa
Acerra
Caserta
Sarro
Capua
Ciazzo
Benevento
Avellino
Policastro
Scalea
S.Marco
Argentano
Scribla
Rossano
Cariati
Catanzaro
Squillace
Gerace
ASROMONTE
Reggio
Sinopoli
Mileto
Nicastro
CALABRIA
Nicotera
Liparto
Messina
Palermo
SICILY

W.Bromage

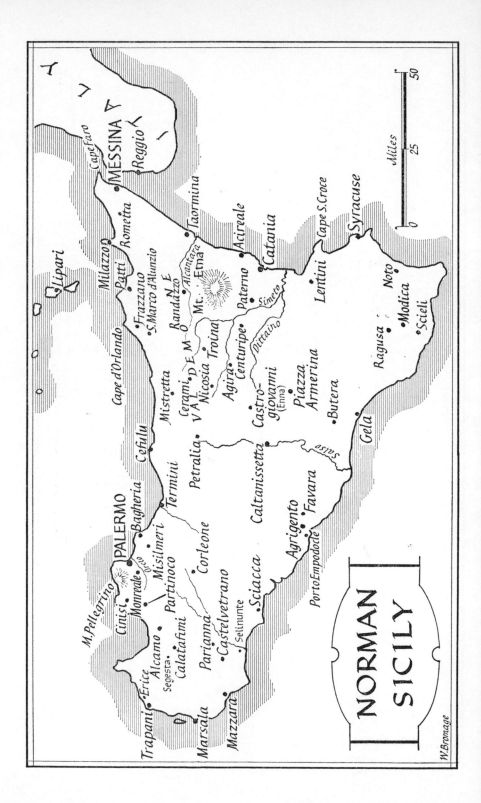

NORMAN SICILY

W. Bromage

ITALY

Cape Faro
MESSINA
Reggio

Miles 50
25
0

Lipari
Milazzo
Patti
Rometta
Frazzano
S. Marco d'Alunzio
N.E.
Randazzo
Taormina
Alcantara
Mt. Etna
Acireale
Catania
Cape S. Croce
Syracuse

Cape d'Orlando
Mistretta
Cerami
Nicosia
Troina
Agira
Centuripe
Paterno
Simeto
Lentini
Noto
Modica
Scicli

M. Pellegrino
PALERMO
Bagheria
Termini
Cefalu
Petralia
V A L
D E M O N E
Castro-
giovanni
(Enna)
Dittaino
Piazza
Armerina
Butera
Ragusa
Gela

Cinisi
Monreale
Misilmeri
Partinico
Corleone
Caltanissetta
Caltavuturo
Agrigento
Favara
Salso

Erice
Alcamo
Calatafimi
Segesta
Parianna
Castelvetrano
Selinunte
Sciacca
PortoEmpedocle

Trapani
Marsala
Mazzara

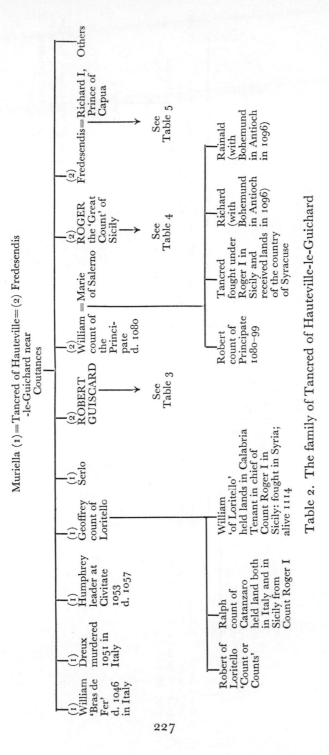

Muriella (1) = Tancred of Hauteville = (2) Fredesendis
-le-Guichard near
Coutances

(1) William 'Bras de Fer' d. 1046 in Italy

(1) Dreux murdered 1051 in Italy

(1) Humphrey leader at Civitate 1053 d. 1057

(1) Geoffrey count of Loritello

(1) Serlo

(2) ROBERT GUISCARD
See Table 3

(2) William count of the Principate d. 1080 = Marie of Salerno

(2) ROGER the 'Great Count' of Sicily
See Table 4

(2) Fredesendis = Richard I, Prince of Capua
See Table 5

Others

Ralph count of Catanzaro held land both in Italy and in Sicily from Count Roger I

William 'of Loritello' held lands in Calabria Tenant in chief of Count Roger I in Sicily: fought in Syria; alive 1114

Robert of Loritello 'Count or Counts'

Robert count of Principate 1080–99

Tancred fought under Roger I in Sicily and received lands of the country of Syracuse

Richard (with Bohemund in Antioch in 1096)

Rainald (with Bohemund in Antioch in 1096)

Table 2. The family of Tancred of Hauteville-le-Guichard

227

Robert I of Grandmesnil=Hawisa, d. = William, count of Évreux
                        of Géré of   s. of Archbishop Robert I
                        Échauffour   of Rouen

| Hugh | Robert II | Arnulf | Adeliza=Humphrey | Judith=Roger I, coun |
| | | | of Tilleul | of Sicily |

Hugh
born c. 1032;
1060 custodian of Neufmarché;
1066 fought at Hastings;
1067–69 custodian of Winchester,
later established at Leicester;
1086 very large landowner in England
died 1088=Adeliza of Beaumont

Robert II
abbot of St Évroul c. 1059;
deposed and went to Italy
followed by many of his monks.
Became abbot of S. Eufemia in
Calabria. Held Vicalvi for
Robert Guiscard. Established
monastic colonies at Venosa
and Mileto; visited Normandy
in 1077; died 1082

Arnulf
went as a
youth to
Italy

Adeliza=Humphrey
of Tilleul
(See Table 9)

Judith=Roger I, coun
of Sicily
(See Table 4)

Robert	William	= Mabel	Hugh	Yves	Aubrey	Others
received the		daughter of	died young in		at Antioch	
Norman lands		Robert Guiscard	1087		1098	

Robert
received the
Norman lands

William
born c. 1060; left for Italy
as a young man; some time
in favour at the imperial
court at Constantinople;
acquired large estates in
Italy; established at Rossano;
1081 accompanied Robert
Guiscard to the siege of
Durazzo; 1098 at Antioch;
died before 1114 in Italy

= Mabel
daughter of
Robert Guiscard

Hugh
died young in
1087

Yves
received English lands
which he pawned to
go on Crusade in 1096;
1098 at Antioch;
returns to Normandy;
1102 leaves for Syria
with his wife.
Dead 1102

Aubrey
at Antioch
1098

Others

232

Table 7. Some members of the family of Grandmesnil, 1050–1100